Surviving and Thriving in Nursing

**WESTERN®
SCHOOLS**

By
Marion G. Anema, PhD, RN

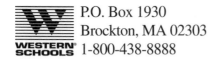

P.O. Box 1930
Brockton, MA 02303
1-800-438-8888

ABOUT THE AUTHOR

Marion G. Anema, PhD, RN is Faculty Chair, Nursing, at Walden University in Minneapolis and Senior Nurse Educator for Sylvan Online Higher Education, Baltimore. She previously was Dean, School of Nursing at Tennessee State University in Nashville. She has written extensively on topics related to nursing education and practice.

> **Marion Anema, PhD, RN,** has disclosed that she has no significant financial or other conflicts of interest pertaining to this course book.

ABOUT THE SUBJECT MATTER REVIEWER

Deborah Papa, EdD, RN, CNAA, is the Department Head of Nursing at Broward Community College and President of Professional Education Network, Inc. She previously was the chief nursing executive at Memorial Regional Hospital in Hollywood, FL and has 20 years of experience in Nursing Administration. She has developed and implemented a number of educational programs. In addition, she has published and presented on topics related to nursing education and nursing administration.

> **Deborah Papa, EdD, RN, CNAA,** has disclosed that she has no significant financial or other conflicts of interest pertaining to this course book.

Copy Editor: Demi Rasmussen, Julie Munden

Indexer: Sylvia Coates

ISBN: 978-1-57801-099-8

IMPORTANT: Read these instructions *BEFORE* proceeding!

Enclosed with your course book, you will find the FasTrax® answer sheet. Use this form to answer all the final exam questions that appear in this course book. If you are completing more than one course, be sure to write your answers on the appropriate answer sheet. Full instructions and complete grading details are printed on the FasTrax instruction sheet, also enclosed with your order. Please review them before starting. *If you are mailing your answer sheet(s) to Western Schools, we recommend you make a copy as a backup.*

ABOUT THIS COURSE

A Pretest is provided with each course to test your current knowledge base regarding the subject matter contained within this course. Your Final Exam is a multiple choice examination. **You will find the exam questions at the end of each chapter.** Some smaller hour courses include the exam at the end of the book.

In the event the course has less than 100 questions, leave the remaining answer boxes on the FasTrax answer sheet blank. **Use a <u>black</u> pen to fill in your answer sheet.**

A PASSING SCORE

You must score 70% or better in order to pass this course and receive your Certificate of Completion. Should you fail to achieve the required score, we will send you an additional FasTrax answer sheet so that you may make a second attempt to pass the course. Western Schools will allow you three chances to pass the same course...*at no extra charge!* After three failed attempts to pass the same course, your file will be closed.

RECORDING YOUR HOURS

Please monitor the time it takes to complete this course using the handy log sheet on the other side of this page. See below for transferring study hours to the course evaluation.

COURSE EVALUATIONS

In this course book, you will find a short evaluation about the course you are soon to complete. This information is vital to providing the school with feedback on this course. The course evaluation answer section is in the lower right hand corner of the FasTrax answer sheet marked "Evaluation," with answers marked 1–25. Your answers are important to us; please take five minutes to complete the evaluation.

On the back of the FasTrax instruction sheet, there is additional space to make any comments about the course, the school, and suggested new curriculum. Please mail the FasTrax instruction sheet, with your comments, back to Western Schools in the envelope provided with your course order.

TRANSFERRING STUDY TIME

Upon completion of the course, transfer the total study time from your log sheet to question #25 in the Course Evaluation. The answers will be in ranges; please choose the proper hour range that best represents your study time. You MUST log your study time under question #25 on the course evaluation.

EXTENSIONS

You have two (2) years from the date of enrollment to complete this course. A six (6) month extension may be purchased. If after 30 months from the original enrollment date you do not complete the course, *your file will be closed and no certificate can be issued.*

CHANGE OF ADDRESS?

In the event you have moved during the completion of this course, please call our student services department at 1-800-618-1670, and we will update your file.

A GUARANTEE TO WHICH YOU'LL GIVE HIGH HONORS

If any continuing education course fails to meet your expectations or if you are not satisfied in any manner, for any reason, you may return it for an exchange or a refund (less shipping and handling) within 30 days. Software, video and audio courses must be returned unopened.

Thank you for enrolling at Western Schools!

WESTERN SCHOOLS
P.O. Box 1930
Brockton, MA 02303
(800) 438-8888
www.westernschools.com

Surviving and Thriving in Nursing

WESTERN
SCHOOLS
P.O. Box 1930
Brockton, MA 02303

Please use this log to total the number of hours you spend reading the text and taking the final examination

Date	Hours Spent
_____	_____
_____	_____
_____	_____
_____	_____
_____	_____
_____	_____
_____	_____
_____	_____
_____	_____
_____	_____
_____	_____
_____	_____
_____	_____

TOTAL ☐

Please log your study hours with submission of your final exam. To log your study time, fill in the appropriate circle under question 25 of the FasTrax® answer sheet under the Evaluation section.

Surviving and Thriving in Nursing

WESTERN SCHOOLS
CONTINUING EDUCATION EVALUATION

Instructions: Mark your answers to the following questions with a black pen on the Evaluation section of your FasTrax® answer sheet provided with this course. You should not return this sheet. Please use the scale below to rate the following statements:

A Agree Strongly	**C Disagree Somewhat**
B Agree Somewhat	**D Disagree Strongly**

The course content met the following education objectives:

1. Identified concepts and strategies related to self-management and time management.

2. Described the elements of chaos and how to use them to improve nursing practice.

3. Incorporated professional expectations for communication and interpersonal interactions.

4. Recognized different types of information and the role of technology in organizing data.

5. Explained essential concepts of organizational cultures and their impact on nursing practice environments.

6. Identified nursing roles related to leadership and management.

7. Differentiated between health and nursing care delivery models and their impact on practice.

8. Recognized the aspects of quality care that are essential to nursing.

9. Explained the impact of transdisciplinary care on patient outcomes and provider roles.

10. Selected alternative, complementary, and integrative healing practices that are useful in care situations.

11. Indicated strategies that support cultural competence and care.

12. Recognized significant workplace issues that impact nursing practice.

13. Explained legal issues and risk management strategies for professional practice.

14. Described ethical principles and how to apply them to nursing practice.

15. Selected a variety of educational offerings that support lifelong learning.

16. Indicated choices that support career management and development for nurses.

17. Identified how nursing roles are changing and emerging career options.

18. Recognized stress reduction approaches to improve individual lifestyles.

19. Specified the role of humor and its value in healing.

20. Indicated approaches to achieving a balanced life, based on a holistic perspective.

21. The content of this course was relevant to the objectives.

22. This offering met my professional education needs.

23. The objectives met the overall purpose/goal of the course.

24. The course was generally well-written and the subject matter explained thoroughly. (If no, please explain on the back of the FasTrax instruction sheet.)

25. **PLEASE LOG YOUR STUDY HOURS WITH SUBMISSION OF YOUR FINAL EXAM.**
    Please choose which best represents the total study hours it took to complete this 30-hour course.

    A. Less than 25 hours

    B. 25–28 hours

    C. 29–32 hours

    D. Greater than 32 hours

CONTENTS

Evaluation v

Figures and Tables xix

Pretest xxi

Introduction xxv

Chapter 1: Self-Management and Time Management 1

   Overview 1

   Critical Self-Assessment 1

      Challenge 1

      Activity Log 1

   Time Wasters 2

   Priorities and Perspectives 2

      Time Awareness 2

      Myths About Time 2

   Time Management Strategies 3

      Time Tools 3

      Application to Nursing Practice 4

   Self-Contracting 7

      Solutions 7

   Conclusion 8

   Exam Questions 9

Chapter 2: Thriving on Chaos 11

   Overview 11

   Coping with Uncertainty and Unpredictability 12

      Challenges 12

      Chaotic Work Environments 12

      Chaos Theory 12

      Application of Chaos Theory to Health Systems 13

      Application to Nursing Practice 14

   Responding to Innovation 16

      Accepting Innovation 16

      Impact on Nurses and Other Health Care Professionals 17

   Managing Innovation to Improve Nursing Practice 17

      Solutions 17

   Conclusion 18

Exam Questions 19

Chapter 3: Communication and Interpersonal Skills **21**

Overview 21

Communicating Effectively, Respectfully, and Compassionately 21

Communication Processes 22

Challenges 23

Effective Communication 23

Respectful Communication 23

Compassionate Communication 24

Application in a Clinical Setting 24

Documenting Patient Care 25

Purposes of Patient Health Records 25

Sources of Patient Information 25

Appropriate Documentation 26

Dealing with Verbal Conflict 27

Application to Nursing Practice 28

Becoming a Voice for Professional Change 28

Application to Occupational and Environmental Health Nurses 29

Solutions 29

Conclusion 29

Exam Questions 31

Chapter 4: Managing Technology and Information **33**

Overview 33

Challenges 33

Types of Information 33

Future Health Care Technologies 34

Information Seeking, Sorting, and Selecting 34

Introduction to the Internet and the World Wide Web (WWW) .35

Business and Institutional Systems 35

Seeking Information 35

Evaluating Web Sites 36

Sorting Information 36

Selecting Information 36

Using Technology to Organize Information 37

Nursing Classification Systems 38

North American Nursing Diagnosis Association (NANDA) 38

Omaha System 38

Home Health Care Classification 38

Nursing Interventions Classification (NIC) and Nursing Outcomes Classification (NOC) 39

Unified Nursing Language System (UNLS) 39

Computer-Based Patient Records (CPR) 39

Application to Nursing Practice 40

Using Information Technology for Education 40

Solutions 41

Conclusion 41

Exam Questions 43

Chapter 5: Organizational Cultures . . . . **.45**

Overview 45

Organizational Culture and Climate 45

Challenges 45

Organizational Culture 46

Organizational Climate 46

Values and Beliefs 46

Types of Health Care Organizations 47

Formal Organizational Structures 48

Informal Organizational Structures 49

Redesigning and Reengineering Health Care 49

Evolution of Organizational Processes 50

Changing Health Care Systems and Nursing 50

Sources of Conflict and Resolution Strategies 52

Resolving Conflicts 52

Solutions 53

Conclusion 54

Exam Questions 55

Chapter 6: Leadership and Management . . . . **.57**

Overview 57

Defining Management and Leadership 58

Challenges 58

Management 58

Leadership 58

Application to Nursing Practice 59

The Synergy Model 60

Comparison of Leadership and Management 61

Empowerment 61

Application to Nursing Practice 63

Decision-Maker 64

Clinical Decision-Making 64

Group Decision-Making 64

Problem-Solver 65

Role Model 66

Solutions 66

Conclusion 67

Exam Questions 69

Chapter 7: Health and Nursing Care Delivery Models **71**

Overview 71

Health and Nursing Care Delivery Models 71

Challenges 71

Delivery of Health Care in the United States 72

Primary Health Care 75

Health Literacy 75

A Systems Approach to Delivering Preventive Health Services 76

Application to Nursing Practice 77

Community-Based Practice 78

Clinical Pathways 79

Choosing a Nursing Care Delivery Model 80

Solutions 81

Group I 81

Group II 81

Conclusion 81

Exam Questions 83

Chapter 8: Quality Care **85**

Overview 85

Challenges 85

Critical Thinking and Clinical Decision-Making 86

Critical Thinking 86

Clinical Decision-Making 86

Case Management 87

Case Management Background 87

Application to Nursing Practice 88

Quality Indicators 88

Dimensions of Quality 88

Application to Nursing Practice 89

Quality Assessment 89

Quality Assurance 90

Total Quality Management 90

Outcome Measures and Quality Assessment 90

    Sources of Data 90

    Donabedian Model 91

    Application to Nursing Practice 92

Evidence-Based Practice 93

    Application to Nursing Practice 93

    Barriers to Implementation 94

Professional Practice Standards 94

    Solutions 94

Conclusion 95

Exam Questions 97

Chapter 9: Transdisciplinary Health Care **99**

Overview 99

Transdisciplinary Health Care 99

    Challenges 99

    Introduction 99

    Background and History of Transdisciplinary Health Care 100

    Pharmacist 100

    Dietitian 101

    Respiratory Therapist 101

    Social Worker 101

    Pastoral Representative 101

    Physical Therapist 101

    Occupational Therapist 102

    Speech-Language Pathologist 102

Collaboration 102

Team-Building Strategies 103

    Nurse-Physician Relationships 104

Planning Patient Care 105

    Solutions 105

Conclusion 106

Exam Questions 107

Chapter 10: Alternative, Complementary, and Integrative Healing Practices **109**

Overview 109

Patient Self-Care Choices 109

    Challenges 109

    Background 110

Reasons for Selecting Alternative Therapies 110

Self-Care Healing Processes 111

Alternative, Complementary, and Integrative Healing Therapies 111

Healing Therapies 112

Healing Traditions 112

Categories of Therapies 113

Alternative Healing Therapies 113

Complementary and Integrative Healing Therapies 113

Classifications of Therapies 113

Dietary Supplements 114

Herbal Therapies 114

Combining Therapies 115

Safety of Alternative Therapies 115

National Center for Complementary and Alternative Medicine 115

Payment for Alternative Therapies 115

Legal Dilemmas 116

Nursing and Combined Therapies 116

Spiritual Nursing 116

Learning about CAM 117

Solutions 117

Conclusion 117

Exam Questions 119

Chapter 11: Cultural Competence and Care **121**

Overview 121

Cultural Competence and Care 121

Challenges 121

Introduction to Cultural Competence and Care 122

Demographic Trends 122

Demographics of Violence 123

Demographics of Health Care Workers 123

Barriers to Nurses Being Culturally Competent 123

Recruitment of Minorities to Nursing 123

International Perspectives on Health 124

Cultural Values and Beliefs 124

International Nursing 126

Caring for Persons from Different Cultures 126

Cultural Assessment - Nurses 127

Cultural Assessment - Patients 127

       Cultural Nutrition Assessment 127

       Communication 128

       Sickness and Cures 128

       Nurses and Ethical Conflicts 128

       Solutions 128

    Conclusion 129

    Exam Questions 131

Chapter 12: Workplace Issues **133**

    Overview 133

       Challenges 133

    Workplace Safety 134

       Employee Safety 134

       Workplace Violence 134

       Sexual Harassment 136

       Latex Allergy 136

       Needlestick Injuries 136

       Back Injury 137

       Physical Environment 137

    Staffing Patterns and Work Hours 137

       Work Environment 138

       Absenteeism 138

       Staffing 139

       Mandatory Overtime 140

    Nurses in Need of Care 141

       Protecting Whistle-Blowers 142

       Recovery 142

       Patient Safety 142

    Collective Bargaining 143

       Formal Negotiations 143

       Pros and Cons of Collective Bargaining 144

       Solutions 144

    Conclusion 144

    Exam Questions 145

Chapter 13: Legal Practice **147**

    Overview 147

       Challenges 147

    Introduction 147

       Defining and Creating Laws 148

Types of Laws 148

Preventive Practice 149

Professional Liability Insurance .150

Common Litigation Issues 151

Risk Management 152

Advance Directives 153

Living Wills 153

Durable Power of Attorney for Health Care 153

Solutions 153

Conclusion 154

Exam Questions 155

Chapter 14: Ethical Practice 157

Overview 157

Introduction 157

Challenges 157

The Ethics of Public and Health Policy 158

Advocacy 159

Professional Advocacy 159

Burnout 159

Moral Distress 159

From Moral Distress to Moral Work 159

Moving from Distress to Action .160

Patient Advocacy 160

Advocating for Patient Empowerment 161

Advocating for Specific Age Groups 161

Nurses Advocating for Each Other 161

Confidentiality and Privacy 161

Participating in Research 162

Ethical Caring 162

Solutions 163

Conclusion 163

Exam Questions 165

Chapter 15: Lifelong Learning 167

Overview 167

Challenges 167

Formal and Informal Education 167

Continuous, Lifelong Learning 169

Readiness to Learn 169

Emotional Readiness 170

Experiential Readiness 171

Knowledge Readiness 172

Educational Designs and Delivery 172

Educational Material Design 172

Educational Delivery Options 173

Solutions 174

Conclusion 175

Exam Questions 177

Chapter 16: Managing Your Career **179**

Overview 179

Where You Are Today 179

Challenges 179

The Beginning 180

At the Crossroads 180

Planning for Your Future 181

Self-Assessment 181

Career Development 182

Professional Portfolio 182

Portfolio Sections 183

Writing a Résumé 183

Résumés 183

Interviewing 183

Strategies for Self-Development 184

Personal Self-Development 184

Professional Self-Development 185

Solutions 185

Conclusion 186

Exam Questions 187

Chapter 17: Changing Roles and Opportunities in Nursing **189**

Overview 189

Traditional and Emerging Nursing Roles 189

Challenges 189

Nursing Roles 190

Managing Changing Roles 191

New Roles 191

Career Opportunities: Where Are Nurses Working and What Are They Doing? 192

NonTraditional and Emerging Nursing Careers 192

Ambulatory Care Settings 192

Special Care Centers 192

Community Nursing Centers 193

Community Education 193

Forensic Nursing 193

Telehealth 193

Business/Corporate Nursing Careers 193

Consulting 194

Nurse Entrepreneurs 194

Advanced Practice Nursing 194

Informatics Nurse Specialist 194

Case Managers 195

Quality Manager 195

Flight Nurse 195

Solutions 195

Conclusion 195

Exam Questions 197

Chapter 18: Stress Reduction **199**

Overview 199

Stress 199

Challenges 199

Stressed Out 199

Defining Stress 200

Mind and Body Interactions 200

Personality, Disease, and Stress 201

Measuring Your Stress 201

Stress-Reducing Options 201

Relaxation Techniques 202

Lifestyle Changes 202

Strategies for Lifestyle Changes 202

Developing Coping Strategies 203

Increasing Stress Tolerance 203

Coping Statements 203

Living With Stress 203

Solutions 205

Conclusion 205

Exam Questions 207

Chapter 19: Humor **209**

Overview 209

    Challenges 209

Value of Humor and Laughter 210

Positive Humor 210

Healing Through Humor 211

Role of Humor in Nursing Practice 211

    Benefits of Humor for Nurses 211

    Benefits of Humor for Patients 212

    Solutions 212

Conclusion 213

Exam Questions 215

Chapter 20: Balancing Your Life — A Holistic Perspective **217**

Overview 217

    Challenges 217

Whole Person Wellness 217

    Wellness Programs 219

    Principles of Whole Person Wellness 219

Mind-Body Connection 219

Achieving a Healthy Environment 219

    Noise Pollution 220

    Joint Work Space 220

Maintaining Total Wellness 221

    Decision-Making Model 221

    Analysis Model 221

    Maintaining Total Wellness in Work Settings 222

    Solutions 222

Conclusion 222

Exam Questions 223

Resources **225**

Glossary **229**

Bibliography **235**

Index **243**

Pretest Key **253**

FIGURES AND TABLES

Chapter 3

Figure 3: Circular Communication Process 22

Chapter 6

Table 6-1: Leadership Traits 61

Table 6-2: Comparison of Leader and Manager Qualities and Behaviors 62

Chapter 9

Table 9-1: Comparison of Patient Planning Activities by Disciplines 105

Chapter 10

Table 10-1: Complementary Therapies Used in Nursing Practice 113

Chapter 17

Table 17-1: Employment Settings 192

Chapter 20

Table 20-1: Decision-Making Model Work sheet 221

PRETEST

1. Begin this course by taking the Pretest. Circle the answers to the questions on this page, or write the answers on a separate sheet of paper. Do not log answers to the Pretest questions on the FasTrax test sheet included with the course.

2. Compare your answers to the PRETEST KEY located in the back of the book. The Pretest answer key indicates the course chapter where the content of that question is discussed. Make note of the questions you missed, so that you can focus on those areas as you complete the course.

3. Complete the course by reading each chapter and completing the exam questions at the end of the chapter. Answers to these exam questions should be logged on the FasTrax test sheet included with the course.

1. Nurses are very busy and must use their time wisely. A positive time-saving strategy is

    a. working very hard to get things done

    b. delaying making decisions until they are really needed.

    c. preplanning activities so there is enough time to accomplish them.

    d. delegating decision-making to other staff and coworkers to save time.

2. A major change in nursing practice is the expectation that nurses

    a. take care of many more patients than in the past.

    b. earn advanced degrees and accept administrative positions.

    c. adapt to uncertainty and unpredictability in the workplace.

    d. learn computer skills to manage patient care information.

3. A contemporary view of communication includes

    a. circular elements that look at relationships.

    b. linear elements that look at relationships.

    c. giving everyone the opportunity to share ideas.

    d. giving experts the opportunity to share their knowledge.

4. Technology has had the greatest impact in the area of

    a. developing new markets for information.

    b. expanding communication channels.

    c. increasing communication options.

    d. generating and sharing information.

5. Practice settings for nurses are undergoing many changes, primarily because

    a. new medications and treatments are available.

    b. redesign and reengineering are altering organizations to assure survival.

    c. nurses are demanding changes in their work environments.

    d. outside agencies are changing requirements for health care organizations.

6. Staff nurses need leadership skills because

   a. of their responsibilities for managing patient care.

   b. they may decide in the future to accept a charge nurse position.

   c. they may need to fill in for charge nurses when they are ill.

   d. it will help them advance on the hospital career ladder.

7. Health care delivery in the United States is unique, compared to other developed countries, because of

   a. a unified approach to providing different levels of care in a variety of settings.

   b. efficient methods that provide cost-effective and quality care.

   c. diverse approaches to providing care, many providers, and huge, complex systems.

   d. the many professionals, with licenses and credentials, who provide care.

8. The American Nurses Association developed a social policy statement for the purpose of sharing nursing's

   a. valuable services rendered to the public in all different settings.

   b. commitment to quality care and positive outcomes.

   c. ability to work collaboratively with other health care professionals.

   d. relationship with society and its obligations to those who receive care.

9. Health care professionals frequently work together to plan and provide care to meet the complex needs of patients. A reason for this collaboration is

   a. patients and family members want everything possible done.

   b. medicine and nursing, as well as other disciplines, are highly specialized.

   c. it is a cost-effective approach to providing different services.

   d. television programs portray many different persons giving care.

10. Alternative, complementary, and integrative therapies are increasingly used by consumers because

   a. Americans like to try new approaches and products to improve their health.

   b. consumers do not like many of the modern treatments physicians recommend.

   c. there is increasing cultural and ethnic diversity in the U.S. population.

   d. old-fashioned remedies are always better than new ones.

11. Changes in population demographics raise questions for health care providers and nurses regarding

   a. the cultural practices that impact health seeking behaviors and the ability to follow treatment plans.

   b. the changes that diverse populations must make in their values and beliefs to fit with Western medicine.

   c. why demographics are changing and how the changes can be slowed.

   d. the impact of changing demographics on global health issues.

12. Nurses face numerous workplace issues such as heavy workloads. The consequences to individual nurses are

    a. hospitals have to pay more for agency nurses.

    b. the ability to make higher salaries.

    c. increased organizational commitment.

    d. burnout, fatigue, and potential patient safety concerns.

13. Nurses prefer to stay out of court and practice legally. One way to do that is to

    a. become an expert on legal matters.

    b. use knowledge and resources to prevent problems.

    c. use coworkers and supervisors to keep you legal.

    d. ask patients and family members if they are pleased with your care.

14. Ethical issues require nurses to determine if they "should" carry out an action. An example of an ethical issue is

    a. giving IV antibiotics when a confused patient yells he does not want it.

    b. following the hospital policy to report patient falls.

    c. supporting a family decision not to resuscitate their child.

    d. giving information about nonsurgical options to a patient who is scheduled for surgery.

15. Lifelong learning refers to the professional responsibility of nurses to keep their knowledge current and to maintain clinical skills. The best way to do that is to

    a. take advantage of different informal and formal educational opportunities.

    b. earn an additional academic degree.

    c. attend all the staff development activities at the hospital.

    d. take advantage of as many online CE courses as possible.

16. Career planning and development are essential for nurses because of the changing health care environment and new role expectations. Nurses need to start career planning when they

    a. are tired of their current job and want to try something different.

    b. find out that coworkers plan to earn certification or another degree.

    c. begin their careers so they have some goals identified.

    d. have worked for 10 years, so they know what they really want to do.

17. Until recently, nurses had limited choices of roles and careers because nurses worked primarily in

    a. settings where they did not have opportunities to have career options.

    b. hospitals as staff nurses doing bedside care or in supervisory positions.

    c. private duty settings where there was no opportunity for advancement.

    d. physician offices where the roles were limited to supporting the physicians.

18. Joyce is a new graduate who is just starting her first job. She felt going to school was very stressful. She now realizes that starting her new job is more stressful because she has to

    a. move and get settled in her new location and apartment.
    b. decide what benefits she wants and how many shifts to work each week.
    c. find where everything is on her unit and in the hospital.
    d. learn how to function in her work setting.

19. Human nature has the capacity for humor; it adds fun and joy to our lives. An additional value of humor is

    a. calling attention others' weaknesses.
    b. helping us get along better with friends.
    c. helping us physically and emotionally.
    d. displaying our skill at delivering jokes.

20. Nurses have a personal and professional stake in achieving balance in their lives because it will help them

    a. make health choices that support wellness.
    b. keep their families happy.
    c. begin to feel better and reduce illnesses.
    d. start a journey to explore the meaning of life.

CHAPTER 1

SELF-MANAGEMENT AND TIME MANAGEMENT

CHAPTER OBJECTIVE

After studying this chapter, you will be able to identify concepts and strategies related to self-management and time management.

LEARNING OBJECTIVES

At the end of this chapter, you will be able to

1. recognize your ability to manage your personal and professional time.

2. select time management strategies.

3. choose strategies to reduce time wasters and increase efficiency.

OVERVIEW

Self-management and time management go hand in hand. In our society today, there is never enough time. Nurses have many competing interests for their time: children, partners, professional activities, church responsibilities, community participation, education, professional development, and many other responsibilities. How do we find more time to do everything we need and want to do? We need to take charge of our time, figure out how we spend it, and find ways to use time effectively.

CRITICAL SELF-ASSESSMENT

Challenge

Susan is married, has two children in grade school, usually works three 12-hour shifts, is taking one class toward a BSN degree, and actively participates in her children's activities. She sleeps about 6 hours each night and finds it difficult to manage her household chores. Her husband is a salesman, travels during the week, and does some of the outdoor chores. She realizes that she cannot continue to live this way. At work, the nurses often face short staffing. They have no control over admissions. She needs more time. One place for Susan to start is to determine how she uses her time. She starts by keeping track of all her activities in a journal. This will serve as the basis for improving how she manages time.

Activity Log

Record your activities periodically each day. Ideally, write them down when they occur. Also, write down how you feel: tired, alert, stressed, or energetic. After a week of keeping track of your activities and feelings, you can analyze what you did and how you felt (Activity logs, n.d.). But first, let us look at time wasters.

1

TIME WASTERS

There are many required tasks we do each day. We may not want to do them or enjoy them. Laundry, cleaning the house, repetitive patient care tasks, and required paperwork are examples. We can find ways to make them more pleasant and do them more efficiently. Time wasters, on the other hand, are tasks that have few benefits and satisfaction compared to other activities we could be doing. Time wasters are categorized as internal or external. Internal time wasters include failure to set goals and priorities, not setting time limits, not listening, making errors, and inadequate planning (Cherry & Jacob, 2002). External time wasters are created by persons and events in our environment. They include numerous meetings, being required to work on tasks that have few positive outcomes, and organizational processes that are not streamlined. We want to manage our time well but often fail.

Brumm (2002a) describes why we fail at time-management. It is because we fall into "time traps." They include

- trying to accomplish too much in too little time.
- lack of self-discipline in accomplishing deadlines.
- personal disorganization; indecision, confusion about priorities, and procrastination.
- too much talk and socializing at work.
- poor communication and poor listening skills.

Our culture, time perceptions, educational, and work experiences, and personality all contribute to how we view and manage time. You have probably observed persons who are very busy and accomplish a great deal. Others have minimal obligations and accomplish very little. Becoming more aware of time will help us avoid time wasters.

PRIORITIES AND PERSPECTIVES

Time Awareness

We are all aware of time. It is discussed every day. Our lives revolve around it. What time do we have to get up, to be at work, to pick children up from their activities, and to attend functions? Nursing practice is extremely time oriented, with many activities scheduled. Professional and general interest media (TV, radio, journals, magazines, and online sources) all address the issue of lack of time.

Myths About Time

Mackenzie, in Cherry & Jacob (2002), studied time management for years by conducting research, lecturing, and writing. Several myths about time management emerged.

- Activity is the way to get things done. The problem is, activity does not necessarily end in results. You can spend time doing the same things over and over without achieving a goal. You keep reading and looking at vacation information but never reach a decision. At work, you keep arranging everything in the nurses station but do not feel it is the best way. The arrangement does not improve efficiency.

- Decisions made at a high level are the best. Ideally, decisions made at the lowest level possible, by those most affected, have the best chance for success.

- Many people find it difficult to make decisions and believe that delaying them will result in better outcomes. The problem is that delaying decisions allows less time. The decisions are more critical. There is less time to correct problems or make adjustments. A panic mode may occur with poor decision-making.

- Delegating decision-making is thought to save time. Effective delegation is useful in the work setting but takes planning. Nurses are responsible for their actions and delegating to others can be hazardous. They have to make the decisions that are critical to patient care and maintaining professional standards.

- Omnipotence is a pathological belief that personally doing an activity will give better results than if someone else did it. It is a myth because no one is indispensable. Current information must be shared so others can carry out procedures at work or share family responsibilities.

- Some people always seem to be working hard and actually are overworking. They do more than others, are always busy with home projects, and stay at work long after the other staff have left. Is that person efficient or effective?

- Efficiency is often tied to effectiveness. If we complete projects with efficiency, are we also effective? The myth is that efficient people are also the most effective. Doing things right is being efficient and effectiveness means doing the right things right. You can very efficiently do the wrong thing. Giving medications on time is efficient but giving the wrong ones is not effective. Treating a clogged drain by pouring something down the pipe may be efficient over the short term but does not effectively address the underlying problem.

- Hard work is an American virtue. Is it true that the harder we work the more we get done? Time spent planning results in positive outcomes. The idea is to work smarter. Planning nursing and home activities means having the resources and equipment ready. It also means having enough time to complete the project. Effective planning and hard work help achieve positive outcomes.

- A nurse manager has an open door policy. The message is that he or she is available all the time. Are his or her communication and effectiveness enhanced? The reality is that he may have many interruptions and his actual work

time is diminished. Planned availability increased productivity.

- Many people believe that defining the problem correctly is the easy part of solving a problem. Actually, the wrong problem may be identified. A great deal of time, effort, and resources are often spent working on the wrong problem. Spend time assessing the situation, get input from others, and be clear about what you need to accomplish.

- We all want to "save" time. It is impossible to put time in a bank. Shortcuts are one strategy used to save time. The problem is that shortcuts may take more time. Communication may be incomplete or actions may be inadequate. The outcome of using shortcuts may be loss of time.

- Time shortage is another myth. We all have the same amount of time. Some people do not use time wisely and therefore do not reach their goals. Preplanning, setting priorities, and being clear about priorities all contribute to using time more effectively.

- We all use the expression "time flies." We envision time having wings and quickly departing. Preplanning helps to schedule enough time for activities.

- Is time against you? Many people are chronically late and complain that time just runs out. They get ready for work, meet friends, or arrive at meetings 15 minutes late. Something always happens that keeps them from getting there on time. It seems to be always beyond their control (Cherry & Jacob, 2002).

Strategies to manage time can be found in many sources. You have to review them and select the ones you can apply to your life.

TIME MANAGEMENT STRATEGIES

Often we need to pay attention to organize how we use our time. When people cannot manage their time, they feel a sense of personal failure. Looking at different ways to organize your time is more objective than blaming yourself.

Time Tools

Brumm (2002a), suggested some time tools.

Put your time in a bank account. For example, there are 168 hours in each week. The time can be broken down to half or quarter hours. Write down how much time you spend each week on all your activities. You can group repetitive things together. If you work five days a week, and it takes you a total of an hour to get to and from work, then that is five hours. Add all your activities and subtract them from the 168 hours. You may find you are over-committed or that you actually have time to do something you enjoy.

Another approach is to equate your time commitments to a cluttered closet. We are all familiar with too much stuff in our homes for the space available. We clean out our closets, have sales, give items to family members, and donate them. Schedules are similar to space. Time is limited, 168 hours in each week. We have too many tasks to fit the time. Organizing your schedule so activities follow one after another or occur on certain days can increase efficiency. Realistically look at how much time a task will take and fit it into the space needed. Spacing it out over time may help. Meeting less often may allow more time for actually working on a project.

A nursing care process (Brumm, 2002b) can be used to analyze your current time management abilities and to develop a new or revised plan if needed. Assess your current/potential time management needs by collecting and organizing information. Develop a plan that includes goals and desired outcomes. Set priorities, develop a timeline, and select interventions. Periodically evaluate what you have accomplished. Change various elements of your plan or add new ones.

This process allows you to monitor yourself and to determine how you are spending your time and what you want to change. Look at your career and professional development goals. Relate them to how you spend your time. If you want to be a nurse practitioner or become certified in a clinical specialty, you need to allocate time. You can also determine what to give up in order to achieve your goals. Many nurses have made efforts to manage themselves so they can manage their time.

Application to Nursing Practice

Bowers, Lauring, and Jacobson (2001) conducted a study to understand how nurses in long-term care (LTC) facilities are affected by their working conditions. Eighteen nurses from two LTC facilities participated in the interviews. Time was a very important factor. The nurses were working in situations where they had too little time and many interruptions. Some strategies they used were: minimizing, prioritizing, pacing, combining, and sequencing.

Minimizing: The LTC nurses tried minimizing the time it took to do required tasks. An important element was to keep the same assignments, so they set up routines. A second approach was to organize their work according to a pattern, such as by task or resident. The task approach supported completing work on time, as when giving medications. Residents saw several different people with this approach, and so there was a risk of fragmented care. The resident approach worked well for the person receiving the care. Some residents had requirements that interrupted the routine, so time became an issue again.

Prioritizing: Prioritizing and reprioritizing work can help. The nurses in this study made judgments about what was most important, what had to be done now, and what could not be done. A resident experiencing severe respiratory problems needs immediate help, so giving medications may have to wait. The visibility of the need may dictate the priority. The nurses wanted to spend more time with the residents, but that became a low priority when time was an issue.

Creating new time, when time is short, was another strategy the nurses used.

Pacing: The pace of work varied, depending on the number of residents and staffing. Nurses felt the day was just "a blur" when they had to work at a fast pace. Their work focused on technical, visible, and urgent tasks. Nurses were frustrated and morale was low when they had to work faster for a period of time.

Combining: Combining or bundling tasks also helped. Nurses combined giving medications with feeding some patients or coordinated some medication schedules, advancing one schedule and delaying another so that medications could be delivered together. The nurses were concerned about the consequences but in the absence of problems, they continued.

Sequencing: Changing the sequence of tasks created new time. When nurses completed their weekly summaries early in the day, they were available if something happened later. Working around what the nursing assistants were doing resulted in fewer interruptions.

Carving out periods of inaccessibility was an effective technique. Verbal and nonverbal messages were sent to residents and family members to indicate that the nurses could not spend time in some situations. Standing outside a room or putting the medicine cart in front to separate themselves were behaviors they used. The nurses did not enjoy communicating inaccessibility. Residents observed those patterns and began lowering their expectations of what the nurses would do.

Another strategy was to convert wasted or down time to useful time. For example, while giving medications, the nurses would do quick assessments of behavior, orientation, or physical status. They also observed the rooms to see that the nursing assistants had done their work. A key to this strategy was that they could not be sidetracked by conversation or other tasks.

The LTC nurses tried to maximize actual time, the time they had to complete their work. Overtime was not an option. Actual time included shift times, off time, and time created by using various strategies. The nurses in this study came to work early, reduced meal and break times, and read required materials at home. Time early in the day was more likely spent with residents than time later in the day. If nurses had only a few minutes at the end of a shift, getting involved with a resident could take too much time.

It was not always possible to create new time. Changing work responsibilities, to even out the work, could be beneficial. Passing work on to other shifts or support personnel did create tensions. Since everyone had time issues, this strategy was not helpful.

Nurses' efforts to manage their time had cascade effects. As they tried different strategies, less time was spent assessing residents, which made it hard to find problems early and affected health outcomes. Legal, ethical, quality, and emotional concerns resulted from the time constraint issue. Work was divided into "must do" and "should do" work. When time was restricted, it was an effort just to complete the "must do" work. Staff felt the consequences of being rushed. They were not doing their work as they wanted. They felt frustrated and dissatisfied. They were concerned about quality (Bowers, Lauring, and Jacobson, 2001).

Staffing needs to be increased in many environments. Nurses must have a voice in what goes into providing quality care. Beyond staff to resident ratios, there are the many time-consuming but valuable activities that promote quality and prevent health problems.

Nurses in home care settings also experience the challenges of managing time. They work in unstructured environments and do not have others to finish their work. New nurses, especially, may find it challenging to organize each workday. Some hints are:

- List key tasks for each day of the week. How long does it take to get ready for visits, what is the travel time, how long do you spend with clients? Estimate the time spent on other activities; finding supplies, charting, telephone tag, and meetings.

- Control your calendar by sketching out the next week or two. Insert time at the end of each day to catch up. When scheduling visits, allow enough time between them for charting. Stick to the time allotted for various activities. Insist that meetings start and end on time. Use technology to communicate, keep records, and complete professional development activities.

- Minimize time in the office to avoid distractions. Have a portable office in your car. Stock it with forms, supplies, and a writing board. As you work through your day, develop a list of specific things you need to get done when you do go back to the office.

- Handle paper only once. Read it, then respond, file, or discard it.

- Simplify documentation when possible. Nurses can work together to develop checklists, flow sheets, and standardized care plans. Computerized record-keeping may be an option. Volunteer to test the new systems so you know if they really meet your needs.

- Include time in your schedule for yourself and others. Be responsive to requests and give complete information. Include time in your schedule for exercise, family responsibilities, and social activities.

- Plan ahead to be ready for the next day or week. Make sure your car is ready. Have office and client supplies ready.

It is estimated that 20% of our activities generate 80% of our results. Better time management means more time for things we really want to do (Sherry, 2002).

When nurses move to new positions, with more managerial responsibilities, they have to look at new ways to manage themselves and others. How they spend their time changes and the demands increase. As managers, nurses must prioritize what is most important for the position. Scheduling all the "must do" activities allows you to see how much time you have for other activities.

Nurse managers especially will benefit from using technology to keep track of schedules. Many nurse managers use personal digital assistants (PDAs). Technology also helps with daily, weekly, monthly, quarterly, and yearly planning. There is software for project planning that may be especially useful for large projects that involve many other departments.

To survive as a nurse manager, start each day by determining what is really important. Do the most difficult in the morning. Instead of putting off less attractive tasks, complete the high priority items and move down the list.

Knowing how to deal with interruptions is an important managerial skill. Keep focused on what you set out to do.

A nurse manager must be a presence for the staff. Create a balance between interacting with people and keeping focused on your essential tasks. Post times on your office door when you are available. Keep the time slots short, 15 minutes each.

Staff can sign up when they are free. Make time for staff on all the shifts.

As a manager, you will have to set limits for interacting with staff. Some people have a lot of needs and will want to share all their problems. Others will try to dump their work on you. Learning to say no is an important skill.

At this level, it helps to work with a mentor to learn new skills. Find support from other managers by networking and attending professional development programs.

A manager provides balance and perspective. Remain objective. Do not get caught up in emotions. Others may become angry or upset. You have to manage yourself, stay focused, and resolve volatile situations.

For the sake of all concerned, always keep a sense of humor. Humor can ease a tense situation. Encourage everyone to share experiences that had a humorous twist. Post humor for the staff to make them chuckle. Be careful that humor does not offend anyone; it must not be directed at individuals (Dunbar, 2002). Finding solutions to our time challenges means actually putting them into practice.

SELF-CONTRACTING

We know that we have to manage ourselves if we are going to manage our time. Self-contracting lets us take control of our time and organize it so we can meet our personal and professional goals, as well as enjoy life along the way.

Solutions

Susan decides she needs to face the time challenges in her life. She started reading information about time management and attends a workshop. With the information from those sources, she starts to plan. She has two goals: one is to have the family participate in a time management plan, and the other is to develop her own plan. The family dis-

cusses their time issues. They agree they have too many scheduled activities, feel pressured to be ready for what they need to do, and are often trying to get organized at the last minute. The family started to develop a plan with a large monthly calendar and list of "must do" things. Once that was developed, they could see how they spent their time.

Routines for school and work days were developed to help the whole family. They planned for their daily and weekly scheduled activities. After dinner, they got things ready for the next day. Books, school items, and clothes were put in the same spot. Breakfast items were planned and organized. Lunches were assembled. The family created a list for items and errands to be added during the week. Whoever was home on the weekend shared household and other chores. The children kept to the same evening and morning routines no matter who was caring for them.

Because Susan and her husband juggle such demanding schedules, the family saw the need to prioritize what was important to each of them. Carpooling helped with schedules. Other parents also had demanding schedules, so monthly driving times were planned.

Over-scheduling was also an issue. The children had added too many activities. The children agreed to complete their current schedule and to be selective about what they would do in the next sessions. Susan was attending school but had not given up anything when she started school. Susan decided to give up one church day and one social activity while she was taking classes. Her husband felt pressure because he was gone four nights during the week and had so much to do when he was home. They reviewed their budget and decided to hire help for yard work.

After a month of using the time management strategies, the family saw the benefits. They were organized for the essential things, felt less pressure, and actually had more free time. Susan started working on her own schedule. She decided not to schedule any extra activities on the days she worked. When she came home, she spent time with the children, got everyone ready for the next day, and relaxed. She went to bed an hour earlier than previously.

Susan also set aside blocks of time to study rather than trying to do that every day, becoming more effective and efficient. She and her co-workers brainstormed about ways to accommodate new admissions and to share unequal workloads. The team efforts made work less stressful, enhanced their interpersonal skills, and improved communication.

CONCLUSION

Susan and her family self-contracted to change how they managed their time. Each month they reviewed what they were doing and actually looked for additional ways to manage time.

Our lives change. There are new responsibilities and opportunities. We can all benefit from assessing our current time and self-management skills and making changes that improve the quality of our lives.

EXAM QUESTIONS

CHAPTER 1
Questions 1-5

1. According to Brumm (2002a), one time trap that may contribute to failures in time management is

   a. trying to accomplish a few projects in a quality manner.

   b. not working hard enough.

   c. working too hard on several projects.

   d. trying to accomplish too much in too little time.

2. The truth about time management is

   a. Activity – "Just Do it"– is the best way to get things done.

   b. Delaying decisions will result in better outcomes.

   c. Decisions made by those most affected, have the best chance for success.

   d. Doing something yourself will give better results than if someone else did it.

3. Betty, a new nurse manager on a busy OB unit, has an open door policy for the staff and finds that

   a. interruptions reduce the work she accomplishes.

   b. some staff check with her at least every hour.

   c. productivity is increased.

   d. effectiveness is increased.

4. Establishing routines such as keeping the same work assignment and organizing work into patterns are examples of the time management strategy

   a. minimizing

   b. prioritizing

   c. pacing

   d. sequencing

5. Nurses in a long term care setting tried managing their time by

   a. helping each other with work assignments.

   b. reducing the number of baths scheduled each week.

   c. converting wasted down time to useful time.

   d. telling the supervisor they had too little time.

CHAPTER 2

THRIVING ON CHAOS

CHAPTER OBJECTIVE

After studying this chapter, you will be able to describe the elements of chaos and use them to improve nursing practice.

LEARNING OBJECTIVES

After studying this chapter, you will be able to

1. recognize the concept of chaos as it relates to uncertainty and unpredictability.

2. examine how chaos influences the adoption of innovations.

3. indicate the positive and negative consequences of adopting innovations.

OVERVIEW

We face uncertainty and unpredictability in the world every day. Is the United States going to be involved in a conflict? Will there be terrorist attacks? Will we keep our jobs? Will our children be safe? How will we cope with the death of our parents? Nurses face these issues in their personal lives and then go to work where they also face similar workplace and patient issues.

Nurses recognize that life keeps changing. Along with change comes innovation; new ways of documenting patient care, improved IV pumps, new medications, and revised policies and proce-

dures. There are many choices, and it is not possible to accept all change. Decisions must be made about when to accept change and how to introduce it. Some nurses are reluctant to change because they are too comfortable with what they have been doing for years. Change is only worth pursuing when it brings added benefits to our society.

Advancements in technology are the major driver of change. Systems are added to a work setting to reduce costs and increase efficiency. The change then filters to everyone in the organization. The business office develops the capability to purchase supplies online, pay bills by direct transfer, and do direct deposit for payroll. Supplies then must be scanned when they are used on the unit and employees are required to use direct deposit.

Nurses need preparation and training so they are ready for the innovations they experience. The world, our society, health care and the nursing profession are in a time of rapid change. Nurses need to be aware of their own skills, values, and ability to adapt. Nursing is more than taking care of patients. It is working within systems that are changing, requiring employees to adapt to uncertainty and unpredictability in the workplace.

COPING WITH UNCERTAINTY AND UNPREDICTABILITY

Challenges

Ten nurses work in a busy outpatient clinic. They primarily work with people who have diabetes. They face two major challenges. The corporate office has announced that a new computer system will be installed in the clinics and the main office. Everything will be networked. The nurses have little experience with computers and dread going through the transition. A review by the quality assurance department indicates that patient outcomes did not meet corporate or national standards. Patients have not been managing their conditions well. They come to the clinic for regular visits but have had episodes of hyperglycemia and hypoglycemia. Some have gone to the emergency room when the clinic was closed. Many patients were found to be unable to verbalize what they were supposed to do to manage their diabetes.

The nurses see the need to be able to predict the outcomes of the patient teaching activities. The patients must be able to manage their care. The patients are from different ethnic and cultural backgrounds; represent a spectrum of age groups; and have a variety of English literacy skills.

In this particular setting, all the nurses teach patients. Each nurse has a set approach to teaching. They may use visual aids or videos, do verbal presentations, or read from the handouts. Nurses who use different approaches each time, depending on their own preferences and the available resources, have varying outcomes. They randomize the initial conditions and get very different results.

A deterministic teaching approach uses the same methods for all patients. Small changes do not affect the outcomes. Chaotic relationships are very dependent on the initial conditions of the system.

The goal with these patients is to predict outcomes. A nurse may carefully structure the initial conditions of teaching for different groups, based on adult learning principles and group characteristics. Evaluation data verifies that the outcomes are mixed. Some patients do well in managing their diabetes and others do not. With the current uncertainty and unpredictability, the nurses feel as if everything is chaotic. How will they meet these challenges? Who will support them as they go through these major changes?

Chaotic Work Environments

Work environments are constantly undergoing change and redesign. The goal is usually to improve quality and reduce costs. Nurses often describe their work settings as stressful and chaotic. It is logical to imagine that a redesign effort that results in improved quality of care would also improve the work environment. Nurses must recognize that chaos is necessary for survival and develop strategies to restructure their own environments.

Chaos Theory

Chaos theory was first described as a mathematical concept in 1975. The work of mathematicians, as early as the 1700s, laid the groundwork. The theory continues to develop and researchers look for a sense of order in seemingly disorganized systems. Scientists and researchers explore relationships that are classified as deterministic, random, or chaotic.

Chaos theory is one attempt to explain how the universe is organized. Chaos theory is still being developed but the principles are useful when looking at environmental changes. The universe is not an orderly place where it is possible to predict what is going to happen. When an organization designs a permanent structure, it will fail if the structure cannot adapt and respond to the changing environment (Robinson & Kish, 2001).

Deterministic Relationships

This type of relationship is predictable because the initial conditions in the system and small changes that occur later do not impact outcomes.

Random Relationships

Completely different results occur with little or no changes in the initial conditions of the system.

Chaotic Relationships

Somewhere between the deterministic and random relationships is where chaotic relationships are found. Long term predictions cannot be made because outcomes depend so much on the initial conditions of the system (Lanza, 2000).

The word chaos is used differently in stressful situations. Emergency rooms in Western Australia were said to be in chaos due to a shortage of nurses. Patients were in the hallways for up to two days before being admitted. The hospitals often had twice as many patients as they could care for and ran out of stretchers. A task force had been set up earlier to find solutions to the problem but it had failed. Some blamed mismanagement for the problem. The chief nurse said the problem was caused by a chronic shortage of nurses (Anonymous, 2002b).

Application of Chaos Theory to Health Systems

For the last 100 years, health care environments have had a machine-like precision approach to organization. Command and control have been centralized with layers of authority. "Chain of command," "chief officers" with assistants, and "charge nurse" are terms that described a paternalistic and inwardly focused organization. Some of these structures are changing as the changing world is mirrored in the increasing complexity of health care systems. Expanding information and access to information has shortened the cycle of change (Herbert, 1999).

Inova Health System

Characteristics of a complex, adaptive system include

- free distribution of information,
- innovation and creativity,
- encouraging learning and adaptability,
- risk taking (Herbert, 1999).

Inova Health System has transformed itself into a complex, adaptive system on the constructive edge of chaos. It started by representing the whole system in one room. Thousands of people were involved in the process. People in the system started working across boundaries of roles, functions, operating divisions, different locations, and disciplines. New communication strategies such as Web pages and e-mail were developed. The people within the system demonstrated the ability to change the system to meet the challenges of the future (Herbert, 1999).

The redesign process reversed assumptions about change. It was not a top-down process, nor was it built on cause and effect. New structures were created that supported collective decision-making and participation. There was a new tolerance for ambiguity. Individuals were challenged to think in new ways by becoming immersed in large group interventions. Transformation occurred at all levels; personal, group, and organization (Herbert, 1999).

Mercer Medical Center

The hypothetical, fictitious case of Mercer presented here illustrates how there is pressure and uncertainty when responding to needed innovations. Mercer Medical Center is a 450-bed community hospital in a metropolitan area. It has been competing with other health care groups to expand its business by developing more managed care partners.

There is the perception in the business community that health care systems do not have the most current technology. A potential customer has inquired about the capability of Mercer's information system. Another hospital group is known to be installing a new information system. Mercer's CEO now indicates they are also going to install the same system very soon.

Mercer did not have a good experience with its attempt to implement a new information management system two years ago, when a nursing documentation system was implemented with little input and agreement from medical, nursing, and other staff. There were many technical problems. A great deal of money was spent on the project, but it was abandoned shortly after it was launched. A newer system was installed and everyone had to learn a second new set of operations.

Facing another change, the medical center wants to do it right this time. Working with the physicians is especially important, since the previous system created such hardships for their practices.

The position of medical director of information is therefore being developed. Kathryn Reed has both medical and informatics expertise. She has worked to create a department that will be supportive and service-oriented. She knows the organization will be stressed because of

- changes in the established work patterns,
- the strict rules of computer system functions,
- the ambiguity of polices as they were being developed for the new system,
- lack of understanding about the value of moving to a new system (Ash, Anderson, Gorman, Zielstorff, Norcross, Pettit, & Yao, 2000).

The information system features are extremely important. Everyone who learns and works with a new systems asks

- Is it fast?
- Is it easy to use, requiring a minimum of training?
- Is help available 24/7, on-line or by telephone?
- Does it have a consistent system interface, and is it reliable?

- Will it have a positive effect on patient care?

An analysis of the case study reveals some of the issues the organization faced when making the change decisions, such as

Their motivation for implementing a new system in a hasty manner is wrong.

- Another failure will have a negative impact on employees, the financial health of the institution, patient care, and perceptions in the community.
- An ethical perspective is needed to address the responsibility to protect patient welfare.
- Scheduling and patient information must be accurate and current. This may not be possible if a system is implemented too quickly.
- Organizational and behavioral changes will be needed to manage a rapid change. Stress will increase.
- The impact on routine work during the change could be severe. (Ash, et. al, 2000).

Application to Nursing Practice

Guidelines for applying chaos theory could be developed to explain nursing phenomena. When they are unable to define and understand relationships, nurses will make assumptions. They will expect outcomes based on the assumptions that were never valid. Nurse managers have a critical role in clarifying such issues during times of uncertainty. As leaders, nurse managers must be strong and visible. Occupational health workers face a great deal of stress and uncertainty in their work. They deal with crises that involve employee health and safety. Serious accidents may happen.

The following behaviors help reduce uncertainty in business and industrial settings:

- Ensuring that your words match your actions. People lose faith when you say one thing and do another.
- Communicating is essential. During uncertain times, rumors fly, and invention takes over

when there is not any concrete information. Everyone needs to know what is happening, even when there is partial information.

- Developing a sense of trust supports open communication.

- Displaying empathy is critical when there is uncertainty.

In occupational health settings, there may be layoffs or downsizing. Nurses can show they are concerned by listening and sharing information about supportive resources (Strasser, 2002a).

We often think about a crisis as being short term. After the September 11th attacks, we have a different perspective. There are long term effects. Strategic planning begins to look at the future. Businesses begin to take a long look at what may happen and how they will manage changes.

Occupational nurses can help adapt to change. Issues may include

- loss of jobs,

- adapting to a new workplace culture,

- changes in management,

- business and plant closings,

- business units and services being combined.

Nurses in occupational health settings may have to do cost analyses to demonstrate the value of their services to the company (Strasser, 2002b). Using chaos theory may help individuals, groups, and organizations through such situations.

Barr (2002) describes the social forces that impact nursing when computer technology is introduced. Nurses see the changes in bedside documentation of patient care, automation of equipment, and transfer of information. The potential benefits for nurses are saving time and improvements in the accuracy, timeliness, and legibility of information. When orders are directly entered into a computer system, the likelihood of error is reduced. Requests are transmitted quickly. Clinical outcome data can

be retrieved. When a change is first presented people may be reluctant to participate. It seems like too much work to change. Barr uses the example of a perioperative unit. In the past, surgical suites were closed units located in one area. Today, these types of services are scattered at different sites. There is a great need to share patient information, schedules, and other resources. A major need was to have efficient ways to enter, retrieve, and share patient information.

In Barr's example, one hospital had a 10 room surgical suite, 3 endoscopic rooms, 6 PACU beds, and 8-day surgery beds. About 6,000 procedures were done there each year. The nursing staff did not have any computer support. When the hospital was brought into a health system, a computer system was purchased. Features included scheduling, documentation, capturing fees, supply management, and utilization reports. Staff were excited about the change. It was installed 1 year and crashed the next. The corporation refused to replace the system. Data was again collected manually. The next year the facility was sold. The new owner had a basic system and agreed to install a new system over the next 18 months. Barr (2002) investigated the social challenges. Would the nurses embrace the implementation of another system? The challenge was to keep staff motivated during this change process.

Three phases of implementation were identified, including

1. Accepting the challenge

   Two factors were essential for people to accept the challenge: commitment and preparation. Everyone needed support through the uncertainty. Identifying the innovators, early adopters, and other categories of persons was helpful in organizing work groups.

2. Knowledge phase

   The leaders in the perioperative units created a sense of trust, shared information, and generated feedback. Training was started at the most basic level to accommodate the individual needs. Initial assessments were done to determine the starting points. Support persons, with great computer skills, were identified for staff.

3. Persuasion phase

During this phase, the nurses started to internalize their computer skills. A video presented the benefits of computer technology compared to current practices. The system was compatible with AORN standards. Selecting nurses with excellent documentation skills to participate in the design and development of policies and procedures helped in this phase (Barr, 2002).

Barr (2002) emphasized that communication is a key factor for adopting technology. Implementing a new system is a time of stress and change. Planning, support, and establishing a vision for the project will help everyone reach the goal.

RESPONDING TO INNOVATION

We have to accept external changes in our lives. Innovation involves introduction of new ideas, processes, and products into our lives. New cars have advanced features that we have to learn in order to drive them. Procedures at work change, and we adapt. We may be interested and ready to try new things on our own. For example, we may purchase theater tickets on the Web to save time. New clothing styles, electronic equipment, and food choices pique our interest. How we go about adapting to innovations has been studied by Everett Rogers for many years (Young, 2000).

Accepting Innovation

E. Rogers studied different ways we respond to change and the rate at which we accept it. He developed categories related to how individuals adopt change

1. Innovators love new things. They have or do things before anyone else. They are risk takers and have inventive ideas. They are not part of the general social system but have an important role in bringing new ideas forward. They may participate in planning groups where their opinions about adopting innovation are valued. They are generally not interested in the actual change processes needed to adopt an innovation. They are looking for the next innovation.

2. Early adopters are part of peer groups and will usually be among the first to accept innovations. They are respected by others and their opinion is valued. They think about adopting an innovation and explore its value before starting. They may be selective about what they adopt. Persons involved in change activities are often early adopters and guide others to accepting change.

3. Early majority adopters wait to see how the innovation will work out. They are followers of the early adopters. While they are not leaders, they communicate with many people and share the innovations. Early majority adopters represent one-third of everyone in the groups.

4. Late majority adopters wait until peer pressure, economic conditions, or work mandates make it necessary. They deliberate a long time and have intense discussions about the innovation. They need a great deal of evidence to convince them.

5. Laggards are the last ones to make decisions about adopting an innovation. When an innovation is introduced, laggards will eventually decide that what everyone else accepts is fine. Up until that time, they wanted to go back to the previous way of doing something. They prefer the past to the future. They may carry out sabotage activities to undermine change (Young, 2000).

We can all give examples of persons in our work setting that fit these profiles. It is important to recognize how the different responses affect the process of change. Each group has contributions to make to the change process. Good leaders identify and use the strengths of each group, for example:

- Innovators are excellent at generating ideas that are needed early in the decision process.

- Early adopters can chair committees and train others. The early majority adopters will respond to the opinions of the early adopters and to training. They will support the implementation of the innovation.

- The late majority adopters will need continued training and support to make the transition.

- The laggards need to have opportunities to express their concerns.

Some may never adapt to change and decide to leave a situation. While it may seem helpful to spend a great deal of time on this group, the other groups are the ones that will make the positive differences for adopting innovations (Young, 2000).

Impact on Nurses and Other Health Care Professionals

Nurses and other staff may not be involved in the initial decisions to introduce innovations into their work setting. but they are affected. The new IV pumps are different. The patient information system may be upgraded. The delivery of medicines from the pharmacy is computerized. Nurses may serve on committees to review the different models of equipment that are available and make recommendations. The final decision may depend on contracts already in place for a health care system and cost.

Nurses are faced with learning how to use new equipment, computer systems, or managing medication administration. Nurses need group support, time to learn new procedures, and a chance to accept the new values and assumptions of the innovation (Young, 2000).

MANAGING INNOVATION TO IMPROVE NURSING PRACTICE

Solutions

In Barr's example, the 10 outpatient clinic nurses discussed their concerns about the computer system with the corporate manager. Two of the nurses were interested in learning more about computers. The company had educational benefits and offered to pay for a course. The manager explained the process for introducing the change. Meetings would be held to keep all employees informed. The implementation process would be done in phases. There was also discussion about the benefits of having information computerized. The nurses in this clinic realized that maintaining patient information would be a big benefit. They also talked about ways to include teaching activities. Training would be scheduled to match each phase of the project. All the nurses in the corporation would have the opportunity to respond to a survey. They could prioritize which functions were most important to computerize first. Nurses who were interested and had computer skills would have the opportunity to serve on a planning committee.

The other challenge for the nurses was patient education. The corporation supplied national and company statistics for patient outcomes. The goal for the corporation was to exceed national standards by 10% with continued improvement each year. The nurses recognized that they used different approaches to patient teaching. They decided to start by reviewing the outcomes of their teaching. The nurses decided to structure their teaching and have two nurses trained to follow a comprehensive teaching plan. Patients would complete a check-off assessment of what they were doing to manage their illnesses. The information from the self-assessment will be scanned into the computer system. Additional teaching aids that use pictures, have simple language, large print, and are in different languages will be available. Patients will be given a compact diary that allows them to fill in and check off what they do every day for a month. When the clinic is closed, patients can call the new corporate help line to get their questions answered before they go to an emergency room. Once the computer network is functioning, the tele-nurse can access the patient records, review their history, and enter the outcomes of the telephone call. Monthly reports will summarize patient clinic visits, daily monitoring of blood glucose, medications taken, and other indicators.

After the system was in place for 1 year, the nurses reviewed the results. They knew many patients had improved outcomes. The previous evaluation criteria were used to make comparisons. The data revealed that

- care standards exceeded the national and corporate benchmarks,
- self-assessment data showed that patients' understanding of their conditions increased by 40%,
- the number of visits to emergency rooms decreased by 60%.

Approximately 20% of the patients accounted for most of the emergency room visits, had a high rate of clinic visits, and knew less about managing their condition than the average patient. The nurses decided to focus on the needs of those patients during the next year.

CONCLUSION

Nurses face changing work environments. There is uncertainty and unpredictability in everyday activities as well as preparing for future changes. Understanding the dynamics of chaos and learning how to manage it has become essential to thriving in nursing and the health care arena. Social changes and technology bring innovation to our work settings. Recognizing the benefits of innova-

tion and developing strategies to move through the processes help us adapt.

The clinic nurses made the transition to using the new computer system. They had a part in developing the patient information system. They felt empowered to make decisions related to re-structuring their work. The positive outcomes gave them confidence to continue on a path of self-development, continued quality improvement, and a sense of fulfillment in their work.

EXAM QUESTIONS

CHAPTER 2
Questions 6-10

6. Chaos theory is defined as looking at systems for signs of

    a. change and redesign in work environments.

    b. constant system movements in a predictable manner.

    c. predictability and order in existing systems.

    d. order in a seemingly disorganized system.

7. Health care environments, for the past 100 years, have been

    a. open systems that adopted new ideas.

    b. organized with machine-like precision.

    c. closed systems that maintained the status quo.

    d. flat organizations with open communication.

8. During a time of crisis, occupational health nurses can reduce employee uncertainty by

    a. suggesting stress reduction classes.

    b. not sharing upsetting information.

    c. having their words match their actions.

    d. maintaining their distance from others.

9. According to E. Rogers, innovators

    a. generate ideas early in the decision process.

    b. like the way things are and do not like change.

    c. accept new ideas once they are accepted by others.

    d. take their time to explore the benefit of new ideas.

10. E. Rogers developed categories related to how individuals adopt change. In the profile of laggards, they

    a. are risk takers and have inventive ideas.

    b. usually will be among the first to accept the innovation.

    c. wait to see how the innovation will work out.

    d. prefer the past to the future and may carry out sabotage activities to undermine change.

CHAPTER 3

COMMUNICATION AND INTERPERSONAL SKILLS

CHAPTER OBJECTIVE

After studying this chapter, you will be able to understand professional expectations for communication and interpersonal interactions.

LEARNING OBJECTIVES

At the end of this chapter, you will be able to

1. define effective, respectful, and compassionate communication.

2. recognize how patient care documentation is a communication tool.

3. choose strategies for dealing with verbal conflict.

4. select communication techniques that promote the nursing profession.

OVERVIEW

Communication is an essential skill in our society. We are faced with many different types of communication:

- verbal,
- written,
- visual,
- auditory,
- subliminal,
- tactile (Tappen, Weiss, & Whitehead, 2001).

The media demonstrates how poor communication can have strange results. Subliminal communication is subtle and tries to get our attention without us being aware. This is used in marketing to encourage us to buy a product. Visual and auditory communication channels are integrated into many aspects of our lives. Television, videos, CD-ROMs, DVD, digital cameras, radio, computer games, educational materials for young children, and toys for children of all ages communicate with us.

Nurses place a high value on communication because poor communication can result in disasters. This chapter addresses four areas of communication that nurses face in their work environment.

COMMUNICATING EFFECTIVELY, RESPECTFULLY, AND COMPASSIONATELY

Nurses have the desire and responsibility to communicate effectively, respectfully, and compassionately. Communication means transmitting information and influencing others. The concepts of effective, respectful, and compassionate communication are part of the historical, caring, legal, and ethical heritage of professional nursing. Nurses work in various settings and interact with patients, family members, colleagues, other staff members, physicians, the public, and the media. It is a challenge to communicate with all these different groups. An understanding of communication processes provides some background.

Communication Processes

Many people are interested in communication. It is studied, critiqued, and used in every aspect of our lives. The five traditional elements of communication are

• Encoder (sender),

• Message (information),

• Method (method of sending the information),

• Decoder (receives the message),

• Feedback (return, indicates understanding of message) (Tappen, Weiss, & Whitehead, 2001).

A contemporary view of communication supports a more circular process. The addition to the five basic elements are the relationships with culture, knowledge, needs, goals, previous experiences, values, roles, and abilities (Tappen, Weiss, & Whitehead, 2001). Figure 3 depicts the process.

FIGURE 3: CIRCULAR COMMUNICATION PROCESS

We communicate by two methods – verbal and nonverbal. Verbal communication includes written or spoken methods for sharing ideas and thoughts. Nonverbal communications are the behaviors we use to communicate messages. This type of communication is often used unconsciously and is difficult to control (Tappen, Weiss, & Whitehead, 2001). You may hear some shocking news and immediately respond by putting your hands to your face and slumping into a chair.

We all observe nonverbal communication because it gives us cues about what the person really feels. The charge nurse may be speaking in a moderate voice, but her hands are clenched, her lips and jaw are tight, and her face is flushed. She says she is not angry about a patient error. There is inconsistency between her verbal and nonverbal messages.

Another component of communication is para-language, which includes speech patterns, pitch, rhythm, rate, and volume (Tappen, Weiss, & Whitehead, 2001). An essential part of communication is listening. How often do we hear someone say; "You never listen? You are not really listening! Listen to what I am telling you." If we are listening we exhibit the following behaviors:

• Make eye contact. In the American culture it is expected, while in other cultures it is not.

• Have positive body language: interested facial expressions, open arms, leaning forward.

• Moderate our voice: pitch, volume, and speed of speech. The voice may change during a conversation, becoming high-or low-pitched, changing from slow to choppy, or moving from quiet to loud (Tappen, Weiss, & Whitehead, 2001).

• Verbal tracking which means actually paying attention to what is said. People may appear to be listening by exhibiting the described behaviors. In reality, they might be miles away and thinking about other things (Tappen, Weiss, & Whitehead, 2001).

Nurses experience many types of communication in their work settings. They have a professional responsibility to communicate effectively, respectively, and compassionately.

Challenges

Over 30 nurses work in a comprehensive clinic that receives federal, state, local, and community support. The patients come from many different cultural backgrounds, are from all age groups, and have chronic conditions. Many patients do not keep appointments or follow their treatment plans. They wait until they have a crisis or need medication. Patient records are incomplete.

Many of the nurses have worked together for several years. Several are new within the last year. A new medical director has just joined the group. The nurses have heavy patient loads, a lot of paperwork, and concerns about clinic funding and policies. They talk about their issues and concerns in small groups but rarely meet as a whole group. They feel they have too much work and that the patients are not cooperative. The new medical director is frequently angry and blames the nurses when things go wrong. They are frustrated and morale is low. The nurses believe that improving communication will improve their work environment.

Effective Communication

 Effective communication is a process where messages are received and understood. We all want and need to communicate effectively. That is, most of the time. People may deliberately be vague about what they are saying. Gossip is based on partial communication with a dash of created thoughts. The daytime television dramas thrive on poor communication. The characters do not have open communication, leave a lot unsaid, and are not necessarily honest. We can all think of instances when communication is less than optimum. The results may be awful. Nurses have had such experiences. Workplace communication deserves attention. Barriers to workplace communication include

• physical barriers, such as noise, activity in an area, and separated spaces.

• psychological issues and different cultural, social, and life experiences, as well as preconceived ideas.

• semantic differences in the way we use words, slang and technical terms, and abbreviations (Tappen, Weiss, & Whitehead, 2001).

In health care settings, it is common to use technical terms and abbreviations. This is confusing to persons without medical and nursing knowledge. Persons for whom English is a second language have difficulty with slang. They understand a literal meaning. When something is "neat," there is a difference between the literal and slang meaning. Another problem area is abbreviations. We use them frequently and expect everyone to understand. We need to verify the meaning, especially when orders are written or communicated. Is the correct laboratory test or procedure actually being ordered?

Respectful Communication

We often discuss the need for a more civilized society. Rudeness is everywhere. We experience it when we drive, go to public places, and interact with others at work. Respectful communication includes the listening skills mentioned earlier. Courtesy is part of the equation. Taking time to hear the entire conversation is one example. Showing appreciation, saying thank you, and acknowledging a person's contribution to a discussion are courteous actions.

Nurses are working with more patients from diverse backgrounds and an aging population. Cultural practices are important for achieving respectful communication. Eye contact in some cultures may be minimal. A male member of a family may be with female patients and be the decision-maker. The eldest member of a family may be the decision-maker. Women may only feel comfortable talking with another woman about their health problems. Nurses need to learn more about cultures that they frequently see in their practice.

The aging population interacts frequently with health care professionals. Physiological and psychological changes in the elderly impact communication. Vision and hearing diminish. Elderly persons may have difficulty reading or hearing instructions (Hogstel, 2001). They may not be able to interpret nonverbal communication. Because nurses and other staff are busy, they may be impatient, believe the patients are non-compliant, and ignore the patients. Cultural sensitivity helps nurses communicate with patients and colleagues respectfully. Caring and compassion are the foundations of nursing practice. How is this communicated to others?

Compassionate Communication

The ethic of caring is part of nursing practice in any setting and with any patient. Caring is interactive and requires involvement. A nurse and a patient develop a relationship that promotes communication. Trust develops over time. This is especially possible when nurses care for patients over long periods. Nurses working in long-term care, home health, clinics, and hospice have the opportunity to develop close relationships. Patients and family members share their concerns and fears. Truth telling is an important part of communication. Maintaining confidentiality also demonstrates compassion (Robinson & Kish, 2001).

Mary Smith is a home health nurse. She has a heavy caseload of patients with chronic illnesses. She has cared for some of the patients for over two years. When she first started interacting with them, she concentrated on their physical needs. Some had complicated care needs. As she became more comfortable with them, their communication expanded to other topics important to the patients. They began asking her to let them know what was really happening to them. They wanted to know the truth about their conditions rather than just being reassured. They had lived with these questions for a long time but had never worked with a nurse who cared about them personally.

The patients also shared confidences with Mary. The patients had stories to share. They had never talked about some bad experiences that happened earlier in their lives. They discussed the poor life choices they had made, some that contributed directly to their current illnesses. The compassionate care and communication these patients received from Mary was therapeutic. This is an example of compassionate communication that met patient needs. Nurses strive to create environments where veracity (truth telling), confidentiality, and privacy are realities.

Application in a Clinical Setting

Gray and Warrington (2002) describe a clinical situation in which communication was an essential element. A nurse described how she was working the evening shift and one of her patient's had a serious, unanticipated incident. Family members were present. They asked many questions and took notes. The nurse felt she was being scrutinized. She was not sure about what information the family needed and thought she had been told that in such situations it was best to say nothing. At the same time, the nurse felt it was her duty to keep the family informed and to offer comfort. The nurse reviewed the hospital policies and spoke with a nursing practice expert.

Breakdown in communication is the most common reason for filing complaints or for legal action. When there is a crisis everyone is fearful, distressed, and anxious. They want to know what is happening. It may not be possible to give in-depth explanations immediately. Share what you can with the family and tell them what will happen next. Nurses can share some information, but everyone involved must participate. Medical information must be communicated by the physicians. They will be making the decisions about the next steps of care. Looking after the family, making them comfortable, and calling on other staff to help will enhance communication (Gray & Warrington, 2002).

Patients and family members have a right to full information after such an event. It may not be possible to give a complete explanation immediately. All the facts must be collected. Nurses should be careful when offering an apology. Admitting fault prematurely is not helpful. The nurse in this situation focused on the family and patient needs. Hospital policy governs who is responsible for disclosing information. If someone else is responsible for sharing information, make sure it is actually done (Gray & Warrington, 2002). That will complete the circle of communication.

DOCUMENTING PATIENT CARE

In the past, documenting patient care was well defined. Most patients were in a hospital or health care setting. The patient record had places for vital signs, medications, and narratives. We used black ink, wrote legibly, filled in all the spaces, and signed the record. Today documenting patient care is more complex, and there are different options.

Purposes of Patient Health Records

Patient health records have obvious purposes. The records

- document patient care,
- provide a single access point for everyone involved in caring for the patient,
- give providers a way to communicate and exchange information,
- is a source of billing information,
- serve as a legal record of the care provided (Young, 2000).

The functions of patient health records continue to expand, based on legislative, accreditation, and professional standard requirements. Patients experience care throughout a system or at different points in multiple systems, expanding record-keeping challenges. Patient health records are another way to examine the consistency and quality of care over time as well as the cost of care.

Information is shared among the many persons who make up the health care team. They can coordinate care, monitor the quality of care, and gain access to current research and drug information. Quality assurance activities are required by federal agencies, third-party payers, and accrediting bodies. The public is also becoming more aware of quality indicators. They can make informed choices about care.

Patient health record information is used as a source for collecting data for research. The use of automated systems that use the same language and classification system will support the combining of aggregate data. The new information would be used to make health policy, funding decisions, and improve health care delivery (Young, 2000).

Sources of Patient Information

When patients enter a health care system, it is essential that data be available. They may be entering a system for the first time or may have had previous encounters for a condition. Collecting and organizing information for each new encounter is time-consuming.

Paper Records

We are most familiar with paper records. Information is gathered from patients and recorded. Additional information from laboratory work, x-rays, pharmacy, and assessments are added. The information elicited from the patient or a family member may be incomplete. The readability of the record may be compromised because of poor writing and faintness of writing on duplicate copies. An advantage of the paper record is that is available and has some history as well as current information. A disadvantage is that information is duplicated. Patients give the same information repeatedly. Providers have to look through numerous pages to find scattered information. One study reviewed 168 outpatient records and found that the data they wanted was not found in 81% of the cases (Young, 2000).

Optically Scanned Records

With optically scanned records, the paper record is scanned and stored electronically on an optical platter. The records can be reviewed by more than one person at the same time. For example, a physician, a nurse, and someone in the billing department can all be looking at the same record. The greatest disadvantage is that it is an image of the original paper document and has the same problems with illegibility. Reading the documents is a slow process. It also is not possible to organize or categorize information (Young, 2000).

Electronic Health Records

Different titles are given to electronic health records (EHR) but they all are electronically stored information about a person's health status and care. It is ideal to capture the information for the person's entire life. A futuristic view of the EHR is that all the information is collected from different sources and presented to the viewer as one record. A variety of media would support displaying the record. The information would come from laboratory reports, pathology, nursing notes, physician entries, and other sources. There is a need for an integrated system. The average hospital has 17 separate sources for patient information. Each department stores it in different ways. The different systems do not interface (Young, 2000).

Bedside or Point-of-Care Systems

Some documentation can happen at the patient's bedside. Wireless systems would allow documentation to occur where the patient is located: outpatient clinic, x-ray department, laboratory, or physical therapy. Data can be entered via voice, touch pen, and keyboard. Handheld and mobile devices are also options. The advantage of these types of systems is that information is entered as the event occurs, and the system is integrated so everyone can view what is entered (Young, 2000).

Appropriate Documentation

Nurses know the saying, "If it is not documented, it was not done." This is a legal stance. Not giving a medication or completing a treatment can open the door to negligence. The following principles pertain to accurately recording patient care information:

- document care at the time it was given
- accurately record what you did
- document what you actually did or observed.

Patient records are open to many persons and may become public records. Documentation should be appropriate (Tappen, Weiss, & Whitehead, 2001). Indicate the source of the information and summarize or put it in quotes.

Guidelines for actually entering the information on the record are to

- completely chart medication information, including time, route, dose, and response,
- chart when a medication was not given,
- chart if a medication was refused and report it.

Record communications with physicians. Note if a call was made but there was no response. Record the details of a message and the physician's response. If you are taking verbal orders, read them back. Record them on the correct patient chart. When recording information, make sure you have the right record and that each page of a paper record has the patient's name.

Organize your charting. Follow the agency system for recording or use the nursing process or problem-based charting. If you chart a symptom or patient problem, include what you did and document the outcome. Chart throughout your shift to show care was given periodically. Specifically include patient and family teaching (Young, 2000).

Patient and Family Teaching

Patient and family education is a vital part of care. The expectations for patient education are based on the American Hospital Association Patient's Bill of Rights. Patients have the right to adequate information about their physical condition, medications, risks and benefits of treatments, and information about alternative treatments. Some state health codes have included those rights. Federal agencies require patient education for facilities that receive Medicare and Medicaid funding. There is extensive documentation required when persons agree to participate in biomedical research.

State practice acts spell out nurses responsibilities for patient education. While documentation is not always complete, patient education is the most undocumented service. Nurses may not recognize and understand the importance of their patient education activities. Not documenting patient education is as serious as not charting medications (Bastable, 2003).

Mrs. Jones was newly diagnosed with diabetes. She was hospitalized for 2 days. She attended classes. Notes in her chart indicated that she attended the classes but gave no information about what was presented or her ability to give her own insulin.

Mrs. Jones also continued classes after her discharge. A record was also kept of her attendance at the outpatient classes. Class materials included the content for each class. Mrs. Jones demonstrated that she could draw up saline into a syringe and give herself an injection.

After she took her insulin each day at home, she felt weak and shaky. After her next office appointment, the nurse had her actually draw up the insulin. She could not see the fine lines on the syringe and was drawing up too much. Additional teaching and practice to ensure she could administer her own insulin was started.

Complete documentation could have avoided this situation. One approach to documenting interdisciplinary patient education is to use a flow sheet that includes identifying information and family education needs. An assessment of barriers to learning identifies areas, such as

- language,
- low vision,
- hearing difficulties,
- speech problems,
- literacy level,
- attention problems,
- physical problems.

A good flow sheet includes space to document who did the teaching, who was taught, what was taught, the methods for teaching, and the patient's response to the teaching (Bastable, 2003).

DEALING WITH VERBAL CONFLICT

We can all think of situations where verbal conflict took over a conversation. Conflict arises whenever two or more people disagree. Verbal conflict is due to poor communication, environmental distractions, or differing perspectives on a situation. Verbal abuse is also used as a tool to attract attention, express anger, increase a sense of power, or reach some other personal goal. Nurses aim to prevent verbal conflict. It is not professional or courteous to demean another person or create a disturbing scene (Cherry & Jacob, 2002).

A nurse may employ a variety of professional responses to verbal conflict

- move the conversation to a more a more private area,
- use a normal tone of voice,
- start comments with "I,"
- maintain eye contact,

- demonstrate positive body language,
- do not back away, unless you are in danger,
- give explanations, not excuses,
- follow up on what you say you are going to do and let the person know you did it (Cherry & Jacob, 2002).

Application to Nursing Practice

The problem of verbal abuse, particularly physician abuse of nurses, is seen in health care settings. Nurses working in operating suites have many stories about verbal abuse by the surgeons and even describe the throwing of instruments. The abuser is trying to gain control. When there is fear, stress, or feelings of powerlessness, the abuse escalates.

Verbal abuse in a hospital setting has the same characteristics as abuse in the public domain. Abuse of any kind should not be tolerated anywhere. Efforts are needed to prevent and reduce verbal abuse. Nurses can refocus the anger by saying "Help me understand what is wrong." Nurses in an operating room (OR) cannot leave the situation but can signal a "code pink", in which other nurses in the OR would stand beside the nurse being verbally abused. In this way they would show support.

Search for solutions. The nurse's goal is to resolve the situation. Provide individual and group support. Support a collaborative practice model, hierarchy is reduced and treatment teams have less conflict. Develop and use policies for reporting and addressing workplace abuse. Organizational commitment and actions help reduce the problem. Let there be peace (Simms, 2000).

BECOMING A VOICE FOR PROFESSIONAL CHANGE

Nurses are patient-focused and concerned about giving quality care. The increasing complexity of health care and shrinking resources make it imperative that nurses become a voice for their profession, for patients, and health care. Political involvement often occurs at different levels. Buy-in is the beginning, when nurses understand an issue and are willing to be part of a solution.

Self-interest may be the major motivator. Nurses may seek to improve working conditions, increase workplace safety, or improve salaries. As nurses become more involved, they learn political skills. They set agendas, accept leadership positions, build coalitions, and participate in political campaigns (Robinson & Kish, 2001).

There are different ways to communicate within organizations and with community and political decision-makers. In work settings, use the channels that are set up to address concerns and issues. Group support increases the attention an issue may receive. Presenting facts sets the stage for discussion. Persistence is important to keep an issue in the forefront of people's minds.

New channels of communication may be needed to achieve goals. For example, the organization may not be addressing the issue of workplace violence. A group of nurses wants to communicate their concerns. They start by gathering facts and writing up the issues. They request a meeting with the chief nursing officer to share their concerns. The process continues until policies are developed, training is done, and evaluation indicates a reduction in violence.

Nurses may want to have a role in political activities to address wider issues. Options for doing that are numerous. A good first step is to join your professional organization and participate in political and legislative activities.

During election campaigns, organizations and candidates hold town meetings. There may be the opportunity to ask questions. Visit elected officials and their staffs. Write up a summary of your issue. Include short examples related to your practice or the impact on patients. Tell the officials why you do or do not support proposed legislation. The time you can spend with officials is very short so be prepared and make your points clear and concise.

Writing letters and sending e-mail is very effective. Legislators listen to their constituents. When a number of nurses communicate, they get attention. There is strength in numbers.

Nursing leaders are asked to testify at hearings. This provides nurses with the opportunity to communicate their concerns, share their expertise, and offer solutions (Cherry & Jacobs, 2002).

Application to Occupational and Environmental Health Nurses

The nursing profession has a social contract with society to shape policy. Nurses in occupational and environmental work settings interface with all kinds of policies

- safety regulations,

- workers' compensation,

- wellness programs,

- health information privacy, and other regulations.

Nurses in these settings are a link between employee health and safety and employer business results. Actively participating in shaping policies and communicating with all parties is essential. Policies that maintain and improve worker health and safety have positive benefits for everyone (Ennen, 2001).

Participating in political activities is one way to learn about the issues and options for communicating. There are different opportunities to get hands on experience. The Nurses in Washington Internship program is one experience. Nurses attend information sessions, network, work with lobbyists, and meet with legislators (Allen & Spera, 2000). They gain new perspectives on what nurses can accomplish in the political arena and skills to communicate their concerns.

Solutions

In the challenge situation, the nurses in the clinic realize they need to change their work environment. They start by communicating with each other. Five of the nurses agree to start organizing the concerns. Nurses write out their priorities for changing the environment. The lists are summarized and the small group identifies the four most important areas

1. Improving communication with patients and families to increase responsiveness and outcomes.

2. Reviewing patient care documentation to reduce duplication and ensure consistency in data collection.

3. Developing a process to deal with the verbal conflict between nurses and the medical director.

4. Seeking additional funding for the clinic through community and political contacts.

The nurses were starting to see that making changes and sharing information would improve their work environment.

CONCLUSION

Communication is a vital part of our lives. Nurses must overcome many challenges to communicate effectively. Understanding the elements of communication and applying them in all areas of their practice will improve interactions with patients and coworkers. Using the available systems for documenting patient care assures compliance with institutional and legal standards. Verbal conflict is part of nursing practice. Nurses need skills to confront the conflict and seek resolutions. Long-term strategies to reduce it are worth pursuing. Nurses, working together, have the opportunity to change the profession and health care. Community involvement and political action are necessary to influence change.

EXAM QUESTIONS

CHAPTER 3
Questions 11-15

11. Workplace communication is affected by a physical barrier such as

    a. not taking time to talk.
    b. lack of information to share.
    c. erratic information systems.
    d. noise and activity in an area.

12. Respectful communication requires nurses to be

    a. informed about many topics.
    b. sensitive to cultural differences.
    c. emotional in sad situations.
    d. humorous in response to patient jokes.

13. When a patient asks the nurse to tell him the truth about his condition, the nurse should respond with specific information that demonstrates

    a. an open exchange of information.
    b. an inability to keep silent.
    c. compassionate communication.
    d. good listening skills.

14. The best approach for the nurse to communicate with the family when a patient suffers an unexpected incident is

    a. giving them a brief explanation and telling them they will be kept informed.
    b. telling them how sorry the staff is and apologizing.
    c. showing them to the waiting room and letting them know the physician will be there soon.
    d. crying so the family knows how upset the nurse is about what happened.

15. A futuristic view of an electronic health record (EHR) includes

    a. scanning written information into a computer.
    b. having one paper record that displays all the patient information.
    c. allowing patients to add their own information to the record.
    d. merging information from different sources into one record.

CHAPTER 4

MANAGING TECHNOLOGY AND INFORMATION

CHAPTER OBJECTIVE

After studying this chapter, you will be able to recognize different types of information and understand the role of technology to organize data.

LEARNING OBJECTIVES

After studying this chapter, you will be able to

1. indicate at least three types of information found in computer systems.

2. recognize processes for seeking, sorting, and selecting data.

3. differentiate selected technologies used to organize data.

4. choose how to apply technology to nursing practice.

OVERVIEW

In the last few decades, we have entered the age of technology. It affects our lives in small and large ways. Buying items on the Internet, online banking and paying bills, communicating by cellular phone, e-mail, and fax are common. The vast amount of information available makes it imperative that we have efficient ways to organize it. Health care institutions have adopted technology to streamline processes, increase efficiency, and make use of new diagnostic technologies. Nurses are part of this change and must be ready to function in this new environment.

Challenges

Jennifer was recently promoted to a nurse educator position at Metropolitan Hospital. Her first project was to update a hospital procedure. She has limited experience in giving presentations or knowing how to find current information quickly. Her supervisor suggested she get on the Internet to find what she needs. Jennifer does use the Internet for personal activities such as e-mail, shopping online, comparing prices, and playing games. She needs to learn how to locate professional information in the shortest time possible.

TYPES OF INFORMATION

 Technology continues to impact health care at a rapid rate. Diagnostic procedures use technology that makes it possible to see inside the body. Images are magnified and enhanced. Automating business systems is possible because of computer technology. Health care environments use technology to

- store and access patient records,

- collect patient information at the bedside,

- automate tracking, delivery, and billing for pharmacy, equipment, and supply materials,

- monitor security, track visitors, and maintain personnel records,
- generate and pay bills,
- direct deposit payroll,
- connect with other institutions, access Internet information, hold conferences, share information, share services, and collaborate (Tappen, Weiss, & Whitehead, 2001).

Perhaps the greatest impact of technology is in sharing information. Decision-making is driven by information (Young, 2000). Physicians, nurses, and other disciplines use information to make patient care decisions. What are the current standards? What are the best practices? What evidence is available to guide practice decisions?

FUTURE HEALTH CARE TECHNOLOGIES

We may think we are entering the realm of science fiction, but many innovations are being tested and introduced. It may be a while before they are commonly used but they are coming.

For example, biosensors can read and transmit physical and chemical body system responses. A biosensor may soon read blood glucose levels and regulate the insulin through an implanted pump.

Home-based technologies may be the primary site for monitoring. Patients can e-mail their symptoms to the physician. A personal status monitor (PSM), worn on the patient's wrist, will transmit vital body information. Possible diagnoses and treatment options will also be shared.

Global positioning satellites can locate a person. This is useful if someone has a chronic condition or is going to a remote site and needs medical care. Waiting rooms could be eliminated (Young, 2000).

The British National Health Service is working on a global electronic patient record system. The record could be accessed from anywhere in the world. It would include the lifetime history of the patient and their current health status. A unique patient identifier must be developed for such a system to work. The biometrics industry is looking at various identification methods. We commonly use fingerprints for identification. Other methods are retinal, iris, and facial imaging, as well as voice recognition (Young, 2000).

Some forms of these technologies are already being used. Pacemakers are checked over the telephone. ECG and x-ray information is transmitted electronically.

Technology will assist with decision-making. Human contact and judgement is always going to be part of patient care. The volume of information and the many ways to use it means we need to have some guidelines for seeking, sorting, and selecting what we want to use.

Information Seeking, Sorting, and Selecting

Literacy is the ability to understand and use language. Computer literacy means having some knowledge of how computers work and then being able to successfully use them. Not too long ago, nurses might have thought that computers would be used to manage supporting hospital systems but would not impact patient care too much. It is obvious that is not the case. All nurses need to have a working knowledge of computers and associated technologies to function in their work. Classes to learn computer skills are easy to find. Once you know how computers work, you can use them to find, sort, and select information.

INTRODUCTION TO THE INTERNET AND THE WORLD WIDE WEB (WWW)

The Internet was started as a network by the U.S. Department of Defense. The goal was to create a communication network that would function even if one part became damaged. Scientists, researchers, and professors were the primary users of the network for many years. The Internet is a new worldwide network of computers that ties systems together.

The Web is a world-wide system of databases within the Internet for people to communicate from different sites. The World Wide Web (WWW) supported communication between researchers who worked in different parts of the world. Since 1991, access has been expanded to general users. The development of software and other tools made it easier for everyone to use the WWW (Cherry & Jacob, 2002).

To access the Web and search for information, computers have to be connected to the Internet. At home, people use telephone lines, cable modems, Web TV, high-speed lines (DSL), and satellite connections (Cherry & Jacob, 2002).

Access to the Internet is delivered by an Internet service provider (ISP). The provider provides the equipment needed to make a connection. Prices and services vary. There may be installation charges. Some services require multi-year contracts. There may be monthly time limits for use. Decide what type and level of services are best for you when connecting a computer from home.

BUSINESS AND INSTITUTIONAL SYSTEMS

Large businesses and institutions do not use stand-alone personal computers. They rely on integrated delivery systems that interface all aspects of the organization. Such systems deliver information across departments and allows use of data for a variety of functions (Young, 2000). The computer on your unit probably has access to different departments and a variety of information. Now that you understand computer basics, you are ready to seek information.

Seeking Information

Using the Web is the most powerful way to locate information. You can find information on any topic. Businesses, individuals, health care systems, governments, libraries, and schools have sites with volumes of information.

Search engines help us locate information on the Web. The search may be done by keywords or concepts. A keyword search is most common. The search looks for the words you enter throughout sites on the Web. If you are looking for articles or health information, the keywords in the entire document will be searched. Programmers set up the keyword parameters (Young, 2000). Metasearching expands a search from one database to many. This option saves times and allows you to see which search engines give you the best results.

You can also search using a subject directory. Selecting a very broad topic such as "diabetes", you will get hundreds, even thousands of listings related to the topic. Narrowing the search produces fewer results. You could search for "diabetes" and "diet." The results focus on that combined topic. Health professionals commonly use the following sites to access medical literature:

- MEDLINE is supported by the National Library of Medicine and lists articles from biomedical journals throughout the world. There are mainly citations and abstracts, but PubMED does have some full text articles. Over 300 nursing titles are listed. The service is free.

- CINAHL focuses on nursing, allied health, biomedical, and consumer journals. Publications from the American Nurses Association and the

National League for Nursing are also included. Citations and abstracts are included. The service is free (Young, 2001).

There are also specialized literature databases. There is usually a fee for using the services as well as for printing articles.

Some nursing journals are online. The Online Journal of Nursing Informatics is free and can be accessed at: http://cac.psu.edu/ndxm12/OJNI.html.

Evaluating Web Sites

Even when you know how to seek information, it is daunting to navigate through all of it. One strategy is to evaluate Web sites to determine which ones give you what you need. Web sites are not controlled, evaluated, or reviewed. Individuals can publish what they want. That is a source of controversy because many sites and information are not suitable for all age groups. There are tools to block sites. Public libraries may want to block certain sites, while others want complete freedom to access any site. When evaluating Web sites look for:

- accuracy,

- reliability,

- correct information (no errors),

- credibility of author and publisher,

- purpose and goals of the site,

- current information,

- ease of access,

- completeness of information.

Compare the Web information to the same information from other sources. For example, if a nursing research journal describes a study and gives information about the limitations of the project, you can compare it to someone's opinion about what to do. Which source of information is more credible? Because there is so much information, you need to spend time sorting it.

Sorting Information

Databases are collections of files that have different types of information, such as text, images, and voice. The data is stored and there are tools to extract and manipulate it. For example, millions of pieces of laboratory data are stored. A laboratory technician could request all the results for one patient or all the results for a specific test done in the last 6 months (Young, 2000).

In our Web search example, once you have the information you requested, diabetes and diet, you still need to sort it. If you are looking for organizations, self-help groups, or chat rooms, you could decide to look at one group or a few from each group. If you searched the literature, the results may indicate how each item fits your query. For example, the results may range from 10% to 100% relevance. You can also sort the articles by year of publication. That is important if you want current information on a topic because you are writing an article or giving a presentation. You may want older information if you are comparing practices at different times in history.

Selecting Information

Some Web sites only have citations or abstracts. That gives you limited information. If you want detailed information, you need to look at full text articles. There are some on-line nursing journals that require you to purchase the articles. Most journal articles have been through a peer review process. That adds support to the accuracy of articles.

Information from professional organizations and associations is usually credible. Nursing association Web sites have current information about legislative activities, issues, trends, and links to other sites. Disease-related associations such as the American Heart Association have current, reliable information and can direct you to other resources. The Federal government is a rich source of information. Health statistics, current clinical research information, access to medical and health information, standards of care, and clinical treatment information. The CDC Web site is a good source for current practices (www.cdc.gov).

The Agency for Health Care Policy and Research (AHCPR) is responsible for promoting research that improves the quality of health care, reduces cost, and expands access to essential services. The agency provides information to health care practitioners, health organizations, and consumers. They also develop practice guidelines.

Using Technology to Organize Information

We know there are many ways to organize our offices, closets, recipes, family pictures, and almost everything else. The large amount of information available from the Internet and other sources still needs organization. Specific words and technical terms are used to put information in different categories.

There are two schools of thought about organizing information. There is a need for both standardized and discipline-specific language (Young, 2000). Medicine, nursing, physical therapy, and occupational therapy share common language related to patient care. Each discipline also has a specialized language. For example, the term "unresponsive" is interpreted differently depending on the environment and context. What did the patient not respond to: pain, a question, or a neurological assessment?

As health care entities continue to merge, they reorganize and collapse services and functions. It is difficult to set up computer systems that can recognize the work of different disciplines and then merge them into standard formats for quality assurance, determining outcomes, and identifying costs. For example, the term "strength of grasp" cannot be categorized because different terms may be used to describe the concept. Is it "hand strength," "finger grasp," or "hand grasp"? When different terms

are used, the data cannot be collected for analysis, explained as part of an assessment, or identified for reimbursement (Young, 2000).

Advantages of Standardized Language

There are many advantages to sharing a standardized language. Information systems can do more than collect and store information. Information is collected from different technologies. A concern is that the different types of information cannot be combined to determine relationships and outcomes. The information should be used for several purposes, to

- advance knowledge by studying different populations and establishing links between diagnoses and outcomes;

- support research findings that could validate diagnoses and selected interventions;

- establish links between practice and education and develop interdisciplinary ties to establish a common language;

- encourage ties between documentation, decision-making, and research in clinical practice;

- accurately predict costs and determine the need for specific equipment, services, and personnel, you need a tracking system;

- build data sets that will influence policy and resource allocation decisions by government, third-party payers, and community groups when planning ways to meet health care needs (Young, 2000, Shneiderman, 2002).

We do need a standard language for all the reasons listed. Classification systems do exist within disciplines. Clinical events are described in the systems. They are useful for practice but are not comprehensive enough to address the broad areas needed to manage complex information. Some established classification systems include

- Diagnosis Related Groups (DRGs),

- International Classification of Diseases, 9th edition (ICD-9),

- Diagnostic and Statistical Manual of Mental Disorders (DSM-IV),

- Health Care Financing Administration Common Procedure Coding System (HCPCS), and

- the International Classification of Impairments, Disabilities, and Handicaps (ICIDH) created by the World Health Organization (WHO) (Young, 2000).

It is apparent that merging all these different classifications would be valuable but almost impossible. Nursing is not in any better position. The need for a common language has been identified for years, but nurses still use different approaches.

NURSING CLASSIFICATION SYSTEMS

Nursing informatics combines computer, information, and nursing sciences. In 1994, the American Nurses Association described nursing informatics as including the

- ability to identify, acquire, preserve, manage, retrieve, aggregate, analyze, and transmit data, information, and knowledge that is meaningful and useful for nurses;

- skills required to understand computers and related technology;

- understanding of concepts relevant to nursing knowledge;

- development of systems to manage nursing information to improve nursing practice.

Gathering and organizing information supports assessing patient outcomes and nursing research efforts. Once we gain the capability to collect nursing data, the question becomes how to organize it.

The American Nurses Association organized a committee to design a national database for clinical practice, the Nursing Minimum Data Set (NMDS). The NMDS supports a common language for describing clinical nursing activities. A computer-ized health record serves as the framework for the data. Examples of information in the NMDS are nursing diagnosis, interventions, type and level of nursing care, patient identifying information, and outcomes.

Issues arose about the interpretation of clinical situations. The Steering Committee of the American Nurses Association (1995b) published information about establishing a single, comprehensive approach to classifying clinical practice.

The efforts of different groups have yielded different classification systems. Commonly used classification systems are described next.

North American Nursing Diagnosis Association (NANDA)

The North American Nursing Diagnosis Association (NANDA) started their work in the 1970s. Their goal was to computerize patient information and categorize it specifically for the discipline of nursing. They communicated with many other nurses and held yearly conferences. They could not agree on a classification design so they agreed to list the nursing diagnoses alphabetically. In 1995, the ANA recognized NANDA as the group charged with continuing to develop a standardized nursing taxonomy (ANA, 1995a).

Omaha System

The Omaha system is used primarily in non-institutional settings. A series of research projects supports its development. It describes and measures patient problems, nursing interventions, and outcomes of care (Tappen, Weiss, & Whitehead, 2001).

Home Health Care Classification

In the early 1990s, a project at Georgetown University sought to develop a system for figuring out the resources needed to provide home care to patients with Medicare. The Home Health Care Classification is the result. The expected outcomes of the services were also described. Many home health and community agencies use the system to measure the outcomes and effectiveness of the services they provide (Tappen, Weiss, & Whitehead, 2001).

Nursing Interventions Classification (NIC) and Nursing Outcomes Classification (NOC)

The Iowa Intervention Project was started in 1987 by a group of nurse researchers at the University of Iowa. Their goals are to develop a Nursing Interventions Classification (NIC) and a Nursing Outcomes Classification (NOC). There is a Web page, list server, and a number of publications related to the project. Over 433 nursing interventions (NIC) are identified and linked to NOC (University of Iowa Web site, 1999).

Unified Nursing Language System (UNLS)

A Unified Nursing Language System (UNLS), to link the different systems, is being developed. The goal is to have nurses accept a common system in order to evaluate the quality and effectiveness of care. Federal agencies and insurance companies have guidelines that establish desired outcomes. That information can also be linked to UNSL for added support. The data that is used in the various systems originates in patient records. The use of records with standard information is vital to supporting systems (Tappen, Weiss, & Whitehead, 2001).

COMPUTER-BASED PATIENT RECORDS (CPR)

The Institute of Medicine developed a description of 12 important features of computer-based patient records (CPR). They include a problem list, rationale for clinical decisions, links to other records, functions to maintain confidentiality, access to input information, and ways to monitor for quality and cost of care. Many health care providers have started to develop computer-based patient records, also known as electronic health records (EHR) and electronic medical records (EMR), but the systems can take as long as 5-10 years to fully implement (Tappen, Weiss, & Whitehead, 2001).

While the issue of a standard language is important to integrating different systems, the health care industry has made great progress in using computer technology to support essential functions. The process for developing computerized information is complex but can start with defining the problem. There may be more than one problem, but identification is critical.

Examples of such problems include:

- Departments not communicating patient information to each other.

- Supplies not being charged to patients.

- Billing processes are done by hand and prone to error.

- Space for storage of paper information is limited.

Another important initial step is analyzing the benefits. This is usually done in terms of time, cost, efficiency, and effectiveness (Young, 2000, Shneiderman, 2002).

We see the application of information systems in every aspect of hospital or outpatient services

- business office,

- food services,

- ordering supplies,

- pharmacy,

- laboratory,

- patient records,

- policies and procedures,

- reports,

- physician orders,

- admission and discharge,

- diagnostic and treatment procedures.

Nursing applications vary by setting, but there are many exciting opportunities. It may take some nurses time to adjust to new processes, but most of the innovations enhance patient care and support nursing activities.

Application to Nursing Practice

Nurses often work in understaffed, high stress, and low morale environments. Information technology can help nurses during a staffing crisis. Simpson (2002) describes how information technology (IT) can help by

- Tracking staffing patterns, which can provide the data needed to determine if mandated patient/nurse ratios are met.

- Linking schools of nursing, libraries, health care organizations, and homes to create virtual classrooms, which allows information to be shared. Students can participate in clinical events. All nurses can move through the various systems, continue their education, and share knowledge without geographic and institutional barriers.

- Having IT personalize care by storing information about patient preferences.

- Allowing required information to be stored, such as advance directives, previous health and admission information, and current problem lists.

- Monitoring all aspects of care, with the help of clinical decision support systems.

- Entering information at the time it happens to ensure timeliness and accuracy, which supports point of care technology.

Personal digital assistants (PDAs) are making their way into clinical settings. PDAs are capable of storing data. Nurses can enter patient care information, be reminded about medications and treatments, and send data to a central system for others to access. Other health care workers, such as dieticians, are using PDAs to track patient outcomes and staff productivity (McCaffree, 2001). The soft-

ware that is installed determines the range of functions, such as

- In outpatient settings, patient information is stored and retrieved. During patient visits, new information is added to the record.

- Up-to-date drug information can be accessed. Some programs will also check for drug interactions on drugs you select.

- Software can calculate drug dosages, IV flow rates, and pediatric doses. An area of clinical practice can be specified to call up the calculations and other information that are focused on that area.

- Diseases are indexed in other software programs. Basic information about the disease, diagnostic criteria, treatment, medications, and follow-up is included.

- Some health care systems are integrating PDAs so nurses can download patient assignments and share change of shift information (Craig, 2002).

USING INFORMATION TECHNOLOGY FOR EDUCATION

Nurses participate in professional development, earn additional degrees, become certified, and keep current in their practice areas. Patient and family education is an essential part of nursing practice. Consumers seek health care and lifestyle information from different sources. All of these activities can be facilitated by information technology.

Rankin (2002) described the experiences of registered nurses who were enrolled in a Web-based course. A survey was used to collect the information from 57 registered nurse°s. Most were satisfied with the course. They were able to access the course from home. In their workplace, access was more difficult because of limited time and computer availability. During the course, they gained knowledge about e-mail, the Internet, keyboard operations, and word processing. Nurses who withdrew from the course identified lack of computer skills and not understanding the work required for the course as the main reasons.

Health care organizations understand the need to apply new knowledge in their clinical settings. The time from innovation to utilization can cover many years. The U.S. Department of Veteran's Affairs virtual learning center is set up to support social learning among staff and to share new knowledge (Charles, 2000).

One project wanted to provide environmental health information to community groups. Computers were set in strategic locations. Participants were trained. Activities were planned based on community needs. High school students in this community were tested for asthma. Students who were diagnosed were taught how to access information for managing their condition. Another community group learned about toxic materials. They were able to bring their concerns about a proposed garbage collection site to community officials (Scherrer, 2001).

Solutions

In our challenge situation, Jennifer talked with the hospital medical librarian. She found out there were self-paced tutorials on the library computers. She completed one that helped her learn about the available sites and databases. The second one focused on how to search the sites. She was ready to get started.

Jennifer completed a search and sorted the information. She then needed to select what she wanted to use.

She had collected more information than she needed. Jennifer thought about the primary purpose for collecting the information but wanted to use all of the information. She went back to her original project. She needed information to update the hospital procedure for maintaining IV lines. The types of information that are most credible include research-based, clinical practice guidelines, and outcome data. She selected those types of information to revise the procedure. She presented the information at staff development sessions. Some of the articles she retrieved discuss cost-effective ways to maintain IVs. She decided to share those in the training sessions.

Two articles addressed safety issues when working with IVs. Jennifer posted them on the staff information board. She added the Web site information so nurses could access additional information. It also demonstrated how the Internet is a resource for information. This strategy may encourage nurses to start finding their own information.

Jennifer gained skills to find sources of current information. She understood that she had just learned the basics and was eager to keep learning.

CONCLUSION

Technology and information continue to expand. The rate of this expansion is accelerating. Nurses must understand how information systems function and how nursing practice is affected. Seeking out educational and training opportunities is the way to start learning. Nurses also should develop plans for keeping current and be open to learning new technologies as they are introduced.

EXAM QUESTIONS

CHAPTER 4
Questions 16-20

16. Advancements in technology will change the focus of monitoring health care from hospitals to

    a. clients' homes.

    b. mobile units.

    c. portable units.

    d. cyber cafes.

17. The Internet was started by the U.S. Department of Defense to

    a. keep different units informed.

    b. create a communication network.

    c. use new technologies that were being developed.

    d. store data in an electronic format.

18. The World Wide Web (WWW) is the

    a. best way to store information.

    b. source of information collected from libraries.

    c. most powerful way to locate information.

    d. most common method of data transfer.

19. Databases are

    a. collections of files with different types of information.

    b. files that store different types of information.

    c. found on the Internet.

    d. saved on computer disks.

20. A purpose for standardized information language is to

    a. allow researchers around the world to share information.

    b. help everyone understand and evaluate what is being said.

    c. develop electronic health records for individual patients and health systems.

    d. encourage ties between documentation, decision-making, and research.

CHAPTER 5

ORGANIZATIONAL CULTURES

CHAPTER OBJECTIVE

After studying this chapter, you will be able to explain essential concepts of organizational cultures and their impact on nursing practice environments.

LEARNING OBJECTIVES

After studying this chapter, you will be able to

1. select at least three common characteristics of organizational cultures.

2. compare and contrast the values and beliefs in different types of organizations.

3. recognize the similarities and differences in centralized and decentralized organizations.

4. evaluate strategies to resolve conflicts and relate them to the different sources of conflict.

OVERVIEW

We deal with many organizations every day. We may file an insurance claim for damage to our car. It may be time to pay Federal income taxes. Our child's school may have a new dress code. When we pick up our dry cleaning we may find buttons missing. Our complaints about interfacing with organizations cover many parts of these interactions.

- There is too much paperwork and the processes are complicated.

- Employees are rude and do not care to solve problems.

- A great deal of time is spent trying to resolve the issues.

- It is difficult to get accurate information.

In this chapter, we look behind the observable parts of organizations. What we see and experience is based on organizational values and beliefs, structures, and processes for preventing conflicts. The first areas of interest are organizational cultures, climates, values, and beliefs.

ORGANIZATIONAL CULTURE AND CLIMATE

Challenges

Several nurses work together on a general medical-surgical unit in a community hospital. The hospital was started years ago by community leaders to provide health care to people in the town as well as to those in surrounding small communities and rural areas. The nurses live in the community and have been part of the hospital since it opened 25 years ago. Patients are family, friends, and neighbors. Staff know each other and have ties outside the work setting.

A health care system is interested in purchasing the hospital because it is profitable and there is no competition. There are community and hospital staff meetings to discuss the proposal. Administrators and managers from the health care system hold informational meetings about their organization and plans for the hospital. They share what it means to be part of a system. The nurses have concerns about how the culture, climate, values, and beliefs will change. They agree to collect information, discuss it, ask additional questions, and determine how their roles may change.

Organizational Culture

 Organizational culture is difficult to define in concrete terms. Young (2000) describes it as a combination of

- beliefs about how to do the work,
- the role of authority in the organization,
- controls and rewards for employees.

Why do we have organizational cultures? When we are part of an organization, we have a sense of identity. Employees will develop a sense of commitment to the organization. The organization's social system helps us make sense of individual and group behavior. We know that things are done a certain way (Young, 2000). Organizational culture is the system that guides employees' thoughts, communications, and actions. The culture is passed on within the company by the emotional and aesthetic patterns of behavior (Robinson & Kish, 2001).

Organizational Climate

Organizational climate defines how others perceive and feel about it. The perceptions may not be accurate and may differ among employees and the public (Robinson & Kish, 2001). It is essential to have the climate accurately reflect the culture and goals. Visible signs of organizational climate include how employees dress. IBM had a strict dress code for male employees: white shirts, subdued ties, and plain suits. Nurses used to wear only white dress uniforms, white hose, nursing shoes, and caps. Many businesses and organizations, such as the military and law enforcement, have standard dress codes.

The physical environment tells us about organizational climates. A school that is in disrepair and lacks resources sends a powerful message to students, parents, teachers, and the public; education is not important. When we go shopping and cannot find anyone to help or have a salesperson who does not know the products or is rude, we tend to not go back.

Health care organizations share their cultures and climates in the physical and environmental conditions we observe. A long-term care setting that is well maintained, odor-free, and accepting of personal items is a sharp contrast to a setting that is drab, has odors, and does not allow residents to have personal items. Where would you like to have a relative stay, and where would you like to work? We make judgements about organizations based on our perceptions and feelings.

Values and Beliefs

Organizational values and beliefs are shared in many different ways. When you walk into a hospital, there may be a display identifying its mission and philosophy. The organization may have a slogan or statement that highlights their most important value, be it quality care, individualized care, providing holistic care, or patient satisfaction. Basing policies on patients' rights is another value.

Organizational goals also give us clues about organizational values and beliefs. We may believe that the goal of health care organizations is to provide patient services. Additional goals influence their values.

Survival may be a goal of the health care organization, which may require conserving resources, reducing the workforce, and discontinuing services.

Growth is another goal of organizations as they focus on finding new patients, adding services, and purchasing new facilities. Resources may be spent on advertising, improving environments, attracting new physicians and other personnel, and acquiring new facilities. Current employees and services may not receive the resources they need or may not be as valued as new employees. Starting salaries may be higher than current salaries.

Profit may be a value that impacts services and employees of a health care organization. Services in this case are evaluated for profitability. For example, a hospital may increase cardiac surgery, reduce pediatric care, and discontinue obstetrical (OB) services.

Status is another value that impacts organizations. There may be a VIP suite and national and international marketing for specialized services. A hospital may be known for its premier heart services. Other services may be minimal because many resources are put into one service. Profitability also increases with status.

Dominance is another goal for some organizations. By increasing or controlling a marketplace or service area the organization may hire physicians and purchase specialized technology and equipment needed for special services. Dominance is also achieved by buying providers and folding them into a larger system. The system could provide a range of services to meet the marketplace needs and be cost effective and profitable (Tappen, Weiss, & Whitehead, 2001).

Cultures tend to support a set of values and become egocentric. When one set of values is promoted, there is the potential for distrust. Persons with different points of view or new ideas may not be accepted. Teams may have difficulty functioning because of different points of view (Robinson & Kish, 2001).

Occupational health nurses are on the front line of reengineering in business and industry. They not only have to respond to organizational changes but also to the stresses employees face. Nurses in these settings must realize that health care is a business.

Having a vision includes both professional and organizational values that support goals. A vision helps structure our priorities. In work settings, having a common vision creates a bond and purpose. Nurses can broaden their vision by asking these questions

- How can nurses add value to the current services they perform?

- Will proposed activities benefit all employees?

- Will management see the impact nurses make?

- What is the benefit of networking with other nurses in the same field?

- Will learning the language of business and industry help connect the work nurses do to the company goals?

Nurses in all settings must recognize that times are turbulent and changing. Having a vision to guide practice is essential; "I am not pushed by my problems, I am led by my dreams" (Mintzer, 2001). Change is constant and organizational structures change in different ways. How change occurs depends on structure, form, sponsorship, and financing.

TYPES OF HEALTH CARE ORGANIZATIONS

There are three main types of health care organizations, including

- Private, not-for-profit organizations were the most common for many years. They were founded by community leaders, charitable groups, and religious orders. Some have existed for many years and continue their work today.

- Publicly supported organizations were started by local, county, state, and federal agencies. County health departments, veteran's hospitals, and public hospitals are examples.

- Private, for-profit organizations have been increasing in recent years. They are often organized in systems with different types and levels of care. For example, they may have acute, long term, and outpatient facilities. Others are organized according to specialty areas such as assisted living, surgical centers, or dental services. They are businesses and expect to earn profits.

Organizations do change. Community hospitals have been acquired by for-profit systems. The proceeds from such sales are put in foundations because they were "owned" and supported by communities and not-for-profit groups. The foundations then support community projects. Today, the differences in types of organizations are not as obvious as in the past for a number of reasons.

For example, all of the providers are competing for the same customers, especially those who self-pay or have health insurance.

In addition, cost constraints affect all types of health care providers.

Finally, many provide services that are reimbursed by the government, such as Medicare and Medicaid. They have to meet required standards. Some organizations and groups do not provide these services because of the low reimbursement rates (Tappen, Weiss, & Whitehead, 2001). In some communities, these services are limited. According to providers, reimbursement levels do not cover the actual costs of the services. Many individuals and families do not have access to health care services in their own areas. They have to travel to find providers who will accept Medicare and Medicaid reimbursement.

Formal Organizational Structures

Formal structures have detailed organizational charts on paper. When we see an organizational chart, we can determine who reports to whom and their place in relation to others. Titles indicate the responsibility and span of control for each person. Typically, the president of an organization is at the top and everyone else reports up the ladder. One view is that the bosses are the brains and the employees are the muscles in an organization.

Large organizations such as the military and educational institutions are examples of formal structures. Formal structures are seen as traditional and bureaucratic for the following reasons:

• Jobs are assigned to individuals or groups based on expertise.

• There is a hierarchy, with everyone at a specific level. Administrators and managers have the highest rankings. Unskilled workers are at the lowest levels. Physicians may be employees of an organization but usually have a parallel structure that supports autonomous medical practice. They are still responsible for following organizational policies and external regulations.

• Written policies are numerous. Memos are frequent and detail what to do and when. For example, a vacation policy outlines how the hours are accrued, length of employment for eligibility, process for approval, when time must be used, and how much time can be accumulated.

• Technical competence is emphasized. In health care settings, that is important (Tappen, Weiss, & Whitehead, 2001).

Nurses know the importance of being competent to provide care. When there is a shortage, nurses are asked to float to different units. They express concern about being competent to care for different types of patients. One strategy to overcome this concern is to provide cross training. For example, nurses in obstetrical units are trained to provide postpartum and newborn care.

In traditional formal organizations, the people at the top have the responsibility and authority to make decisions, approve the budget, determine goals, and hire or fire people. It is a fact that the organization could not function without the people on the lower rungs of the organizations. They are all needed if organizations are going to survive and thrive.

Restructuring and redesign are common in the complex organizations of today. Goals for doing so are cost savings, recognizing that people are the most important resource, and making it possible for organizations to adapt to changing environments (Tappen, Weiss, & Whitehead, 2001). The formal organizations begin to develop informal structures.

Informal Organizational Structures

Smaller organizations do not have complicated layered levels of administration. They may have started very small and retained those characteristics. New organizations that thrive on creativity and innovation tend to have flat and informal structures. An organizational chart will show who is in charge but have few layers for reporting. It might also indicate that teams, rather than individuals, are responsible for certain functions and outcomes. Managers are there to provide resources, coordinate efforts across groups, and plan strategies to meet the company goals. Employees self-regulate their activities. Informal structures support adaptability and creativity. These characteristics are needed for organizational survival and growth. As innovations and changes appear, an organization with informal structures is ready to respond and adapt (Tappen, Weiss, & Whitehead, 2001).

Organizations with different departments or divisions may have subcultures. For example, the technical people may dress informally and work independently. They focus on implementing new products and keeping everything running. They work across organizational layers. Vice presidents of different divisions are mindful of their roles and responsibilities. They stay within the formal structures and do not intrude on others' territories.

Another type of informal structure is the "experts" throughout an organization. They are consulted because they know the history and understand how to navigate the system to get results. They understand the limits of acceptable behavior. A dress code may be very specific but

deviations are sometimes ignored. For example, there is often one maintenance person who can fix problems. That person is called even if he is not directly responsible for the area.

Nurses may have networks in the different departments. If something is needed immediately, the nurses call on others. The expert nurse is also a resource for other nurses who have questions.

Experts close the gap between how things are really done compared to what is formally stated. There may be issues with this approach. Nurses need to follow policies, maintain standards, and practice legally and ethically.

REDESIGNING AND REENGINEERING HEALTH CARE

All types of organizations in business, industry, and health care must pay attention to costs, efficiency, effectiveness, and outcomes. The health care industry faces the following challenges:

- The cost of providing health care continues to increase.

- Reimbursement from third-party payers and governmental sources does not cover costs.

- Many people do not have insurance and yet need care.

- The health care needs of the aging population continue to increase and take a large share of the resources.

Redesigning health care focuses on who does what jobs and how to get work done more efficiently. Reengineering health care allows organizations to change processes to accomplish tasks (Tappen, Weiss, & Whitehead, 2001).

The question is, how are health care organizations going to survive, provide services, and keep current with technology, practices, and standards? There is agreement that fundamental, radical, and dramatic changes are needed. Industry and business have been applying these concepts. There is doubt that the same processes will work in health care. Reengineering requires rethinking and radical redesign of processes (Robinson & Kish, 2001).

Evolution of Organizational Processes

Adam Smith, in 1776, wrote about the division of labor. The idea was that many workers would each do one step in a complex process. Productivity and uniformity was increased. Henry Ford adapted this concept by dividing work into tasks that were repeated. Overseeing the numerous workstations required managers. After World War II, there was great growth in business and industry. Managing all the processes became more complex. An organizational hierarchy was established (Robinson & Kish, 2001).

Companies now realize that the previous processes do not work. Change has replaced repetition of activities. Three influences that are driving organizations today are customers, competition, and change.

The first driving force is customers. They have expectations and demands and want quality, value, and service.

Second, competition is fierce. Companies compete in global markets, so technology is required to stay competitive.

Third, Americans have accepted the idea of change as normal. Consumer products, fashion, food, automobiles, housing, and lifestyles change every day. Technology related products change rapidly. We want new computers, video games, cameras, cars, and home products. By the 1980s, the automobile industry, Disney, and Harley Davidson had all changed, based on the three driving forces (Robinson & Kish, 2001).

The health care industry has some characteristics of business and industry but is also very different.

Mismanagement of health care can have catastrophic results. Patient needs are unpredictable. There are many entry and exit points in health care. Can reengineering be adapted to health care systems?

Changing Health Care Systems and Nursing

The goals are to transform organizations, improve profits, and decrease costs. Employees at all levels participate. Nursing shortages, starting in the 1980s, served as the focus of redesign. The purpose was to ensure that nursing care survived, in spite of the inhospitable work environments.

As the shortage of nurses becomes a greater issue, work environments must uphold legal and ethical standards of the profession. For example, mandatory overtime is an issue. Nurses have gone to court, and legislation now mandates patient/nurse ratios and other workplace rules. The American Nurses Association has increased its efforts for workplace advocacy. Workplace safety, work environment issues, and legal practice concerns are part of the agenda (Robinson & Kish, 2001).

Process of Reengineering

All members of an organization must change how they look at their work. Employees are usually comfortable in their current roles. They may not want to give up what they have or take on additional responsibilities. Cooperation with a cross-section of persons will support success. Training a change team or core group to understand the challenges is essential. As the process continues, employees will begin to see benefits, such as

- greater ability to make decisions and exercise individual judgement,

- job descriptions that include strategic responsibilities,

- individuals being responsible for solving problems,

- members demonstrating continuous quality improvement skills,

- cooperation and collaboration through teamwork being expected and offered,

- appreciation that change is part of work and the organization showing willingness to respond (Robinson & Kish, 2001).

A driving force in reengineering is technology. How patients interact with health care providers has changed. Computers track their visits, diagnostic tests are automated, and information is shared between physicians. Patients in rural areas have broader access to care. In large organizations, employees are cross-trained to provide a variety of services. When health care workers can provide more than one service, costs are contained and efficiency is increased (Robinson & Kish, 2001).

Ray, Turkel, & Marino (2002) believe the traditional organizational values have changed with reengineering tactics. In the past, the ideal included commitment to workers, investment in professional development, and fair pay. The new focus is getting employees to do more with less. Nurses' salaries have barely kept pace with inflation, and nurses are sometimes seen as liabilities. Some are disillusioned with working conditions. Nurses need preparation, through education and support, to face the reality of workplace changes. For example, nurses may believe that management can and will solve all problems. Nurses need to learn skills and form communities to implement change and resolve conflicts. Change is synonymous with reengineering and redesign.

Impact of Change

Even when we know change is needed, it may be difficult to accomplish. We may be comfortable with our work situation, know what we are doing,

and feel competent. In redesign, it is essential to understand why change is needed. A positive approach to change, realizing the impact it will have on the organization, and preparation will help. Sometimes organizations jump into change. Rapid and continuous changes can cause psychological and physical overload. People may barely get used to one change before another one happens. Employees get tired and may not have the energy to cope with subsequent change. Nurses feel the impact of rapid change in some settings. They experience burnout and leave nursing or find new practice settings (Robinson & Kish, 2001).

Time spent in planning and sharing information is vital to success. Continuous and ongoing evaluations measure how the process is moving forward. They also allow for corrections as indicated. Theories of change are found in the literature. Lewin's theory of change is well known and can serve as a framework for implementing change. It includes

- Stage 1 – unfreezing, which requires that the need for change be recognized and planning to begin. The restraining and driving forces are identified. The driving forces must be more dominant than the restraining forces for the redesign to succeed.

- Stage 2 – implementing the change. Skills needed include anticipating problems, communication, and focusing on the outcomes.

- Stage 3 – refreezing, which happens when evaluation and modifications happen as needed. At this point, the change is in place, and all the participants have adopted the change and own it (Robinson & Kish, 2001). The expectation and hope is that implementing change will be a positive experience. The reality is that whenever there is change, there is the potential for conflict.

SOURCES OF CONFLICT AND RESOLUTION STRATEGIES

Nurses work in stressful environments. Caring for patients and providing quality care are stressful and challenging to nurses. Sanon-Rollins (2002) describes a situation in which a nurse exchanges strong words with a physician and still has to make rounds. Code team members disagree about procedure, and the patient is dying. Conflicts happen when two incompatible events occur together. Sources of conflicts are varied

- Tensions between groups due to positions, gender, ethnic backgrounds, education, age.

- Increased workload along with fiscal constraints, perception that others are not working hard, absenteeism.

- Multiple role demands, including more roles and higher expectations.

- Threats to professional identity and territory, unclear boundaries.

- Threats to safety and security, such as layoffs, economic security, increase in stress.

- Scarce resources related to inadequate pay, few pay increases, and limited help, equipment, and supplies.

- Cultural differences on beliefs and values about work, approaches to work, and willingness to do certain tasks.

- Invasion of personal space, crowded conditions, and constant interruptions (Tappen, Weiss, & Whitehead, 2001).

A combination of conflicts can interfere with work. Nurses have a variety of responses when they experience conflict on the job

- Disbelief, especially when values are an issue.

- Disconnectedness after the initial shock.

- Obsession, the nurse is constantly thinking about the conflict.

- Frenzied activity to reduce the frustration.

- Self-evaluation that leads to resolving the conflict or facing burnout, apathy, and withdrawal.

- Distancing self from the source of the conflict, which supports self-preservation.

- Actual resolution, creating a positive outcome and skills to use in future situations (Restifo, 2002).

Resolving Conflicts

Conflicts happen at all levels within an organization. Two persons may have difficulty working together. Groups may want to use different strategies to resolve issues. Organizations can have conflicts with external groups. Health care environments encounter mergers, downsizing, reengineering, and redesigning. Employees face psychological, social, and physical consequences when working in conflicted situations. Patients seek help because of problems and bring conflicts to the health care environment (Smith, Tutor, & Phillips, 2001).

Some people try to resolve conflicts from a game perspective. Someone needs to win, someone needs to lose, or the situation is deadlocked in a tie. This approach does not resolve conflicts. Nurses in three hospitals were surveyed about how they handled conflict. Avoidance was the most common strategy used. Other strategies were compromise and accommodation.

Rather than relying on a strategy that is comfortable, select one that fits the situation.

- **Accommodation** is a lose-win strategy that helps preserve relationships. Nurse managers may have to share resources, and one has to be willing to do so on a given situation, making accommodation an appropriate strategy.

- **Competition** is a win-lose approach that may be the only way to make a change. An emergency may require using this strategy.

- **Avoidance** is a lose-lose technique but can be

effective. Ask someone else to take over in a volatile situation.

- **Compromise** is a win-lose/lose-win situation in which everyone gets something. Often this is a temporary resolution.

- **Collaboration** is a win-win approach. Persons working together can find solutions that are impossible for individuals to accomplish alone (Sanon-Rollins, 2002).

Circumstances influence the impact of conflict. Open opposition between two persons or groups is disruptive not only to those involved but also to everyone in the work setting. Conflicts cost time and resources. Productivity drops, nurses resign or request transfers, and absenteeism increases.

There may be barriers to resolving conflicts. Facility policies, poor staffing, inadequate supplies, or time issues all contribute conflicts that are difficult to resolve as individuals or small groups. Collective action, by larger groups, is needed.

Nurses can share their concerns and provide possible solutions to eliminate conflicts. Administrative action can address organizational and disruptive behaviors (Smith, Tutor, & Phillips, 2001). For example, there are persons who hunger for power and want to control everyone and everything. Settling such issues requires sustained effort and creative solutions. Outside help, such as counseling is an option. Moving nurses to other units, giving them different assignments, or firing them are also considerations.

McElhaney (2002) recommends looking forward when trying to resolve conflicts. Alternative positioning is a negotiation principle based on the merits of the situation. The four strategies are

1. Separate the problem and the people.

2. Recognize that the position one has in the conflict is less important than the interest in resolving it.

3. Consider several options before making a decision.

4. Results are based on objective criteria.

This approach results in win-win situations. Conflict is part of our lives. Resolving issues can improve interpersonal relationships and positively change work environments.

The goal is to work together more effectively. Strategies include negotiation and settlement. One process for resolving conflict has the following steps:

- Identify the problem or issue. When people are in conflict, they may not be objective about the real issues. They often have only their personal view of the situation. It is essential to clearly understand the issue before trying to solve it.

- Generate several possible solutions. It is a mistake to quickly suggest and implement a solution. Take time to explore several possibilities.

- Evaluate suggested solutions. Take time to discuss why they would work or not.

- Choose the best solution. Look for the best one, not a perfect solution.

- Implement the selected solution. This is the true test if it will work. Give it enough time, and do not jump from solution to solution.

- Verify that the problem is resolved. Did the solution really solve it? (Tappen, Weiss, & Whitehead, 2001, Sanon-Rollins, 2002).

Solutions

Using an organized process to identify and resolve conflicts increases the chances of success. The nurses at the community hospital in our challenge are working to identify potential conflicts and prevent them if the organization changes.

The nurses on the medical surgical unit start meeting informally and list their questions and concerns. Other nurses want to participate. The nurse administrator sets up a Web site for them to post their questions. Nurses can also put their questions in a secure box by the time clock. The hospital has updated announcements on the information system and posts new information on bulletin boards. The nurses' concerns are primarily related to potential changes in

• staffing, length of shifts, and work schedules;

• salary and benefits;

• organizational culture and climate;

• redesign efforts;

• governance and participation in decision-making.

As the probability for the change increases, nurses talk with staff at other hospitals in the system to gain more information. The nurse administrator facilitates meetings with nursing administrators from the health care system. The community hospital nurses feel they have sufficient information to make decisions. Generally, they plan to remain at the hospital until after the change, work with the new system, and evaluate outcomes after one year.

CONCLUSION

Nurses in all work settings deal with unique organizational challenges. Changes in structure, mission, culture, ownership, and functions all require rethinking how nursing is practiced. As the complexity of organizations increases, conflict is evident. Nurses have the ability to recognize what is happening and to find ways to adapt to new opportunities.

EXAM QUESTIONS

CHAPTER 5
Questions 21-25

21. Organizational culture includes

    a. controls and rewards for employees.

    b. beautiful and aesthetically pleasing sur-
        roundings.

    c. having employees from different ethnic
        backgrounds.

    d. making sure all employees enjoy their
        work.

22. Organizational climate judgements are based
    on

    a. what others tell us about an organization.

    b. individual likes and dislikes.

    c. what is printed in the annual report.

    d. perceptions and feelings.

23. Formal organizational structures are seen as
    traditional and bureaucratic because

    a. jobs are assigned to individuals based on
        "who you know" not "what you know".

    b. there is an informal flat organizational
        chart with few layers for reporting.

    c. there are few written policies and employ-
        ees self-regulate their activities.

    d. technical competence is emphasized.

24. In large organizations, employees are cross-
    trained to provide a variety of services. The
    outcome of workers providing more than one
    service is

    a. costs are contained and efficiency is
        increased.

    b. costs are contained but efficiency is
        decreased.

    c. increased expenditures but increased effi-
        ciency.

    d. increased expenditures and decreased effi-
        ciency.

25. One way to achieve a win-win solution to a
    conflict is through

    a. individual effort to change what is happen-
        ing.

    b. assigning blame to the persons responsible
        for the conflict.

    c. collaborating with others to achieve group
        solutions.

    d. leaving the job and finding one where there
        is no conflict.

CHAPTER 6

LEADERSHIP AND MANAGEMENT

CHAPTER OBJECTIVE

After studying this chapter, you will be able to understand nursing roles related to leadership and management.

LEARNING OBJECTIVES

After studying this chapter, you will be able to

1. specify different leadership and management styles.

2. identify at least two professional benefits of empowerment.

3. indicate different decision-making models.

4. select problem solving strategies that have the potential for application.

5. recognize positive role modeling characteristics and behaviors.

OVERVIEW

Nurses face many challenges in their work settings. Patient care, collaborating with team members, addressing the needs of family members, and dealing with staff and supply shortages require time and attention. In many settings, nurses feel they do not have a voice, are not allowed to make patient care decisions, feel they are constantly "putting out fires," and cannot meet professional standards. They want to broaden their practice,

implement creative solutions, and continue their professional development. New skills are required to survive in the changing work environments and to grow professionally.

Nurses may believe leadership and management skills are only needed for those types of positions. Nurses work independently in many settings. In complex, large organizations, they have a high level of individual responsibility for patient care.

Nurse leaders are responsible for making sure that the resources needed for patient care are available, that staff members have the knowledge and skills needed to provide quality care, and that there are opportunities for continued professional development. The organizing principles and implementation of policies contribute to defining nursing practice. All nurses have an interest and stake in leadership and management practices in their organizations.

In this chapter, we explore the different meanings of leadership and management, the various components, and the outcomes for nurses. First, leadership and management are defined and compared.

DEFINING MANAGEMENT AND LEADERSHIP

Challenges

Jane and Beverly have worked together for 6 years on an acute care psychiatric unit. These registered nurses primarily complete admission assessments, administer medications, and coordinate discharge planning. The facility is undergoing changes because it needs to increase profitability, increase its market share, and become known for its quality care. The new chief nursing officer is interested in reorganizing nursing services. Part of the plan includes empowering all nurses to become leaders. Jane loves her work and is comfortable with the routines. She is caring and firm with patients. She follows the rules and policies. She is very thorough in her documentation and works cooperatively with her coworkers and the other staff. Jane attends in-house staff development sessions and goes to a clinical conference once a year.

Beverly also enjoys her work but is looking for more challenges. She is completing her BSN degree from an online university. She reads several nursing journals and finds new information on the Internet. In addition to her routine duties, she spends time with the patients. This is important to her, the reason she chose nursing. She attends the same group sessions each week and actively participates.

Jane and Beverly look forward to attending the information sessions about the nursing changes. They want to know what will change and how they are affected. How will their roles and responsibilities change? What support will be available to help them through the changes? They know everything will be different. They will wait to make decisions until after they have all the information.

Management

 In the early 1990s, management was defined according to broad functions: planning, organizing, commanding, coordinating, and controlling. Management functions focused on employee work. The functions did not really describe what managers do. In the 1980s, the functions of managers were defined as doing whatever was necessary for employees to do their work. Included are interpersonal, informational, and deci-

sional actions. A current view is that effective managers can bring out the best in their employees in terms of commitment, loyalty, creativity, productivity, and continuous improvement (Tappen, Weiss, & Whitehead, 2001).

Management Theory

Early work on management theories looked at behavior styles of the manager and followers. The styles change, based on the control needed in different situations. Attributes were described according to the degree they were present:

- autocratic and authoritative,
- democratic and participate,
- laissez-faire or hands-off.

Nurse managers may use all three management styles. Situational management responds to what is needed at a particular time. Employees expect more involvement in decision-making. A democratic style is associated with job satisfaction (Cherry & Jacob, 2002).

Leadership

The ability to influence others is the core of leadership. The role of a leader is to help people understand their interdependence and to work together effectively. A leader understands the organizational goals and helps people focus on them. Leaders can influence others to work toward the goals. They can inspire and share a vision (Tappen, Weiss, & Whitehead, 2001). Nurse leaders may focus on continuous quality improvement in care, cost-saving strategies, professional development, and maintaining standards. Are leaders born or do they develop? There is a great deal of research related to that question. Leadership and management are different.

Leadership Theories

There is no clear answer to the question of what makes a leader. Traits that leaders exhibit are intelligence and initiative. They also are creative and willing to take risks. The research has not supported that persons are born with these traits.

Behavioral theories address what leaders do and how they do it. They may be authoritarian, democratic, or laissez-faire.

Leaders may focus on tasks or relationships. Achieving balance between the two contributes to effective leadership.

Situational theories address the complexity of the work environment and take into account a variety of factors. Situations are different, and leaders must understand the different factors that are important (Tappen, Weiss, & Whitehead, 2001).

Although research does not support a specific theory, certain observable qualities and behaviors are common to leaders. Effective leadership qualities are integrity, courage, initiative, energy, optimism, perseverance, balance, self-assurance, and the ability to handle stress (Tappen, Weiss, & Whitehead, 2001).

Leadership goes beyond traits and requires actions. Effective leader behaviors include thinking critically, problem solving and listening to others. Skillful communication requires listening, exchanging of information, and giving feedback (Tappen, Weiss, & Whitehead, 2001).

Application to Nursing Practice

The concept of shared leadership was implemented in an organized care delivery system in eastern Wisconsin (George, Burke, Rodgers, Duthie, et al, 2002). Self-directed teams and shared governance models were recognized to increase staff leadership behaviors and autonomy in practice. The anticipated result was improved patient outcomes. The chief nursing officer developed partnerships with the nursing staff to create an environment for autonomous nursing practice and excellence in clinical nursing. The staff nurses were required to actively participate in proposing ideas and solutions. Risk-taking behaviors were support-

ed. A shared vision was essential for this transformation.

In this setting, several assumptions were basic to creating a shared vision

- nurses who provide direct care must have autonomy and decision-making skills,

- autonomous nurses can provide quality, cost-effective care,

- the professional commitment of nurses is recognized and honored,

- autonomous decision-making promotes speed and accuracy and ensures quality practice.

- shared governance must incorporate peer review (George, Burke, Rodgers, Duthie, et al, 2002).

The successful implementation of shared governance required shared leadership training. A shared leadership concepts program (SLCP) was created. For shared leadership to work, certain competencies described in the literature were required, including

- negotiating win-win solutions,

- facilitating change,

- influencing follower changes,

- using a systems framework for thinking and problem-solving,

- empowering others to embrace a shared vision and act responsibly,

- using shared leadership concepts in decision-making situations (George, Burke, Rodgers, Duthie, et al, 2002).

Over 700 nurses have been trained in the leadership program. Nurses are evaluated on their leadership behaviors. Clinical experts serve as mentors, Colleagues and coworkers observe each other. Nurses complete an assessment of their own leadership behaviors.

<u>Study Results</u>

Because of the time and money put into the program, it was essential that desired outcomes were evident. Three different research projects were conducted between 1995-1999. The following conclusions were shared:

- Participation in the program increased nurses' leadership behavior and autonomy.

- The growth was sustained for at least 6 months.

- Nurses who participated in the program had increased leadership behaviors compared to those who did not participate.

- Nurses had significantly increased leadership behaviors when measured before and 6 months after participating in the program.

- There were improvements in patient care outcomes that were linked to increased leadership behaviors.

This health system was the first regional system in the United States to receive Magnet status. The linkages between quality patient outcomes and the care delivery processes were recognized (George, Burke, Rodgers, Duthie, et al, 2002).

The Synergy Model

Nursing leaders do not provide direct care but can create organizations and structures to support professional practice. The desired future for the organization is envisioned, then the building blocks to achieve it are implemented. Organizations pursuing synergy go beyond building the future from the present reality. Synergy is a dynamic development that is observed when nurses work together in positive ways to reach a common goal. The American Association of Critical Care Nurses led the way in developing the model.

There are three levels of outcomes: patients, nurses, and system. Outcomes cover different factors at each level of the synergy model and include

- Patients come into health care systems with variations in stability, vulnerability, level of decision-making, care needs, and resources.

- Nursing competencies are clinical judgement, advocacy, caring, collaboration, responses to diversity, and clinical inquiry.

- Systems must survive, provide high quality care, reduce readmissions, and deliver clinically effective care.

The synergy model emphasizes how patient care is organized to help patients through all the interdepartmental challenges. The model also supports infrastructures for patient assessment, nurses' career advancement, and interdepartmental collaboration (Kerfoot, 2001).

Another area of research (Wieck, Prydun, & Walsh, 2002) tried to determine what younger nurses and nursing students want in their leaders, compared to nurses already working in the profession.

The next generation of workers (born between 1963-1977 and called Generation X) is the smallest entry pool in modern times. They are the emerging work force. Their parents, the baby boomers, are 44 million strong. Generation X has grown up with technology and creative thinking. They are focused on having time for personal and goal-directed activities. They are not interested in meetings, are not joiners, and have little patience with process.

It is essential that leadership approaches can recruit, employ, and retain them. The study wanted to determine if Generation X nurses and "baby boomer" or entrenched nurses had congruent ideas about desired leadership traits. The "baby boomer" nurses will be the leadership models for Generation X (Wieck, Prydun, & Walsh, 2002). Over 350 surveys were completed by nurses representing the two groups.

<u>Study Findings</u>

Both groups, the younger generation nurses and nursing students and the entrenched nurses, had similar expectations for leaders. The leadership traits are ranked from highest to lowest (Table 6-1).

TABLE 6-1 LEADERSHIP TRAITS	
Emerging Nurses	**Entrenched Nurses**
Honesty	Honesty
Motivate others	High integrity
Team player	Fair
Receptive to people	Same
Positive outlook	Same
Good communication skills	Same
Approachable	Same
Knowledgeable	Empowering
Vision	Friendly
Risk-taking	Available
Sense of humor	
Adapted from Wieck, Prydun, & Walsh, 2002.	

Comparisons to other studies show that the emerging workforce is different from personnel at magnet hospitals. For example, being a visionary leader was ranked at the top by personnel in magnet hospitals but one of the least important traits for the emerging workforce in this study.

While some of the desired leadership traits between the two groups were similar, the general approaches to work and careers will have a major impact on attracting new nurses to the profession.

The emerging workforce wants entrepreneurial opportunities, short-term employment, and balance in their lives. The emerging workforce may not be attracted to health care careers and more importantly, to leadership positions (Wieck, Prydun, & Walsh, 2002).

Nurses will benefit from developing a broad view of their roles. They need the qualities and the behaviors of leaders. For example, providing negative feedback is difficult, but doing it in a positive manner is possible. Positive feedback helps

employees know that they are doing what is expected. Nurse leaders have the essential role in setting goals and sharing a vision.

Comparison of Leadership and Management

Leaders do not need formal positions and authority to influence change. Martin Luther King, Jr. changed the course of history because he shared a common goal with many people. He did not hold an elected position or have formal power to carry out his dream of equality for all.

Leaders may not be good managers. They may inspire and influence others, but some are not interested in doing the day-to-day activities required to reach organizational or nursing unit goals. Table 6-2 compares the qualities and behaviors of leaders and managers.

All nurses need leadership skills to effectively care for patients, to promote high quality nursing practice, and to contribute to the advancement of the nursing profession. Nurses who function in managerial roles need additional skills to perform all the required responsibilities. Empowerment is one approach to change nursing practice.

EMPOWERMENT

The concept of empowerment is changing the work environments for nurses. Health care systems are commonly structured to manage employees from a technical, hierarchical perspective. This approach is derived from earlier industrial models, when employees needed close supervision to carry out specific tasks. Nurses are professionals who want to practice in settings that recognize and support them. Nurses expect to be valued as professionals. They want to use their leadership skills and have collaborative relationships with coworkers.

Power can be defined in terms of our ability to recognize our resolve even when others are resis-

TABLE 6-2 COMPARISON OF LEADER AND MANAGER QUALITIES AND BEHAVIORS			
Qualities of Effective Leaders	**Behaviors of Effective Leaders**	**Qualities of Effective Managers**	**Behaviors of Effective Managers**
Integrity	Critical Thinking	Leadership	Monitoring Activities
Courage	Problem Solving	Clinical Expertise	Resolving Conflicts
Initiative	Respect for Individuals	Business Knowledge	Representing Organization
Energy	Listening		
Optimism	Supporting Exchange of Information		Networking
Perseverance	Providing Feedback		Rewards and Punishments
Balance	Goal Setting		
Coping with Stress	Sharing a Vision		
Self-awareness			
Continued Development			Employee Development

Adapted from Tappen, Weiss, & Whitehead, 2001.

tant. Using our power requires actions. A nurse manager has the power to schedule work hours. Because two nurses are ill, the manager will change the schedule although the nurses on that unit resist the changes. Empowerment refers to our feelings about competence, control, and entitlement. For nurses to feel empowered, they need a voice, recognition, and respect (Tappen, Weiss, & Whitehead, 2001).

Kanter describes empowering work environments that make information, resources, and support available. There are also opportunities for learning and developing. The structure of work environments has the greatest impact on employees' perceptions of their empowerment and work behavior. Empowered nurses have access to

- opportunity for advancement within an organization and the profession

- mobility and growth by having new experiences, receiving rewards, and continuing their professional development

- resources such as supplies, time, equipment, and support to complete work

- information, which includes technical knowledge, data, organizational policies and goals, and the broad vision

- support for feedback, guidance from managers and hands-on assistance (Almost & Spence-Laschinger, 2002).

Empowered employees function as team members, contribute to making decisions, and control their work. Nursing leaders and managers have the authority and responsibility to create empowering work environments. There are many ways to create new environments.

Nurse managers have the challenge of being the "leader of leaders." Professional nurses expect leaders and managers to treat them as peers and equals. Collegial relationships are the norm. The talents of individual nurses are valued and supported. Coaching and building team relationships are essential for empowered organizations. An example is the change in how performance evaluations are done. Instead of an annual evaluation done by the manager, performance is reviewed and discussed by peers on a regular basis. Nursing leaders must recognize they do not have to know and do everything. The ability of nurse managers to recognize and use the talents of all nurses can move the organization forward and increase job satisfaction. Effective managers encourage leadership among staff nurses who are equal and unique.

Empowered organizations have peers, collaborators, colleagues, and coworkers. Instead of traditional supervisors and managers, there are mentors, coaches, and persons who can inspire (Kerfoot, 2002). Coaching can occur on nursing units. Communication and critical thinking are essential coaching techniques. Using them at the bedside can improve results in

- patient care outcomes,
- retention of nurses,
- increased clinical performance,
- negotiation skills,
- staff empowerment (Detmer, 2002).

Application to Nursing Practice

Mischenko (2002) describes a setting in England where community nurses had 4 years of experience with self-management. The Nursing Development Unit began exploring a self-management process as they prepared for accreditation. Nurses worked in teams. They developed critical thinking skills and heightened political awareness. The accreditation was a success and helped the nurses gain confidence in their own abilities. They became dissatisfied with the management structure that was hierarchical. They began to negotiate for self-managed status. The move to self-management was planned by a group of empowered nurses. The outcomes of self-management in this setting included

- little absenteeism,
- continued extension and integration of roles,
- greater flexibility,
- increased productivity (Mischenko, 2002).

Many executive nurse managers have visited the unit to understand how self-management is implemented. A question they all have relates to performance evaluations and capability issues. Empowerment is based on employees using internal rules and values to manage their performance.

There are programs available to learn how to lead empowered organizations. Leaders are encouraged to move away from hierarchical organizational structures (Mischenko, 2002).

Changes in the workplace require empowering all staff and improving communication (Shaw, 2002). Leaders and managers can increase empowerment in an organization by sharing the sources of power and including others in decision-making. The three main sources of power in an organization are

- resources (money, materials, and human help),
- support (including authority to act without getting permission),
- information (about organizational goals and activities).

Nurses also need opportunities to grow professionally, involvement in decision-making, and opportunities to move ahead in the organizational structure (Tappen, Weiss, & Whitehead, 2001).

Nurses can empower themselves by

- participating in interdisciplinary conferences and projects,
- attending professional conferences,
- reading professional journals and books,
- accessing Internet information,
- participating in research projects,
- organizing clinical conferences and discussions groups in the work environment,
- observing how expert nurses practice,
- earning additional credentials and degrees (Tappen, Weiss, & Whitehead, 2001).

DECISION-MAKER

Nurses make many critical decisions as they care for patients and function within organizations. How we make decisions affects outcomes of patient care. The basis for making decisions is also important because we draw on prior knowledge and experiences. The classic decision-making process relies on

- using personal clinical experience,

- relying on previous knowledge from the basic and social sciences,

- reviewing references such as texts and unit-based materials,

- asking experts and coworkers for information (Young, 2000).

The information obtained from these sources is useful, but it may not be complete or current. The movement to evidence-based practice is discussed in Chapter 8. Clinical decision-making is an essential skill.

Clinical Decision-Making

Clinical decision-making is defined as the process of selecting interventions and actions that help patients reach a specific outcome. Nurses use their judgement to draw conclusions about the interventions and actions. The goal is to have the conclusions match the desired outcome. An example is making decisions about interventions and actions to promote wound healing. Possible conclusions and their match to outcomes are

- a perfect match, with the wound healed

- a partial match, with wound healing evident

- no match, with the wound looking worse (Pesut & Herman, 1999).

Nurses then will be able to examine the results and make some more decisions. The clinical nurse should formalize what was done when the wound healed. This involves collecting data about the variables present (such as age, length of time wound was present, medical conditions, and nutritional status). To share and continue the effective interventions, the clinical nurse then can use a transdisciplinary approach to share the results with other nurses and providers.

With the outcome of partial healing, nurses should consult health care team members, review the literature, and revise the interventions. Collecting data about what happens with the new strategies may lead to an effective set of interventions.

With no wound healing, a team approach is needed to review all the elements of the interventions and develop new strategies to achieve the desire outcome.

Group Decision-Making

Group decision-making requires additional skills because of differing values and perspectives. All the nurses on a unit may have a voice in determining the staffing patterns. These nurses have diverse needs; some want 8-hour shifts and others want shifts set at 12 hours. The nurses discuss patient care delivery methods and how staffing is affected. Some believe having nursing assistants assigned to registered nurses is cost-effective and helps maintain quality care. Others like to work alone in a primary care mode.

Group decisions require consensus. Negotiation and consensual skills are needed. Ground rules for discussions, clear goals, and collaboration contribute to achieving group decisions. Group leadership is equally distributed, and conflicts are handled constructively (Rideout, 2001). Nurses are empowered when they work together and make constructive decisions. Problem-solving skills require analysis of situations so that decisions result in positive outcomes.

PROBLEM-SOLVER

Analytical skills such as critical thinking and problem-solving are essential for nurses, personally and professionally (Bastable, 2003). Personal problems and how we resolve them affect our professional lives. For example, a nurse and his family decide to move an hour's drive from work in order to be in a better school district. Supervised care is not available before and after school. Resolving that problem will certainly affect the parents' professional responsibilities.

We all know people who cannot seem to make positive decisions. Something always happens, and there is one crisis after another. How do those individuals function at work? Do they continue to make poor decisions, have crises, and demonstrate poor organization of their work? The same problem-solving skills are used in all aspects of our lives.

Nurses think of problems in terms of patient issues. We use patient problems when assessing and determining what is needed. A broad definition of a problem that can apply to many situations is a query, puzzle, or question that requires an answer or resolution (Rideout, 2001).

Persut and Herman (1999) describe several thinking approaches that contribute to solving problems, such as

- **Prototype** identification, which uses a model case as a beginning point for comparative analysis.

- **Hypothesizing,** which determines an explanation, based on a set of facts that are further investigated.

- **If-then thinking,** which links ideas and consequences in a logical sequence.

- **Reframing,** which involves giving different meanings to the content or context of a problem. The new meanings are based on past experience and knowledge.

Nurses use a variety of strategies because clinical and organizational problems are complex. For example, a patient acts in a belligerent way. The first thought is that the patient is angry with the nurse. Reframing the problem requires looking at the context: news about a poor prognosis, the illness of a family member, reactions to medications, or intense pain.

Using the problem-solving process allows the nurse to determine the cause of the behavior. Different solutions are required, depending on the cause. Following an organized process helps assures that all aspects of the problem are considered, including

1. Identifying the problem or issue. Discussing and exploring an issue helps focus on the real problem. People do not necessarily share their concerns. A nurse who works nights may state she cannot sleep much during the day. The discussion may focus on sleep strategies. After some exploration, the nurse reveals that she has to care for her two young children during the day. The child-care center they previously attended has closed. That problem requires different strategies.

2. Generating a number of possible solutions. Thinking creatively is essential. What is usually done or what has been done in the past may not resolve this new problem.

3. Evaluating suggested solutions. This is an essential step but may be difficult, especially when groups are involved. Interdisciplinary team members, because of their different perspectives, may have difficulty agreeing on a resolution related to one discipline.

4. Choosing the best solution. This decision must include all the parties involved. Patients, family members, staff nurses on all the shifts or one unit, administrators, or the community will be part of the solution.

5. Implementing the solution. This is the true test; does it work? Allow time to see if it works. Sometimes a good solution is discarded before it is truly tested.

6. Determining if the problem is truly resolved. It may take multiple tries to resolve some problems (Tappen, Weiss, & Whitehead, 2001).

A matrix can help organize potential solutions so they can be reviewed objectively. The criteria for the solution are placed across the top and coded according to importance. The solutions are placed down the left side. The solution receiving the highest ranking is selected (Robinson & Kish, 2001).

The problem sometimes is just shifted to someone else or to another area. For example, the night nurses in ICU are short-staffed and cannot do the number of baths they had in the past. It is decided that the day shift nurses will do more baths. The day shift nurses are also short-staffed and have many more people to deal with during the day. They do not have time to do more baths. Therefore, the problem is not solved. Nurses need supportive work environments to use problem-solving skills.

Empowered work environments encourage nurses to address and resolve problems. Individual nurses or groups can tackle problems on their units or within organizations. Encouragement can include rewards, incentives, and supportive policies. Nurses who demonstrate skill in problem-solving often are experts in the problem area, are creative, have a broad knowledge base, and have experience in research procedures. Nurses do have skills and experiences to contribute to organizational change and patient care improvements.

ROLE MODEL

A team of clinicians, educators, and researchers developed a theory of modeling and role modeling. They based the theory on their personal experiences, clinical practice, nursing education, social sciences, and research. The nurses conducted research on the theory and applied it to nursing practice. Over the years, they mentored many students and colleagues. The theory was also applied in diverse practice settings with people of different ages (Robinson & Kish, 2001).

Modeling and role-modeling (MRM) is recognized as 1 of 8 theories that can serve as a foundation for holistic practice. Modeling and role modeling are two major nursing roles. Role modeling is the actions of nurses as they work with patients to promote health, growth, and quality of life (Robinson & Kish, 2001). The components of the theory are useful for nurses as they interact with coworkers and others in their work settings.

Nurses can use themselves as role models. This is one teaching strategy. We can all think of a nursing instructor or coworker who demonstrated outstanding professional or clinical behaviors. Our admiration lead us to acquire those same characteristics. We identified with that person. Socialization theories explain how we acquire new behaviors and attitudes. Role-modeling behaviors include

- competency in performing skills, ✓

- positive interactions with others,

- personal examples,

- enthusiasm and interest conveyed (Bastable, 2003).

The motto "actions speak louder than words" is relevant to nursing practice. Modeling and role modeling benefit everyone in a work environment and have positive benefits for patients.

Solutions

The nurses on the acute care psychiatric unit in our challenge situation are learning more about the changes planned for the facility. Jane and Beverly attend informational sessions and are reading the printed material. They still have questions, but it is evident that expectations for nurses will include

- training, over 6 months, to learn leadership skills,

- working in interdisciplinary teams to develop communication and problem-solving pathways,

- participating in unit-based groups to develop empowerment and self-management strategies,

- serving as role models and mentors for other nurses, if selected,

- developing a plan for professional goals and determine development needs,

- participating in peer review processes.

Jane and Beverly frequently discuss the changes. They talk with other nurses on their unit and their friends on other units. Jane is very uneasy about all the proposed changes. She never thought her work environment would change so much.

Beverly is intrigued by the proposed changes. The changes fit her care philosophy and her goals for professional development. She is aware of the literature about changes in work environments, empowerment, and leadership and management principles.

After 6 months, Jane has left and gone to a new position that is similar to her old one. Beverly is involved in the several change projects, feels energized, and is taking a leadership position in the organization.

CONCLUSION

Nurses focus on their primary jobs. Most are giving direct patient care. They must make sure they are meeting patient and family needs and be able to maintain and improve their clinical skills, function within changing organizations, and meet their personal obligations. Unless they are looking to advance their careers, they may not think about leadership and management as part of their daily practice.

Understanding and applying leadership and management principles to clinical practice is essential. Nurses act as leaders in the care they provide. They must manage their time and resources. Nursing care is complex and requires excellent decision-making skills and problem-solving competencies. Nurses can find colleagues who are experts and demonstrate the best of nursing practice. Changing health care environments rely on empowered workers. All nurses have the opportunity for leadership, in any position or setting. The challenge is for nurses to continue their own professional development, share their knowledge and skills with others, and become active participants in societal and organizational change.

EXAM QUESTIONS

CHAPTER 6
Questions 26-30

26. A broad description of managers' responsibilities includes

    a. all of the formal and informal assignments that are part of the job.

    b. whatever tasks and projects are assigned by their supervisors.

    c. whatever is needed to help employees do their jobs well.

    d. all of the required daily paperwork and reports.

27. In a work environment structured to support self-managed nursing, empowered nurses have access to

    a. opportunity for advancement within the organization.

    b. many high level administrators.

    c. adequate staffing and expert physicians.

    d. a work-friendly physical layout of patient care units.

28. Nurses in the OR who want to use a group decision-making approach to decide how to reorganize the layout of the surgical areas will

    a. schedule many meetings to review options.

    b. select a leader to make the decision.

    c. negotiate and reach consensus.

    d. ask that a consultant help them.

29. When caring for a patient who is angry and belligerent, the nurse decides to reframe the problem and

    a. ask the patient and family members what is wrong.

    b. look at the context of the problem.

    c. look at the patient's previous behavior.

    d. ask the night shift nurses what happened to the patient.

30. A mentor's role-modeling behaviors include

    a. demonstrating leadership skills.

    b. competency in performing skills.

    c. working on a team with licensed practical nurses and nursing assistants.

    d. being aggressive with physicians and nursing managers.

CHAPTER 7

HEALTH AND NURSING CARE DELIVERY MODELS

CHAPTER OBJECTIVE

After studying this chapter, you will be able to differentiate between health and nursing care delivery models and their impact on practice.

LEARNING OBJECTIVES

After studying this chapter, you will be able to

1. recognize significant elements of selected health and nursing care delivery models.

2. discriminate different health and nursing care delivery models.

3. identify at least three nursing issues with selected delivery models.

4. select a delivery model that is congruent with your current practice area.

OVERVIEW

The delivery of patient care varies by organizational philosophy, setting, staffing mix, external requirements, reimbursement regulations, and resources. Health care delivery in the United States is a huge, complex, fragmented business. Historical events and the continuation of traditional approaches are important factors in how care is delivered today. Nurses often do not have a voice in determining delivery systems implemented in practice settings. In settings with shared leadership, nurses

have a voice in decisions. This chapter highlights several health care delivery models. The strengths and weaknesses of the models are explored as well as the impact on patient care and the nurses who are providing the care.

HEALTH AND NURSING CARE DELIVERY MODELS

Nurses provide care in many different settings to patients with a wide range of needs. We talk about systems of care, but the issues are complex. A synopsis of the features of health care in America provides some insight into how nurses function in the many organizations that deliver care.

Challenges

Janice manages a rural health clinic that is funded by the state. She is a family nurse practitioner. Denise works in the emergency department at the small private hospital in the rural community. Barbara is a school health nurse. The three nurses are serving on a local committee to address health care issues in their rural community. The committee is made up of local leaders in business, church, education, and community organizations. The town council members identified several problems and issues related to health services in their rural community. They are

1. The hospital is part of Premier Health System. Community Hospital is losing money.

2. The community is growing, with families moving into new housing developments. The local school budget is stretched, and it is difficult to fund additional health services.

3. The community has a growing number of long-time residents who are retired.

4. A new plant is dumping industrial waste into the river. There are also concerns about the health of employees.

The committee is to review the assembled information and make recommendations. Public informational meetings will be held. The final recommendations will be given to the community officials. They will work with others to implement strategies that will maintain and improve health services.

Delivery of Health Care in the United States

 The approach to delivering health care in the United States is different than in most developed countries. A common feature of health care in most developed countries is universal coverage because there is a national health care program.

Health Care Delivery Systems in Other Countries

Most developed countries share certain health care delivery characteristics

* national health service or socialized insurance;

* ownership is private or public;

* reimbursement for hospitals is done on a global basis or per diem payment;

* reimbursement for physicians is based on negotiated fee for services or salaries;

* consumer payment out-of-pocket is negligible (Robinson & Kish, 2001).

The merits of such systems are not discussed in this chapter. There are issues and concerns with all

the systems. The features of health care delivery in the United States are

* different entities are responsible for providing care;

* health care is privately run;

* reimbursement for hospitals varies: diagnostic related groups (DRG), negotiated fees for services, per diem, and capitation;

* reimbursement for physicians varies: using plans such as resource-based relative value scales, or fee-for-service;

* consumer payment varies from small to significant (Robinson & Kish, 2001).

Strengths and Weaknesses of U.S. Health Care Delivery

Strengths of the U.S. health care system include

* excellent medical, nursing, and allied health education,

* use of technology,

* research focus,

* focus on treating illness,

* free market,

* no central agency governing all aspects of delivery,

* licensing and certification set standards for care (Robinson & Kish, 2001).

Weaknesses in the U.S. health care system include

* fragmented collection of services and providers,

* complex and huge,

* expensive, not cost effective,.

* access based on ability to pay and insurance coverage,

* private financing primarily through employers,

* legal rules regulate practice behaviors,

- focus on illness care rather than health promotion and maintenance,

- health plans are the buyers of services in the open market,

- high administrative costs for billing, collections, and debts (Robinson & Kish, 2001).

The United States does not have a "system" but rather have a collection of fragmented pieces (Shi & Singh, 1998). Health care is delivered by a variety of providers, including

- over 700,000 physicians,

- almost 2 million nurses,

- 187,000 dentists,

- 158,000 pharmacists (Shi & Singh, 1998).

There are many other groups of providers, including

- physical, speech, and occupational therapists,

- medical social workers,

- OR, radiology, respiratory, and laboratory technicians,

- nutritionists and dietitians,

- organizations (focusing on patient education),

- medical transcribers.

The sites for delivering care are numerous, including

- 6,580 hospitals,

- 16,700 nursing homes,

- over 5,000 mental health facilities,

- over 60,000 facilities for mentally retarded persons,

- 19,000 home health and hospice agencies.

There are almost 800 primary care programs sponsored by different levels of government (Shi & Singh, 1998). Services are delivered by different types of institutions and organizations.

Hospitals

Hospitals may provide a wide range of services or may be specialized. They are licensed, have a staff of physicians, and offer 24-hour nursing care that is supervised by registered nurses. In the mid-1850s, hospitals provided custodial care and were avoided if possible. Most of the hospitals in the United States were founded by physician, philanthropists, and community leaders. In contrast, most hospitals in Europe were founded by religious orders and later became tax-supported, government institutions. Most (85%) of hospitals in the United States are nonprofit, voluntary, short-term, general hospitals. Public hospitals are the next most common, followed by for-profit and federal hospitals (Robinson & Kish, 2001).

Hospitals may be not-for-profit (voluntary) or propriety (for-profit). Voluntary hospitals have a single mission, usually to provide service to the community. Many voluntary hospitals are community-based, started by persons in the area. Many church-sponsored hospitals were started in the late 1800s. Catholic sisterhoods established the first church sponsored hospitals in the United States. Voluntary hospitals share a number of characteristics, such as

- offering open and unrestricted use of emergency services,

- providing emergent care without considering payer status,

- having tax-exempt status,

- demonstrating fiscal ability to meet their mission,

- developing for-profit services, such as adult day care, childcare centers, and pharmacy services,

- being the largest group of hospitals in the United States (Robinson & Kish, 2001).

Characteristics of proprietary hospitals include

- operating as a business, with tax cuts, benefits, and write-offs,

- offering multiple facilities, in addition to hospitals, such as nursing homes, clinics, home health agencies, and outpatient services,

- being exempt from providing humanitarian services, but may feel pressured by the community,

- providing of emergency services to stabilize patients before transferring them to other facilities (Robinson & Kish, 2001).

Rural health agencies have unique problems in providing health care services. They may not have access to technology, expenses often exceed revenue, and there are shortages of personnel. The majority of persons needing care in rural areas are poor or elderly. Almost 50% of rural hospital revenue comes from Medicare. Nurse practitioners and physician assistants substitute for physicians. Rural hospitals may be associated with a health care system. If the hospital is not profitable, it may be turned into a primary care center. If it is investor-owned, it may be closed (Robinson & Kish, 2001).

Outpatient services do not require an overnight stay. Most outpatient visits occur in a provider's office. Outpatient services include home health care, urgent care, dental care, optometry, women's health care, and alternative care. Hospitals have started providing outpatient services in areas such as lab and diagnostic services (Robinson & Kish, 2001).

Public health care agencies have legal requirements to provide specific services and conduct certain activities. They may provide direct services, collect health information, set standards and qualifications for providers, conduct research, and inform the public of health issues. The scope of services varies by local or state requirements. Some common services include well-baby care, sexually transmitted disease clinics, family planning, tuberculosis screening, and mental health services (Robinson & Kish, 2001). Public agencies are also becoming more involved in health-related anti-terrorist initiatives.

Public and voluntary clinics are a "safety net" for persons who do not have access to other types of care. Services are provided in communities of need, schools, day care centers, elderly housing, homeless shelters, migrant worker settings, and senior centers. Federal programs and voluntary organizations support the clinics (Robinson & Kish, 2001). A recent type of service is parish nursing, which targets persons who are affiliated with a church or who live in the community the church serves.

Long-term care includes not only nursing homes but also care provided by family, foster care, custodial care, and room and board services. Elderly, chronically ill, and disabled persons often need care on a long-term basis. They may require different levels of service at different stages of illness. The shift from inpatient to outpatient services requires that a variety of options be available (Robinson & Kish, 2001).

The programs and services previously described are not delivered through a system of interrelated parts that work together. The essential elements of a system — financing, insurance, delivery, and payment — are not standardized and exist in many different forms. The goals of the players are different. For example, private insurance companies seek to make a profit and set the rules to help achieve that goal. Governmental programs seek to provide services to specific populations; they do this by providing funding to state and local entities to actually provide the services. The federal government does provide direct services to some groups, such as veterans (Shi & Singh, 1998).

The mingling of these different approaches has resulted in multiple financial arrangements to pay for services. There are numerous insurance providers with differing requirements to help minimize their risks. Multiple payers set their individual rules for reimbursement. There are also scores of settings where services are delivered and countless consulting organizations, experts, and policy makers that plan, fund, and regulate the delivery of health care (Shi & Singh, 1998).

Primary Health Care

Nurses experience the impact of the health care delivery systems in the work settings everyday. Primary health care focuses on preventing disease or injury. Examples of primary health care activities and programs include:

- immunizations,
- family planning,
- well-child care,
- smoking cessation,
- healthy living,
- alcohol and drug prevention,
- automobile safety,
- environmental protections (Hunt, 2001).

In this country, we still focus on illness care and the use of technology to treat complex conditions. Preventive services are more effective in reducing human suffering and supporting a high quality of life. In an era of cost containment, preventive services can reduce or even eliminate illness care. An example is HIV-related care. The lifetime care costs for HIV patients were $155,000 in 2000. Before the advent of new diagnostic and treatment tools, the cost was about $55,000. Persons were treated for symptoms and died early. The cost of illness care for HIV will continue to rise as life expectancy increases and new therapies are approved. In contrast to providing care, prevention activities cost very little (Hunt, 2001).

Preventive care is provided in ambulatory, outpatient, school, workplace, and community settings. Nurses who work in these settings function quite independently. They have to make sure there is funding for the programs. Developing budgets and writing grants are part of their responsibilities. Expert knowledge related to the programs they teach is also required. Along with this knowledge is the ability to plan, implement, and evaluate the programs. Are they making a difference? What needs updating? Are the programs targeted to meet the needs of different populations? Leadership and management skills are essential. Nurses manage the work settings as well as all aspects of care: communication, physical care, and teaching (Hunt, 2001).

Health Literacy

Individuals in the community now assume a great deal of responsibility for their own health care. They must understand how to take their medications, manage chronic conditions and disabilities, care for family members, and seek help when needed. The ability to read and understand directions is vital. Andrus & Roth (2002) raise the concern about illiteracy and its impact on health care. Literacy means the ability to read and write English. Functional literacy means the ability to use English and computation skills at levels required for everyday life situations, job functions, and to meet life goals. Functional health literacy is defined at the ability to read, understand, and carry out health instructions.

A National Adult Literacy Survey (NALS) was published in 1993. It showed that 48% of English-speaking Americans had inadequate functional health literacy. Medicaid enrollees had a mean reading level of 5th grade. Another study included English and Spanish populations in Atlanta and Los Angeles. At least 33% of the patients did not understand directions about preparing for radiological exams. Another 20% could not understand information about routine appointments. Approximately 75% could not interpret the information on a standard informed consent document (Andrus & Roth, 2002).

Patients not only struggle with written education materials but also with understanding how to correctly take medications. In one study, the directions to take a certain number of tablets each day were well understood, but the medications were not necessarily spread out over the entire day. The readability of 21 common, over-the-counter drugs labels was also studied. Only one product required less than a 7th grade reading ability. The majority of labels required 20/50 vision. About 100 million Americans require vision corrections and cannot read the small print (Andrus & Roth, 2002).

The consequences of functional health illiteracy include

- lack of knowledge and decreased comprehension about medical conditions.

- decreased comprehension of medical information.

- poor compliance with health care regimens.

- lack of understanding about preventive health care options.

- increased use of outpatient and inpatient services.

- increased health care costs (Andrus & Roth, 2002).

Finding Solutions to the Problem

Patient education and health information materials are written for proficient readers. There are complex words and long sentences with several thoughts. All patients prefer simple instructions. Patients with limited skills take words literally, do not look at the context, ignore unfamiliar words, and do not read long sections of information (Andrus & Roth, 2002).

There are many efforts to create solutions to literary barriers to health information. The Maine Area Health Education Center (AHEC) Literacy Center trains health professionals to create easy-to-read materials. Several national organizations have developed low-literacy materials. There are pro-

grams to identify exactly which words in a text may cause difficulty. Software programs calculate the readability of documents.

As an example of these efforts, the Centers for Disease Control and Prevention produced a series of redesigns for their polio immunization pamphlet. The original pamphlet had 16 pages at a 10th grade reading level. A later version had just 391 words presented in a Q&A format with a 6th grade reading level (Andrus & Roth, 2002).

Many items that need assembling have directions with numbered pictures and little text. With this approach, it does not matter where patients live or what languages they speak. This innovation fits with a global market economy and is useful in health care.

Nonwritten materials are useful. Many persons with low literacy rely on television for health information. One study compared two groups' understanding of sleep apnea after looking at a video and a reading a brochure. The group who saw the video had greater knowledge (Andrus & Roth, 2002).

It is also useful to measure patients' understanding by asking them to repeat the instructions, write them in their own words, and accept follow-up calls. Continue to work on simplifying patient education and instructional materials.

Nurses are supporting and advancing research by collecting data in clinical settings and collaborating with other professionals. Compiling evidence about the problem, documenting outcomes, and sharing results in the literature and at conferences helps provide solutions.

Promote health literacy by supporting local, regional, and national efforts to erase illiteracy. Talk with elected officials and community leaders. Develop partnerships with educational and community groups (Andrus & Roth, 2002).

A Systems Approach to Delivering Preventive Health Services

Jackson (2002) describes a systems approach to delivering clinical preventive services. Research supported that preventive services were not being provided in clinics, even though the clinicians were aware of recommendations. Reasons for not providing services included

- not enough time,
- uncertainty about what to do because of conflicting information,
- lack of commitment to prioritize services,
- inadequate reimbursement,
- lack of a system for integrating preventive services into regular patient care.

The essential elements of a preventive care system were identified and include

- assessing staff and providers to determine their beliefs and values about preventive health care services.
- assessing current preventive health care services from clinic and individual provider perspectives.
- developing preventive services procedures, documentation, and responsibilities.
- implementing a preventive health services plan.
- evaluating the services provided.
- making adjustments as indicated.

Following a plan increases the likelihood that preventive services will be offered as part of regular care. Nurses, in primary care settings, have many opportunities to improve care, help patients learn about prevention, and provide support for patients who need to manage their chronic illnesses.

Application to Nursing Practice

School nurses focus on primary care. They work in educational settings from preschools through college. Our memories of school nurses probably include receiving first aid, being weighed and measured, and going home when we were sick. Legislation, passed in the 1970s, has dramatically changed school nurse practice. The Rehabilitation Act of 1973 and the Individuals with Disabilities Act of 1975/1997 require schools to provide education and services for children with disabilities.

Schools now use a multidisciplinary approach to meeting children's needs. In addition to physical and developmental problems, there is concern about "at risk" children. They are diagnosed with psychiatric conditions and experience mental, emotional, substance abuse, pregnancy, and behavior issues. There are also children coming to school with acute health problems. Poverty in the school population requires additional services such as providing food and clothing. Homeless children may miss school or change schools. Foster care and custodial custody raise issues of legal guardianship and consent for care (Wolfe & Selekman, 2002).

School nurses face daily challenges, for example:

- A 10-year-old child, with diabetes who just had an insulin pump inserted. The nurse is told the child can monitor herself without any help.
- A parent tells the nurse that Jim can resume normal activity since it is 48 hours after his appendectomy.
- A child states he was in the ER during the night for an asthma attack. He now is short of breath, and the nurse determines he is wheezing.
- A 15-year-old is exhibiting manic behaviors. There is no record of her having problems. The parents decided not to share information about their daughter's hospitalization and told her not to tell anyone about the medications she is taking (Wolfe & Selekman, 2002).

All of these examples demonstrate the complexity of caring for children in school settings. Nurses need pediatric, mental health, community health, and managerial skills to function effectively in that role. School nursing is truly different today than in the past.

Another approach to getting the message about preventive care is to go directly to the public. Wakefield (2002) believes there is not enough emphasis on preventive care. Nurses see the results of inadequate exercise, poor eating habits, smoking, and other high-risk behaviors. She calls nurses to action. Become involved in shaping policy decisions and alert the public to preventive efforts. Wakefield herself acted by participating in two radio talk shows and highlighting chronic disease issues. Every nurse can join the effort to reduce preventable diseases.

Community-Based Practice

Nurses who work in community settings must know the community. One definition of community is people, location, and social systems. The focus is on meeting the needs of groups by providing services.

Diversity is found in most communities. Nurses become knowledgeable about communities by getting to know people and reviewing vital statistics and demographic information. Family structures give flavor to a community and define health needs. Young families have different needs than in established communities. The types of families – nuclear, extended or older – also dictate the types of services needed (Hunt, 2001).

Culture affects health. It defines health needs, practices, and patterns of use. Families may not seek help from Western-type health care. They may use traditional methods of herbs, laying on of hands, and spiritual guidance. They may only use modern medical services in emergencies. Language differences may discourage them from attending preventive health programs (Hunt, 2001).

The boundaries of a community are formally defined by governmental lines. These boundaries define what services are available and who is eligi-

ble. County and state health departments provide services defined by their laws. Nurses need this detailed information about their areas of service.

Some problems are not defined by boundaries such as air pollution. This problem is not contained in one area and groups have to work together to solve the problem. Some boundaries are defined but become fluid if health problems occur. School boundaries are defined but when students from different schools have been together at a sporting event and there is an outbreak of meningitis (Hunt, 2001), the situation exceeds the boundaries.

In a community, there are economic, educational, religious, welfare, political, and safety systems. These social systems impact the health of a community. Transportation to services makes them accessible. Preventive programs reduce costs and improve the quality of life in a community (Hunt, 2001). Nurses must meet the needs of different populations in their communities.

Models for Care

The practice settings for community-based care are numerous. They are categorized by age group, type of service, and type of problem. Examples are

- adult foster care, residential centers, board and care homes, and skilled nursing facilities;

- ambulatory care, day surgery, and rehabilitation centers;

- detoxification facilities, homeless shelters, business and industrial sites, and schools (Hunt, 2001).

Hartley (2002) describes using a survey in ambulatory care settings to measure patient satisfaction. The 51 items on the Primary Care Assessment Survey (PCAS) were derived from the Institute of Medicine's (ICM) definition of primary care. The major areas are

- access,

- continuity of care,

- comprehensiveness of care,

- clinical interactions,

- interpersonal treatment,

- trust.

The patient's perspective is important. The 51-item PCAS is completed while patients wait for appointments. Literacy was taken into account. Patients who cannot read are taken into a private room, and the survey is read to them. Wording is adapted to specific groups. For example, in an Appalachian setting, patients were confused about the term "doctor" because most of the care is provided by nurse practitioners. The PCAS has a 5th grade reading level and takes about 10-15 minutes to complete. This is one example of an effort to measure patient outcomes.

In community settings, nurses participate in collecting service outcomes and spend their time differently compared to nurses working in hospitals. Nurses who practice in community-based settings also spend more time in their consultant role (teaching and communication) and their management role compared to acute care nurses. In hospital settings, nurses spend the most time in patient care activities (Hunt, 2001).

Partnership Model

The partnership model is also called co-primary nursing. A registered nurse is paired with a licensed vocational nurse or nursing assistant. The pair works together consistently. The registered nurse can encourage growth in the partner. It is more cost-effective than true primary nursing, but it may be complicated to maintain the same work schedule for the partners. Registered nurses may also find it difficult to delegate activities (Cherry & Jacob, 2002).

Modular Nursing

Modular nursing focuses on patients in a particular geographic area of a facility. It may be a unit or wing of a larger area. The same staff provide care to the patients in that module. The team of staff is smaller compared to other delivery methods. Communication is enhanced. A nurse is leading the team and has responsibility for planning and coordinating care. The modules should contain all the materials and supplies needed to provide care. Efficiency is increased. The physical layout of a facility is important in support modular nursing, long corridors do not work well (Cherry & Jacob, 2002).

This approach is useful in settings where patients stay for long time. Modular nursing has teams with different types of caregivers. Modular nursing improves utilization of nurses. This is important during times of nursing shortages.

One study explored patient and family members' perception of caring when nursing delivery was changed from primary to modular. There were no differences in perceptions of caring between patients who experienced primary nursing care and patients who experienced modular nursing care. It was interesting to note that when patients stayed longer in the setting, their perceptions of caring increased (Carruth, et al., 1999).

Clinical Pathways

Clinical pathways were developed to respond to the need to quantify quality, cost-effective care. The initial concern was the time patients spent in acute care settings. In 1983, Medicare moved from cost-based reimbursement to prospective payment. Instead of paying for the actual costs of services, payments for specified services were developed. There are almost 500 Diagnosis Related Groups (DRGs). Hospitals receive a set amount for each patient, based on their DRG. For example, treating patients with congestive heart failure is reimbursed at a set rate. Hospitals were charged with making sure patients received the care they needed. It was equally important that the services were efficiently provided so patients could achieve the expected outcomes in the approved timeframe. Patients who stayed longer than the expected time cost the hospital money, and patients who recovered in a shorter timeframe contributed to the institutions profitability (Cherry & Jacob, 2002).

Because there are many other factors that determine the actual costs of care, there are mechanisms to account for them. Adjustments in reimbursements are made. Some of these factors include

• geographic differences in salaries,

• location of the hospital,

• providing medical education and being a teaching hospital,

• new technology,

• productivity,

• service to large numbers of low-income persons (Shi & Singh, 1998).

It was imperative that systems be in place to monitor all aspects of patient care and progress.

Clinical pathways specify the type and amount of care patients need for a condition. It is evident that the amount and type of treatment financially impacts organizations. Pathways are roadmaps to follow. They guide the caregivers and patients toward recovery. Patients who move through the pathways ahead of schedule benefit the hospital. There is concern when patients progress more slowly than expected. The reasons for their lack of progress are examined, and all the interdisciplinary team members develop strategies to overcome the problems and move the patient forward on the path (Cherry and Jacob, 2002).

Clinical pathways are developed to cover a number of goals, including to

• identify patient and family needs, based on individual characteristics,

• set a timeframe to achieve quality patient outcomes,

• reduce the length of stay and minimize inap-

propriate use of resources,

• determine the best care settings, providers, and timeframe for interventions (Cherry & Jacob, 2002).

Professional nursing standards for care serve as the foundation for developing clinical pathways. Clinical pathways are usually developed for the most common conditions seen in a facility. For example, if many of the patients have congestive heart failure, hypertension, and diabetes, clinical pathways are developed for those conditions.

Choosing a Nursing Care Delivery Model

Because of the many options for nursing care delivery, it is essential to review all the elements in work environments that are impacted. Nursing managers, empowered staff nurses, new technologies and equipment, and consumers all affect decisions about how care is delivered. Think about the changes in obstetrical units. Many rooms look as if they belong in expensive hotels. Deliveries are done in the rooms where women labor. Family members, including children, participate. Significant others are in the OR during cesarean-sections. Television captures the experiences. Why did these changes occur? Public demand, competition among providers, a more natural approach to labor and delivery, realization that health and safety were not compromised, and a philosophy that family support is beneficial.

A nursing care delivery model must fit with the setting, the patients' needs and expectations, the type of care provided, and available resources. Combinations of models may meet the desired outcomes best. For example, in a long-term care setting, a functional approach to medication administration supports safety. A primary care approach meets patients' needs for continuity of care.

A nursing care delivery model must offer safe, well-organized, and focused patient care. The model must aim to achieve good outcomes measured by safety, cost-effectiveness, and quality. Nursing care delivery then is organized for the satisfaction of patients, family, and all levels and types of staff (Cherry & Jacob, 2002).

Solutions

In the challenge, a group of people in a rural community are striving to find solutions to several health issues. The committee met several times, reviewed all the information, and held information meetings. They would like to divide into groups to further work on the issues. They are making the following recommendations to the town council and have prioritized them.

Group I

1. Meet with Premier Health System administrators to determine the exact financial status of the hospital: what services are losing money, what services are profitable, and what options would be considered for continuing services.

2. Contact the state agencies responsible for environmental and worker safety. Share the concerns and monitor actions and outcomes.

Group II

1. Survey the persons over age 60, go to meetings, and talk with them. Compare the available services to what they are currently using and what they identify as needs.

2. Work with the parent-teacher association to develop a specific list of needs for health services. Develop a plan to recruit volunteers to help. Find out if there are nurses in the community who would volunteer on a regular schedule. Find sources for grants to support health services. Complete projections for health services needed for enrollment growth. Present findings to the school board before the next budget hearings.

The committee realizes that there have to be ongoing mechanisms to identify, address, and evaluate community-related health needs.

CONCLUSION

Health care in the United States is extremely complex. Nurses require knowledge and skills to function effectively in many different settings. Leadership and management skills are necessary to organize, implement, and evaluate nursing and health care services. Clinical pathways are one approach to making decisions about the types of services and the timing of them. The importance of health literacy is not usually addressed but is important. Patients and family members make significant health care decisions every day. They also must manage their illnesses. Having understandable educational materials increases patient awareness. The emphasis on cost-effective care mandates that nurses examine delivery models to determine what is useful in certain types of settings. Nurses have many opportunities to expand their practice to settings outside of hospitals. Additional skills and knowledge help nurses adapt to new area of practice.

EXAM QUESTIONS

CHAPTER 7
Questions 31-35

31. The essential elements of a health care delivery system are

    a. personnel, facilities, services, and programs.

    b. financing, insurance, delivery, and payments.

    c. facilities, patients, delivery methods, and billing.

    d. funding, programs, insurance, and evaluation.

32. Course materials for a group of newly diagnosed patients with diabetes who have low literacy, are from different cultures, and use English as a 2nd language could be

    a. presented by interpreters so participants would understand the material.

    b. developed and written in each language.

    c. presented verbally so the patients' limited reading ability would not be a problem.

    d. presented primarily using media such as video tapes and television.

33. Compared to nurses working in acute care settings, community nurses spend more time in

    a. direct patient care planning, nursing interventions, and evaluation.

    b. developing and implementing education programs.

    c. consultant (teaching and communication) and management roles.

    d. mentoring (working with new staff) and leadership roles.

34. The goals of a clinical pathway for a patient with congestive heart failure are to

    a. help set the budget items needed for the operation of the clinic.

    b. educate staff about the essential nursing actions when providing care.

    c. determine quantity, quality, and cost-effectiveness of care.

    d. access patient satisfaction, compliance, and number of hospitalizations.

35. When nurses choose a delivery care model, it must fit with

    a. staff experience and preferences for providing care.

    b. the strategic plan and goals of the organization.

    c. community expectations, cultural diversity, economic conditions, and patient choices.

    d. the setting, patient needs and expectations, type of care provided, and resources.

CHAPTER 8

QUALITY CARE

CHAPTER OBJECTIVE

After studying this chapter, you will be able to recognize the aspects of quality care that are essential to nursing.

LEARNING OBJECTIVES

After studying this chapter, you will be able to

1. recognize the significance of critical thinking and clinical decision-making in nursing practice.

2. identify the elements of case management and its role in demonstrating quality care.

3. identify outcomes measures and evidence-based interventions found in your practice setting.

4. specify the role of professional standards in achieving quality outcomes.

OVERVIEW

Quality care for patients is a core value of nursing. Nurses must rely on critical thinking and clinical reasoning skills to provide care that has positive outcomes.

The changing health care environment requires the concept of quality to be examined from health policy, institutional, system, payer, provider, and consumer perspectives. The focus of care is shifting from treating health problems based on experience and individual preferences to standardized practices with specific outcome measures and quality indicators.

This chapter focuses on the different definitions and elements of quality care. The rationale for moving to outcome measures is presented. Case management is one response to the shift. The concept of quality is defined and the evaluation indicators and measures are discussed. The sources for identifying quality, evidence-based, and professional standards are highlighted.

Challenges

RNs at the Sunnyside Home Health Agency are attending the monthly staff meeting. The nurse manager reports that the costs for treating COPD patients are extremely high compared to state, regional, and national data. The nurses spend some time sharing the issues they encounter when caring for this group of patients. They know they spend a lot of time with the patients who have frequent physician visits and are often hospitalized. Further discussion reveals the nurses use different approaches to care. They base their decisions on a patient's condition, their own experience, physician preferences, and the patient's willingness to comply with treatment. The nurse manager knows a plan is needed to standardize care, improve outcomes, and increase quality.

CRITICAL THINKING AND CLINICAL DECISION-MAKING

 In 1980, The American Nurses Association (1995a) developed a social policy statement. The policy's purpose is to set forth nursing's relationship with society and its obligations to those who receive care. The statement provides support for the importance of thinking and reasoning. Essential features of nursing practice include the ability to think critically and use clinical reasoning.

- Nursing science requires critical thinking to understand and resolve patient problems.

- Scientific methods use defined reasoning processes to examine information.

- Nurses must rationally select courses of actions.

The Pew Health Professions Commission (1991) identified 16 competencies for health professionals in the 21st century. Some related to

- problem-solving and thinking independently,

- managing large volumes of scientific and technical information,

- providing health care services.

Critical Thinking

Critical thinking is the discipline of thinking. Critical thinking makes it possible to look at information and situations fairly. We must explore our own feelings and opinions, as well as those of others. When we think critically, we do not make judgements until all the evidence is evaluated (Rideout, 2001). Thinking strategies include the following areas:

- Knowledge Work – Actively reading, reviewing research, and learning the clinical language.

- Self-Talk – Expressing thoughts and ideas to ourselves.

- Prototype Identification – Using models for comparative analysis.

- Hypothesizing – Selecting an explanation to support facts and continuing to investigate the information.

- If-Then Thinking – Connecting possible actions and outcomes in a logical progression.

- Reflexive Comparison – Comparing a patient's status at different time observations.

- Reframing – Looking at the context or content of a situation from a different perspective.

- Reflection Check – Use self-reflection and self-correction of critical thinking strategies to examine clinical reasoning (Pesut & Herman, 1999).

In clinical settings, nurses interact and communicate with patients. They must integrate the social, cultural, and political environments of the patients and the organization to objectively evaluate health situations. Nurses may need to examine their assumptions about patients and organizations and look for alternative explanations to events (Rideout, 2001).

Clinical Decision-Making

Clinical decision-making is the foundation of nursing practice. One study found that clinical decision-making is a complex cognitive process. For example, nurses in clinical practice used a variety of approaches to make decisions. They used detailed description when they recorded required information. The nurses reviewed the information, and selected the clinical information. When decisions were made, the nurses used inference. Then, synthesis was the process used when the nurses incorporated multiple sources of data to accomplish nursing actions. Nurses also went back and verified the effectiveness of their previous actions. An outcome of this study was developing examples of thinking processes and a vocabulary to describe cognitive processes (Smith-Higuchi & Donald, 2002).

CASE MANAGEMENT

Critical thinking and clinical judgement skills are essential for case management. Case management is not a new method, but it is increasingly important. Changes in health care delivery require processes that support cost-effective, quality care with positive patient outcomes.

Case Management Background

Case management is a new name for an old approach to providing care. In the early 1900s, nurses were working in settlement houses. Their duties included

- listing family needs,

- establishing a method for follow-up,

- helping with the delivery of services,

- ensuring that families and services were connected (Hunt, 2001).

In the 1970s, insurance companies started to use case management to monitor and control claims. The focus was primarily on disastrous accidents and illnesses. Today, case management programs are found in most every health care provider and payer group. Case management is both clinical and business focused and works with set outcome goals (Cherry and Jacob, 2002).

Case management is also referred to as care management and care coordination. The goals are to balance quality care and cost. Quality is achieved by an emphasis on maintaining and re-establishing health. Costs are decreased by empowering patients and families to assume responsibility for self-care. Professional satisfaction is enhanced by collaborative practice and providing coordinated care (Hunt, 2001).

With the emphasis on cost effectiveness, managing care is an important role. Case management

includes gate-keeping. This function is extremely important when patients have complex problems. Patients with chronic problems often need different levels of care and move through various levels of a system. They may be managed with community-based care for a long time, then need secondary and tertiary care. A case manager can provide continuity of care in all the stages. Managed care organizations (MCOs) employ nurses with advanced education and experience to manage care across settings (Shi & Singh, 1998).

Gate-keeping functions include monitoring, coordinating, supporting, and informing. These functions are carried out in the context of utilization review. Each case is reviewed with the goal of selecting the appropriate settings and services. The review may be done prospectively, concurrently, or retrospectively.

Prospective review is done before care is given. Decisions are made about referring patients to specialists, or patients can call the insurance plan administrator for pre-authorization. An objective is to prevent unnecessary or unsuitable care. Discharge planning can start early.

Concurrent review happens when the services are used. When a patient is admitted to an inpatient facility, a certain amount of time is authorized. If a longer stay is needed, a review is done. The longer stay may be authorized or not. Discharge planning is essential.

Retrospective review comes after the care is given and a case may be reviewed. Reviews include assessments of individual cases, checking for billing accuracy, and looking at utilization patterns. Statistical data supports corrective actions and monitoring care (Shi & Singh, 1998).

Nurses are responsible for discharge planning. It is ideal to have a plan started at the beginning of care. It takes time to get approvals for different types of care. For example, patients with hip replacements need rehabilitation and some services at home. The rehabilitation center may generally have a high census, so a space must be reserved. If space was not available, the patient would stay in an acute care setting longer than necessary. That is not cost-effective. Organizing care in advance provides seamless services.

Application to Nursing Practice

Occupational health nurses use a case management approach to work with employees who are ill or have work-related injuries. A more proactive approach is tracking absences. Tracking absences can trigger case management. Early intervention can reduce days away from work. One example is an employee who is paid $20/hour or $800/week. Indirect costs each week are estimated at $4,000 for a total of $4,800 for 1 week of absence. Employee absences are costly to employers.

A nurse can track absences to determine variations in a diagnosis or individual patterns. For example, are there differences in absence patterns among employees with the same chronic illness, such as diabetes? Do individual employees have patterns of absence on Mondays and Fridays or frequent absences for low back injury? These patterns can be addressed prospectively and cost-effectively. Collaborating with other departments identifies what is impacted: discipline, family leave, safety issues, and productivity. Trend analysis of absences identifies problem areas and supports interdepartmental planning (Kalina, Haag, Tourigian, & Wassell, 2002).

QUALITY INDICATORS

Health care delivery focuses on three areas: access, cost, and quality. Quality has not received as much attention as access and cost because it is difficult to define. As concerns about cost have increased, professional groups have worried about the effect on quality. The Institute of Medicine defined quality as the use of professional standards and health services to increase the chance of positive outcomes. All health care professionals have the goal of providing quality services (Robinson & Kish, 2001).

Customers define quality. When you buy a product, you define the quality. It includes the materials, how it is made, how it looks, and its features. Outcomes, in the business sense, are not the same in health care. When we purchase a car, the desired outcomes include a good-looking vehicle that is reliable, safe, and affordable. With health care outcomes, we want our health to improve or be maintained and to have access to services that are affordable. Quality is embedded in all of these elements.

Dimensions of Quality

One approach to examining quality is to consider both micro and macro dimensions. A micro-view considers the services provided and how the services affect the persons receiving them. A macro-view looks at quality from the perspective of the entire organization or system (Shi & Singh, 1998).

The micro-view looks at the clinical and technical aspects of care. Different criteria are used to measure quality. Criteria include facilities, qualifications of personnel, efficiency of services, and effects on patients receiving care. Variations in all categories do occur. One of the main areas of variability is in physician practice (Shi & Singh, 1998).

The micro-view also looks at the interpersonal aspects as being important from a patient's perspective. Because patients do not have technical expertise, they cannot judge specific treatments or therapies well, so they judge the technical aspects of care indirectly, by commenting on provider interest, concern, and interactions. Patient satisfaction positively contributes to the success of treatments. Satisfied patients are willing to comply and will keep seeking care. Providers who express hope and compassion help increase patient satisfaction.

Organizational quality is also affected by patient satisfaction. Lasting impressions are created in the community. Employees with satisfied patients feel positive about working in an organization. Patients value their association with the organization (Shi & Singh, 1998).

Quality of life is receiving attention today because of the growing number of persons with chronic illness or disabling conditions. New technologies and treatments make it possible to prolong life. Patients, often the elderly, live with declining health for many years. Two types of quality of life are defined. The first, general quality of life, is affected by chronic diseases. There are limitations in physical, social, and mental functioning. Access to community resources and job opportunities are limited. Personal happiness suffers. The second type, disease-specific quality of life, persons with a specific disease focus their lives around the care they need. They are concerned about medications, treatments, and recurrence of the illness (Shi & Singh, 1998).

Institutional quality of life is an increasing concern because many persons spend years in such settings. Indicators of quality are cleanliness, safety, noise, odors, air quality, autonomy, and freedom to voice concerns. How residents are treated by staff and accommodating their individual preferences are also important (Shi & Singh, 1998).

The macro-view is broad and focuses on system quality, such as

- cost,
- access,
- population health,
- life expectancy,
- low-birth weight,
- cause specific mortality,
- prevalence of specific illnesses and conditions.

The dichotomy is that we believe in universal access to quality care but are forced to reduce costs. To meet that goal we need a national health care policy (Shi & Singh, 1998).

APPLICATION TO NURSING PRACTICE

Pindus and Greiner (1997) reviewed literature and research to determine how changes in the health care industry impacted workers and the quality of patient care. They found that nurse staffing characteristics are associated with reduced hospital mortality rates, length of stay, cost, and morbidity. The literature related to other caregivers was limited. They also found a positive relationship between nursing staff and resident outcomes in nursing homes. There is more evidence for nursing homes than for hospitals. There is little research on structural work measures and their relationship to outcomes. Because quality of care is a new science, additional research is under way to look at staffing ratios.

Since this project was completed in 1997, there have been continuing efforts to find patterns in quality care, cost-effectiveness, and patient outcomes.

Quality Assessment

Quality assessment and quality assurance are two terms used in the literature but are not always differentiated. Quality assessment refers to measurement of quality by using standards. The process includes

- defining how quality is determined,
- determining which quality indicators to measure,
- collecting data,
- analyzing the data,
- making sense of results by interpretation (Shi & Singh, 1998).

It is essential to share the results within the organization, with consumers, and with professional colleagues. Successes are helpful to others. Areas for further improvement are identified. Weaknesses are corrected. Quality assurance expands the quality assessment process. Since the project was completed the concept of quality has evolved from assessment to assurance to total quality management.

Quality Assurance

Quality assurance goes beyond quality assessment. It is the commitment of an institution or system to continuously carry out quality improvement activities. Earlier, external standards governed the definition of quality. For example, nursing homes were required to meet Medicare, Medicaid, and state minimum standards. Some variation in meeting the standards was acceptable, but major variations were punishable by fines or removal from the programs. That approach was simple routine monitoring of quality (Shi & Singh, 1998). True quality assurance is derived from the principles of total quality management.

Total Quality Management

The Total Quality Management (TQM) movement started when Deming and Juran, two engineers, went to Japan after World War II to help rebuild the economy. They used statistical methods to control quality. Before World War II, manufactured goods were of poor quality. The quality greatly increased by the 1960s. As the competition for Japanese goods impacted U.S. manufacturers, TQM was accepted in this country (Robinson & Kish, 2001).

The key features of TQM are as follows:

• The concept of quality is part of the entire organization. All the functions of an organization are engaged in quality activities. Organizational leaders must provide visible support.

• The commitment to quality is continuous. Once quality standards are met, they are reviewed. The goal is to achieve a zero error rate. It is obviously impossible to achieve perfection, but that is the goal.

• All the members of an organization are actively involved in achieving quality.

• TQM emphasizes the need to exceed standards. Every process is reviewed, and small changes are made to improve quality.

• The TQM process is customer-driven. Customer satisfaction is important. In health care organizations, internal customers are the nursing units as they interface with other departments. Communities and patients are external customers.

The implementation of TQM has reduced lengths of stay, enhanced clinical outcomes, and increased patient satisfaction (Shi & Singh, 1998).

OUTCOME MEASURES AND QUALITY ASSESSMENT

Measuring quality is difficult because the elements are subjective and qualitative. Scales are developed to quantify the information. The data collected must be useful. For that to happen, the measurement scales must be

• Valid tools that measure what they are actually intended to measure. For example, if patient satisfaction is being measured, the tool must have items that are logically related to patients and their satisfaction with services, interpersonal interactions, and other areas.

• Reliable tools that demonstrate similar results each time they are used. If a tool is used in similar settings, over time, there should be similar results (Shi & Singh, 1998).

Tools to collect data include written or telephone surveys. Standard templates exist to record occurrences of events such as patient falls, medication errors, and deaths. Recording and organizing the information on a computer also makes it easy to track, evaluate, and compare data to other settings and to national outcomes.

Sources of Data

The majority of data is collected from billing records. The records do not contain information about how the services were delivered and the outcomes achieved. The coding of information is designed for billing and payment. National uniform standardized data sets could track and monitor care for everyone, with all of the data being organized and processed into useful information. The U.S. government is sponsoring some data collection projects on the national level. They include the

- National Hospital Discharge Survey,

- Current Medicare Beneficiary Survey,

- National Health Interview Survey.

The data helps inform and guide clinical and epidemiological research agendas in this country. Larger national samples are needed. Private providers and states are moving forward more quickly than the federal government. Kaiser Permanente is working on a completely computerized patient record. Several states are developing minimum core data sets for mandatory reporting of hospital discharges.

The public expects nurses to provide quality care. Nurses are accountable for their actions because of their profession. A characteristic of professions is the responsibility for setting standards. Various sources contribute to professional standards: state boards of nurses, laws, professional organizations, health care providers, and society in general (Shi & Singh, 1998). Collecting standardized data from large, national samples will move the processes for measuring quality forward.

Donabedian Model

The Donabedian model is a well-known approach to defining and measuring health care quality. In this model, there are three elements. The elements complement each other and are used together to measure quality. All the elements are related to patient care outcomes. The three elements are structure, process, and guidelines.

Structure includes all elements that are in place before any interaction with patients. Examples include facilities, staffing levels, administrative organization, staff credentials, and equipment. Accreditation and approval commonly rely on structural elements to measure minimum standards. An example of improvement in quality is the training of personnel. A macro-view of the quality of structure includes the number of physicians in an area, the number and type of beds per a population unit, and the blend of primary and specialized providers (Shi & Singh, 1998).

The second element, process, is the manner in which care is provided. Process examples are diagnostic tests, correct prescriptions, waiting time, type and quantity of care received, and interpersonal interactions. Quality improvement projects have focused on the process element. Some of the projects are related to clinical practice guidelines, cost-efficiency, critical pathways, and risk management.

The third element, clinical practice or medical practice guidelines, set standards for treatment. The format is a clinical plan to manage a specific condition, based on evidence. Originally, in 1989, there were about 700 sets of guidelines. Today, there are about 1,700 sets of guidelines developed by 75 national organizations. The Agency for Health Care Policy and Research was directed by Congress to facilitate the distribution and evaluation of guidelines. Over 35 million guidelines have been distributed for conditions such as pressure ulcers, otitis media, depression, urinary incontinence, and low back pain. Critics of clinical guidelines believe the purpose is to reduce the use of services. Proponents argue that the results are lower cost and better outcomes. A weakness is that the value of the guidelines is not supported by research (Shi & Singh, 1998).

Cost-Efficiency

Cost-efficiency is also referred to as cost-effectiveness. A cost-efficient service is one in which the benefit received is greater than the cost of providing the service. At the beginning of a service or treatment, the benefit is usually greater than the cost. At some point, optimal quality is reached when services are not under- or over-utilized. For example, patients are not receiving the services they should (under-utilization) or they are receiving services they do not need or that are not beneficial (over-utilization). Inefficiency is regarded as potentially unethical because patients are not receiving what they should. When Medicare introduced the Prospective Payment System, patients were discharged "quicker and sicker." It was feared that quality of care would decrease. As hospitals improved their processes, quality increased and mortality rates decreased. The principles of cost efficiency indicate that it is possible to increase quality care and lower costs (Shi & Singh, 1998).

Risk management is concerned with preventing harmful events in clinical practice and facilities management. A target area is preventing malpractice. Physicians today practice defensively. The results include more diagnostic tests, specialist consultations, and longer hospital stays. Risk management incorporates standard practice guidelines, critical pathways, and cost-efficiency (Shi & Singh, 1998).

Application to Nursing Practice

LaDuke (2002) states that nurses who see risk management as preventing lawsuits do not see the complete picture. Risk management is an institutional concern but should also be part of nurse's professional plan. Litigation, professional misconduct, or a criminal conviction can ruin a career and a life. The following steps can prevent problems.

- Keeping current with standards of practice, joining specialty organizations, reading professional literature, and attending conferences.

Focus on information that will help you in your practice area.

- Following institutional policies and going through channels to update them if necessary.

- Maintaining your own liability insurance coverage. Do not assume your employers' coverage will protect you.

- Minimizing your chance of injury by following policies and getting help when needed. If you sustain a back injury and did not use equipment or get help, the facility may claim they are not liable.

- Keeping communication with patients, families, colleagues, physicians, and others open.

- Taking threats of legal action seriously. Discuss the threat with an attorney.

Health care continues to become more regulated, and nursing is more complex. Nurses must protect themselves.

One study aimed to determine the quality of care and patient satisfaction with care in 25 critical care units. Standardized instruments were used to collect data from patients, nurses, and physicians. The data was analyzed on a unit basis and then summarized. Physicians rated quality of care the highest, and nurses rated it the lowest. Patients and nurses had similar view of patient satisfaction. Physicians overestimated patient satisfaction. There were wide differences in physician and nurses responses within and between units. Physician and nurse views of quality and satisfaction were related to the level of doctor-nurse collaboration and nurses' job satisfaction (Shannon, Mitchell, & Cain, 2002).

Quality Report Cards

There is continuing concern about quality as managed care has expanded. Managed care incorporates the incentive to cut costs. There are efforts to develop quality report cards to be used by employers and employees to select plans. The

National Committee for Quality Assurance developed a tool called the Health Plan Employer Data and Information Set (HEDIS). HEDIS covers 71 indicators of performance in eight different areas: effectiveness of care, access and availability of care, satisfaction with care, stability of health plan, use of services, cost of care, informed choices, and descriptive materials. Health plans must use the standard definitions and procedures to collect HEDIS information.

Outcomes

Outcomes measure the effectiveness of an institution or system after all the services are delivered. Examples are rate of postoperative infection rates, iatrogenic illnesses, and rates of re-hospitalization. Patient satisfaction, ratings by consumers, and enrollment of Medicare beneficiaries into managed care are also important (Shi & Singh, 1998). Quality care needs a base of evidence such as outcomes rather than decisions made on experience, preference, and habit.

EVIDENCE-BASED PRACTICE

Clinical decisions are based on both expert clinical decision-making and the optimum external evidence. Practitioners must critically analyze research and information before using it. The following steps are useful to determine the value of evidence:

- Precisely define the process or patient problem. You may want to find information about developing standard of care or seek evidence to support treatment of specific conditions.

- Search recent literature and other information.

- Separate the information that is most useful.

- Check the validity and usefulness of the evidence.

- Use the information to resolve a patient problem.

- Evaluate the outcomes (Young, 2000).

Precise definitions of patient problems are essential for evidence-based practice. Skills in doing literature searches, accessing other sources of information, and subscribing to specific information sites will prove valuable.

Application to Nursing Practice

A clinical example of evidence-based practice involves a patient who had a grand mal seizure. It was his first seizure, and several tests were done in the ER. Nothing definitive was found. Discharge instructions were given to the patient based on the usual practices: no driving, take medications as prescribed, and see the physician for follow-up visits. The patient was concerned about having more seizures. The nurse conducted a literature search on MEDLINE. The search indicated that the risk of recurrence after 18 months of no seizures is less than 20%. The patient felt better because he had some idea about his future.

Dykes and Wheeler (2002) describe how nurse practitioners are using evidence in their practices. They do this by

- renewing their commitment to research,

- participating in educational seminars,

- developing tools to validate the relationship between nursing interventions and client outcomes,

- using clinical pathways and other outcome-based documentation to support integration of new information in each step of the nursing process,

- using research-based interventions,

- sharing outcomes with colleagues. The aggregated data, over time, establishes the significance of interventions.

Evidence-based practice allows nurse practitioners to positively impact standards of patient care in managed care markets.

Tingle (2002) writes in the *British Nursing Journal* that clinical mistakes happening today were also happening 10 years ago. The current report from the Health Services Ombudsman identifies the same errors cited in previous reports, such as

- unsatisfactory care and treatment of a patient who had a pacemaker implanted.

- failure to detect the recurrence of cancer and to provide continuity of care.

- failure to make a correct diagnosis.

- failure to manage care with sufficient urgency.

The common error in these and many other cases is that staff do not think reflectively about the care they are giving and about ways to improve it. Proactive case management is needed. The providers are required to demonstrate evidence-based and reflective health care practices.

Nurses in England are addressing issues related to clinical governance that include clinical effectiveness and evidence-based practice. The goal of clinical governance is to ensure that health care organizations develop systems to place quality of care at the center of business, at every level. There are now guidelines for practitioners. Clinical governance includes audits, effectiveness, and risk management. Quality assurance and staff development are the other elements. Clinical effectiveness mandates that nurses acquire the skills and knowledge needed to practice from an evidence-based perspective (Cranston, 2002).

Barriers to Implementation

Clinical paths and patient care outcomes came about in an effort to reduce variability in practice, contain costs, and enhance patient outcomes. The fact that guidelines exist does not mean they are being used. Disseminating the information is a frequently cited problem. Nursing literature has, for a long time, identified the difficulties of putting them into practice. The data is available but must be transformed into knowledge. Nurses need to cogni-

tively process the data, create associations, and gain experience with data sources to turn data into useful knowledge (Young, 2000).

PROFESSIONAL PRACTICE STANDARDS

The public expects nurses to provide quality care. Various sources contribute to professional standards: state boards of nurses, laws, professional organizations, health care providers, and society in general (Tappen, Weiss, & Whitehead, 2001).

There are different types and levels of standards. Registered nurses take the National Council Licensure Examination for Registered Nurses (NCLEX-RN) examination. The purpose of this examination is to determine that a nurse meets minimum standards for practice. Each state has a board of nursing that is legally responsible for maintaining standards. The boards define professional practice through its rules and regulations (Tappen, Weiss, & Whitehead, 2001).

Institutions also develop internal standards for practice. They are found in policies and procedures. For example, certain training is needed to administer chemotherapy. There are distinctions in practice for registered nurses, licensed vocational nurses, nursing assistants, laboratory technicians, and all other types of personnel (Tappen, Weiss, & Whitehead, 2001).

The American Nurses Association members developed Standards of Clinical Nursing Practice. The standards cover all areas of practice and are used by students, nurses, policy makers, providers, and legal personnel.

The Code for Nurses was also developed by the ANA and highlights the responsibility nursing has to the public. The code also supports self-regulation within the profession (Tappen, Weiss, & Whitehead, 2001). Nurses, individually and collectively, keep the public's trust and meet their responsibility for providing quality care when they practice within professional standards.

Solutions

The nurses at Sunnyside Home Health Agency are ready to make quality improvements. The nurse manager reviews literature, looks at professional standards, finds best practices on the Internet, and compares quality indicators for other conditions. She prepares a draft document for the nurses. At the next meeting, the nurses discuss the document, share their ideas, and agree to use a template to record what they do for their patients for 1 month. They will also write narratives to determine the reasons for physician and hospital visits. They develop

- a time line for staff development,

- adapt a standard clinical pathway,

- a process for data collection,

- the desired outcomes.

The nurses will work with clients, family members, physicians, pharmacists, and respiratory therapists to make quality, cost-effective care a reality.

CONCLUSION

Nursing practice, along with health care delivery systems and other professions, has entered the age of quality care outcomes. Nurses must understand that their actions directly affect patient and organizational outcomes. Relying on past experience is not sufficient. Careful choices are required to ensure that patients are receiving the care they need. Efficiency and cost-effectiveness are required. Nurses can achieve the desired outcomes by relying on critical thinking and clinical reasoning skills. Case management is one approach to meeting quality care expectations.

The concept of outcomes is translated into indicators and measures. The basis for practice in all health care disciplines is finding evidence for decision-making and relying on professional standards to guide practice.

EXAM QUESTIONS

CHAPTER 8

Questions 36-40

36. Critical thinking strategies include

    a. a high level of competence in doing nursing tasks.

    b. asking coworkers for their ideas for solving problems.

    c. challenging physician orders when making rounds with them.

    d. actively reading research and learning clinical language.

37. Jean, an occupational health nurse, uses case management for workers who have injuries or chronic problems and is interested in starting to track absences because

    a. management wants to know which employees are absent a lot.

    b. it is easier to keep employee records up to date.

    c. early intervention can reduce days away from work.

    d. she likes to try new systems to see how they make her job easier.

38. The goals of health care outcomes are to

    a. help patients and families use more services and see physicians more often.

    b. improve health care and provide access to affordable health care.

    c. make more services available to people in every community.

    d. cut costs and services so money can be used for other societal needs.

39. Nurses in a community-based clinic plan to adopt an evidence-based practice model including the essential step of

    a. using clinical pathways to support integration of new information into the nursing process.

    b. having a committee plan all the steps they need to include in the model.

    c. using current information and policies to develop an evidence-based practice model.

    d. getting advice from nurse administrators and physicians about how to start.

40. Professions set standards that are based on

    a. legal cases, minimum levels of practice, and common practice.

    b. state boards of nursing, laws, and professional organizations.

    c. community expectations, history, and new technologies.

    d. usual nursing practice, policies, and governmental regulations.

CHAPTER 9

TRANSDISCIPLINARY HEALTH CARE

CHAPTER OBJECTIVE

After studying this chapter, you will be able to explain the impact of transdisciplinary care on patient outcomes and provider roles.

LEARNING OBJECTIVES

After studying this chapter, you will be able to

1. recognize the importance of transdisciplinary health care in the current delivery environment.

2. indicate the role of collaboration in transdisciplinary health care delivery.

3. specify critical elements of team-building and its value to transdisciplinary health care.

4. select elements of team-building that are useful for planning patient care.

OVERVIEW

Health care delivery is complex. We know patients receive only a small part of their care in acute or inpatient care settings where they have access to all the needed services. Patients and their family members must provide some care at home. Care needs may be short-term or continue for a lifetime. It is still essential that services not be duplicated, are cost-effective, are appropriate for patient needs, and meet quality standards. One professional issue described in the literature is physi-

cian and nurse working relationships. Different disciplines, working together as transdisciplinary teams, can achieve both professional and patient-identified goals.

TRANSDISCIPLINARY HEALTH CARE

Challenges

The nurses working in the OR at a large teaching hospital are frustrated by the verbal abuse they experience from a few surgeons. Two surgeons throw instruments when they get angry. The nurses talk with each other about the daily abuse but are not sure what to do about it. They meet with the nurse manager. He knows about the problem but believes it is a part of working in a high-stress OR area. The nurses are not satisfied with the answer. They discuss their next steps.

Introduction

Many health care disciplines typically participate in meeting the needs of patients, family members, and communities. There is a high degree of specialization within health care. Physicians and nurses, in the past, provided the majority of care, with family members helping to meet basic needs. Today both medicine and nursing are specialized. Many other recognized professional and paraprofessional groups contribute significantly to patient care. Some background information will help us understand the concept of transdisciplinary health care.

Background and History of Transdisciplinary Health Care

Health care professions have examined and supported an approach that brings people together to support patient care. The professions commonly included in this approach are

- medicine,
- nursing,
- pharmacy,
- dietary,
- social services,
- physical therapy,
- occupational therapy,
- speech pathology, and
- pastoral care (Cherry & Jacob, 2002).

Multidisciplinary health care is based on bringing the skills of multiple disciplines to meet all of the patient's needs. Interdisciplinary care has added the concept of coordinating care among the disciplines. The disciplines are dependent on each other to meet patient needs. An example is the complex care of a critically ill patient with head trauma. The patient has needs that require medical and nursing care. Nutritional support, drug therapy, and respiratory care are also essential. Social services and pastoral care are needed to help the family come to terms with the patient's situation. If the patient survives, all types of therapy and rehabilitation will be needed. It is evident that all the members must rely on each other to share information, carry out necessary activities, and communicate so the best outcomes are achieved.

Transdisciplinary health care includes both multidisciplinary and interdisciplinary care and adds a new concept of shared roles. There are elements of healing and caring that are relationship-

centered. The total results of the actions or outcomes are greater than the sum of each discipline's area of concern (Cherry & Jacob, 2002).

Transdisciplinary health care has emerged because of changes in health care delivery. Managed care and case management are examples of approaches that build on transdisciplinary care. Transdisciplinary health care overlaps with the concepts of collaborative care, work redesign, discharge planning, and patient-focused care (Cherry & Jacob, 2002).

The Joint Commission on Accreditation of Healthcare Organizations (JCAHO) recognizes the concept of transdisciplinary health care in the following definitions:

- multidisciplinary health care uses information from several areas of expertise at once;
- interdisciplinary health care refers to the involvement of two or more academic disciplines in planning.

It is evident that JCAHO supports interactions between disciplines. One example is in the JCAHO Patient Education Standards, which state that collaboration between health profession contributes to success in patient education (Cherry & Jacob, 2002).

Cherry and Jacob (2002) believe it is only a matter of time before transdisciplinary health care is incorporated into standards of practice.

Pharmacist

Until recently, pharmacists were mainly responsible for making medications available. Technology and the inclusion of technicians make it possible for pharmacists to spend more time on patient-focused care. Some of the services a pharmacist provides in transdisciplinary health care are:

- drug information services,
- patient and staff drug education,
- patient monitoring,

- consultation services,

- pain management and nutritional support,

- concurrent drug evaluation,

- reporting adverse drug reactions,

- participating in research (Cherry & Jacob, 2002).

Dietitian

Dietitians are responsible for helping patients meet their nutritional needs. Technology and new therapies have increased the complexity of care. Patients may require nutritional support for many years. Nurses, patients, and family members may manage the therapy for months or years. Areas of dietary responsibility that contribute to transdisciplinary care are

- making nutritional resources available in home settings,

- providing members to the nutritional support team,

- examining drug and food interaction,

- educating staff, patients, and families,

- calculating metabolic nutritional needs and developing formulas for nutritional support (Cherry & Jacob, 2002).

Respiratory Therapist

Respiratory therapy is a new allied health profession, first recognized in 1997. The services range from oxygen administration to complete ventilation support. Technology has made this profession an integral part of health care. Respiratory therapists provide the following types of care in all settings where patients have needs:

- arterial and other types of blood sampling,

- pulmonary function tests,

- sleep studies,

- cardiopulmonary function tests,

- sputum testing (Cherry & Jacob, 2002).

Social Worker

Social workers provide services to patients and families in a variety of settings, often for many months. Services provided include

- patient, family and staff education;

- discharge planning and assessment of living arrangements;

- referral to community services;

- coordination of treatment plans;

- completion of advance directives;

- evaluation of behavior and mental disorders, coordinate care (Cherry & Jacob, 2002).

Pastoral Representative

Pastoral representatives may practice a specific faith, but in health care settings they serve all patients. The focus of their care is addressing the spiritual and emotional needs of patients and family members. Services include

- pastoral counseling and support,

- sacramental ministry,

- religious celebrations,

- follow-up spiritual guidance (Cherry & Jacob, 2002).

Physical Therapist

Physical therapists provide care in different settings. They evaluate patients' ability to stand, sit, walk, use their range of motion and muscle tone, and other abilities related to walking and moving. They provide services such as

- wound care,

- identifying assistive devices,

- developing plans of care to restore or maintain function,

- providing therapies to improve functioning,

- developing plans to improve physical fitness (Cherry & Jacob, 2002).

Occupational Therapist

The goal of occupational therapy is to help patients carry out daily activities of daily living (ADLs) independently. They work in many settings. Activities include

- training disabled patients learn ADLs,
- training disabled patients to manage home and family responsibilities,
- assisting with return to work skills,
- facilitating access to community resources.

Speech-Language Pathologist

Speech-language pathologists have different roles. They provide direct services and carry out consultation. They work with patients who have speech, language, voice, swallowing, or cognitive problems. Activities include

- evaluating speech and related problems.
- developing treatment plans.
- providing specific services.
- monitoring and evaluating outcomes (Cherry & Jacob, 2002).

It is obvious that, in addition to physicians and nurses, other disciplines are needed to provide transdisciplinary health care. Nurses have a significant role because they are with patients and families on a regular basis and because of their broad backgrounds. In all settings, nurses use the nursing process to organize care. Within transdisciplinary care, they often carry out case management, develop clinical pathways, and monitor outcomes for quality (Cherry & Jacob, 2002).

COLLABORATION

Collaboration includes considering patient needs and preferences and helping them reach positive health outcomes. It involves planning care with significant others, setting realistic goals, and ensuring that necessary resources are available.

Sharing accountability with other disciplines in collaboration also includes demonstrating mutual respect for patients and team members (Tappen, Weiss, & Whitehead, 2001).

Collaboration means working together on joint assignments. Patient education is an activity that requires collaboration. Disciplines have different roles. Physicians focus on diagnosing and treating. They have legal and professional obligations to explain treatments, potential side effects, and possible outcomes. Pharmacists are alert to drug allergies and interactions. Nurses practice holistically and can fulfill the educator role by considering all the complexities of teaching patients (Bastable, 2003). They can take complicated information and make it understandable for patients. They can use a variety of teaching and learning principles to enhance patient comprehension. Transdisciplinary health care also requires working in teams.

Nurses work with many different disciplines. They must avoid becoming aligned with specific groups so that others do not feel like outsiders. This strategy maximizes the cooperation and influence of everyone involved.

Negotiation is part of collaboration. It includes discussion, conferencing, and making bargains (Cherry & Jacob, 2002). When transdisciplinary teams meet and plan care, not everything will be done exactly as team members desire. Prioritizing and setting time lines for outcomes are part of negotiating. Everyone on a team wants to deliver quality, cost-effective care that meets professional standards. Negotiation makes that possible.

Nurses can take specific steps to ensure that collaboration really makes a difference in patient outcomes.

- Monitor the patient's condition and let team members know what is happening.
- Coordinate activities, treatments, and home visits for maximum benefit of services.

- Integrate services from the different disciplines to increase effectiveness of services.

- Plan sessions with transdisciplinary team members, clients, and family members to jointly solve problems (Hunt, 2001).

Advanced practice nurses work closely with physicians, where a high level of collaboration is needed for successful patient care. It takes time and effort by both parties to achieve a partnership. Respect is highly valued. Medical and nursing education programs should include content on collaboration, conflict avoidance, and conflict resolution (Howard-Ruben, 2002).

At the Mayo clinic, there is a physician liaison program throughout the hospital. Nurse managers and physicians assigned to each unit collaborate on issues such as specific performance improvement, reducing supply expenses, increasing patient satisfaction, and developing procedure-specific guidelines for activities that previously required an order.

Other hospitals, across the country, are using similar approaches. Collaborative efforts can succeed with open communication and respect for each other (Steefel, 2002).

TEAM-BUILDING STRATEGIES

Team-building strategies are necessary for transdisciplinary health care to make a positive difference. Team-building has intrapersonal, interpersonal, and intragroup benefits. Working in teams raises challenges for the individuals to

- learn how to work together,

- be supportive of others,

- deal with apathy, tension, conflict, control, and competition, and

- develop trust, increase productivity, and promote mutual decision-making (Rideout, 2001).

When teams are actually meeting and trying to make patient care decisions, a number of techniques are useful.

Brainstorming is a technique used to produce ideas. Group members just throw out ideas. It is very spontaneous. Brainstorming is used to identify problems, strengths, weaknesses, and solutions. Ideas are written out for everyone to see. There is usually a time limit so everyone knows to come prepared and quickly share their ideas.

Nominal group technique works with brainstorming but allows everyone to participate. The group facilitator uses an orderly process to get responses. Persons may "pass" if they do not have comments and wait until the next turn. When all the participants pass twice, the session ends.

The Multi-voting technique is used with the other techniques to select topics. The topics may include deciding on problems, determining information to collect, or how to define outcomes. Each member is given a set number of points to use for voting. They decide how many points to use for each vote. When all the points are used, the solution with the most points is selected. The process is repeated for each decision made (Robinson & Kish, 2001).

There are different approaches to team building. The common goal is to reach a consensus and provide patients with the care they need. Planning patient care requires all the skills discussed.

Teamwork is being emphasized today in health care because it can lead to more comprehensive care, reduce costs, and improves decision-making. Many disciplines are specialized. They assume responsibility for only certain aspects of patient care. Effective team functioning is built upon the following strategies:

- Setting clear goals and timelines that are defined in the first few contacts.

- Periodically evaluating progress. It is necessary to reconsider how to do activities if goals are not being met. Change what is needed to achieve the desired outcomes.

- Planning meetings in advance, knowing the purpose of getting together, and summarizing your decisions.

- Using individual talents. Ask team members to volunteer for tasks they do well or something in their area of expertise. For example, a team member may have skills in doing literature searches or taking notes on a laptop computer.

- Be clear on individual roles to avoid overlap and gaps in patient services.

- Share leadership as the team continues to work together. This allows everyone to develop new skills (Wenckus, 2002).

The words we choose when communicating can make a difference in how team members accept what we are saying. Use "I" statements to express your thoughts, rather than critiquing what others are expressing by using "you." Recognize team members' feelings, but do not tell them you know how they feel (Wenckus, 2002).

Nurse-Physician Relationships

Many nurses have had bad experiences with physicians. Nurses and physicians are supposed to work as a team. Danis, Forman, & Simek (2002) ask if the nurse-physician relationship can be saved. The history of the problem is based on several factors:

- Each profession looked at the other from their own professional perspective.

- Authoritarian relationships prevailed, with physician dominance and nurse reverence.

- Throughout history, nurses have been portrayed as handmaidens of physicians.

- Nurses learned in school to respect physicians.

- Nurses became accustomed to taking and carrying out orders. In a 1968 study, 21 out of 22 nurses gave an unknown drug (placebo) at twice the dose on the label because a physician ordered it.

While history impacts relationships, other factors also influence them. Poor relationships are a major source of stress for nurses. Men are accustomed to taking on power roles and the genders are concentrated in health care professions – males in medicine and females in nursing. The media sometimes depicts nurses as not too intelligent and unable to make clinical decisions. Some nurses resist advancing their education. Professional respect is gained by increasing knowledge and skills (Danis, Forman, & Simek, 2002).

Changes are happening. Nursing positions are decreasing, technicians are assuming responsibilities, and non-physician providers, such as nurse practitioners, are providing more care for patients. Collaboration and team building are necessary to change the scenario. Nurses need to

- Address conflicts as they occur; do not be angry or sarcastic. Seek to resolve difficult situations.

- Be assertive.

- Encourage mutual respect.

- Practice from a holistic, rather than a task, perspective.

- Develop your professional skills and demonstrate professional excellence.

- Recognize the nursing profession can impact health care and be involved in policy and decision-making (Danis, Forman, & Simek, 2002).

Cook, Green, & Topp (2001) explored the impact of physician verbal abuse on perioperative nurses. Verbal abuse was the most common form of aggression in the OR. Generally, verbal abuse from patients and physicians is widespread. The negative effects of verbal abuse, identified by the 78 nurses in the study, were

- relationship with physicians,

- job satisfaction,

- feeling of well-being at work,

- trust and support in the workplace, and

- self-esteem.

Strategies are needed to eliminate verbal abuse and make it understood by everyone that it is not tolerated. Policies that support reporting and interdisciplinary efforts make a difference. The most important challenge is for nurses to confront the abuser (Danis, Forman, & Simek, 2002).

PLANNING PATIENT CARE

A transdisciplinary team involves all the disciplines previously mentioned, as well as any others that are needed. The patient's age, gender, and physical problems may require specialists. Table 9-1 depicts how transdisciplinary team members participate in care. Communicating with other disciplines is essential when planning patient care. Nurses are responsible for integrating, coordinating, and communicating with other disciplines. Communication includes:

- giving physicians information about a patient's condition;

- recording food intake and sharing problems with the dietitian;

- contacting a social worker to participate in discharge planning so the patient will have the needed resources at home;

- connecting family members with a pastoral representative when they express a need to talk (Tappen, Weiss, & Whitehead, 2001).

Solutions

The OR nurses in our challenge are pursuing their issue of physician abuse with a goal of enhancing collaboration and team functioning. They meet with the nurse manager, the Vice Presidents of Human Resources and Nursing, and the Medical Director of OR services. The nurses present a document that outlines their issues and some possible solutions. They want and expect the verbal abuse to stop, now.

There is a great deal of discussion. Everyone contributes their views. The VP of Human Resources is specific about the policies regarding a hostile working environment. The outcomes of the meeting focus on clearly communicating the standards and options.

TABLE 9-1: COMPARISON OF PATIENT PLANNING ACTIVITIES BY DISCIPLINES

	Nutrition	Medication	Ambulation	Wound Care	ADLs	Manage Pain	Education
Pharmacist	X	X		X		X	X
Dietitian	X			X			X
Respiratory Therapist	X	X			X		X
Physician	X	X	X	X		X	X
Social Worker							X
Pastoral Representative					X	X	X
Physical Therapist	X		X	X	X	X	X
Occupational Therapist	X				X	X	X
Speech-Language Pathologist	X	X			X	X	X
Nurse	X	X	X	X	X	X	X

Adapted from Cherry & Jacob, 2002.

- The Medical Director and the VP of Human Resources meet with the two physicians to discuss the problem. Information, detailing the objectionable behaviors is presented in writing.

- Another meeting is set up with the nurses to make sure everyone had the same understanding of what behaviors are acceptable.

- Counseling for assertiveness training and anger management is made available.

- Physicians are informed that they will be required to take anger management classes if the behaviors continue.

- The nurses complete the assertiveness training and use the techniques when needed.

- The nurse manager attends leadership sessions to improve effectiveness in dealing with difficult situations.

Over time, all the parties must work to create a positive work environment based on respect, collaboration, and team support.

CONCLUSION

Nurses work in environments where many disciplines have a stake in patient care. Nurses have major responsibility for providing direct patient care in different settings. They provide the coordination necessary to achieve positive patient outcomes. Transdisciplinary health care is an approach that recognizes the relationships of the various disciplines. Collaboration means that the disciplines work together and contribute their expertise. Because of the complexity of care and the length of time some patients require care, several disciplines may be involved. Team-building is essential for successful collaboration. When teams function effectively, they can plan patient care that is cost-effective, high quality, and likely to achieve positive outcomes.

EXAM QUESTIONS

CHAPTER 9
Questions 41-45

41. Transdisciplinary health care is based on a new concept of

    a. multidisciplinary health care.
    b. interdisciplinary health care.
    c. shared roles and relationships.
    d. discipline-specific responsibilities.

42. Nurses have a significant role in transdisciplinary care by

    a. working with physicians to ensure that patients receive quality care.
    b. integrating, coordinating, and communicating with others.
    c. consulting other disciplines when they determine there is a need.
    d. deferring to other disciplines when they make patient care decisions.

43. When John, a middle-aged man, is newly diagnosed with diabetes, the nurse working to get him ready for discharge coordinates a collaborative effort to

    a. educate John about all the areas of care he needs.
    b. help John accept his condition.
    c. tell the dietitian to explain his diet.
    d. share with John's physician his readiness for discharge.

44. Teamwork is emphasized in health care today because it can

    a. make the work environment less stressful and more pleasant.
    b. result in reduced costs and improved decision-making.
    c. help all the team members know exactly what they should do.
    d. meet patients' demands for specialized care from several disciplines.

45. The history of problems between physicians and nurses started with

    a. physicians being under a great deal of stress but not meaning to be abusive.
    b. work environments that bring out the worst in people.
    c. nurses being taught to respect the authority of physicians without question.
    d. lack of ethnic and gender diversity in the nursing profession.

CHAPTER 10

ALTERNATIVE, COMPLEMENTARY, AND INTEGRATIVE HEALING PRACTICES

CHAPTER OBJECTIVE

After studying this chapter, you will be able to select alternative, complementary, and integrative healing practices that are useful in patient care situations.

LEARNING OBJECTIVES

After studying this chapter, you will be able to

1. recognize selected alternative, complementary, and integrative healing practices.

2. differentiate factors in patients' decisions to explore and use healing therapies.

3. choose healing therapies that are compatible with patients' health needs.

4. select educational approaches that enhance patients' ability to make informed choices.

OVERVIEW

Americans in large numbers are turning to alternative, complementary, and integrative healing therapies. Today, consumers are more informed about health care options than in the past. The cultural and ethnic diversity of the population is one reason for this shift away from modern Western medicine. Healing therapies are not new to other cultures and have been practiced for thousands of years. The challenges for nurses are to learn more about alternative therapies, work with patients who want to use them, and help patients understand how to make informed choices. Nurses have the opportunity to gain new knowledge and meet the distinctive needs of individuals and populations.

PATIENT SELF-CARE CHOICES

Challenges

Brad and his partner, Kevin, both are being treated for HIV/AIDS. They started treatment 7 years ago and have maintained their health. They are now on a comprehensive drug regimen. Brad has the common side effects, while Kevin feels quite well and has few side effects. They attend a support group once a month. At one session, other participants shared how they were using herbs and other products. They were buying them in Mexico, and the cost was minimal compared to other drugs. They said they felt the same as when they took the standard medications. When Brad and Kevin went to the AIDS clinic for their next regular appointments, they discussed the use of other therapies with the nurse practitioner.

Background

 Everyone makes choices about their own health. The decisions include medical treatments and what we do for ourselves every day. *Healthy People 2010* (U.S. Department of Health & Human Services, 2000) provides information and knowledge about improving health. The emphasis in this document comes from mortality and morbidity statistics. Many pathological conditions are preventable or can be minimized by early recognition and intervention. The purposes of *Healthy People 2010* are to

- increase quality and years of healthy life

- eliminate health disparities.

Healthy People 2010 covers 28 focus areas. Several of the areas directly address

- injury and violence prevention,

- nutrition and obesity,

- physical activity and fitness,

- sexually transmitted disease prevention,

- substance abuse,

- tobacco use.

Consumers have become more active in determining their health care. People seek health care but may not necessarily carry out the simple activities that have a major impact on their health. We all make choices about the areas listed above. If we consistently followed positive guidelines, we could be healthier and prevent or reduce health problems (Hunt, 2001).

What we are experiencing is a paradox. Health care costs rise every year. Deaths from major diseases continue to drop. We should be healthier, but we are not. For example, obesity is a national epidemic. It contributes to the onset of several chronic diseases.

Obesity is defined as being at least 20 pounds over ideal body weight. At least 60% of Americans are in this category. The number of children with weight problems is rapidly rising. Obesity is a major cause of mortality, killing more than 300,000 persons a year. What are we doing about the problem? Spending $33 billion a year on weight loss products and services (Keegan, 2001). It is obvious that we are not doing well in managing our weight. Self-care emphasizes the need for individuals and families to accept responsibility for their health.

Health care takes place more and more outside acute care settings. People are living many years with chronic illnesses. The media presents nonmedical therapies that promise great benefits or cures. Increasing cultural diversity in the United States brings new perspectives on health care practices. People make health care decisions from their cultural perspectives (Hunt, 2001; Keegan, 2001). Before the advent of organized Western medicine in this country, people relied on home remedies they had used for years. Today, it is estimated that 42% of Americans use complementary therapies and spend over $21.2 billion a year. Half of that amount is paid out of pocket (Chambers-Clark, 2002a). There are many choices for nontraditional therapies. Nurses have a responsibility to help the public become empowered to make informed decisions.

Reasons for Selecting Alternative Therapies

People have different reasons for exploring and using alternative therapies, including

- Being dissatisfied with modern medicine and health care. People want personal care, choices, and participation in making decisions.

- Reluctance to accept health limitations. In the past, people lived with symptoms and accepted a diagnosis of death. People now want to try many different therapies. They believe that alternative therapies may provide new benefits.

- Many people travel, read about other cultures, and gain new knowledge from the Internet.

Their interest in food, customs, and lifestyles, including health practices, expands.

- Research support for the effectiveness of non-traditional therapies. The media reports research findings for herbs, mind and body work, energetic and Eastern therapies. For example, people who have stress-induced headaches may have tried conventional therapy by taking medication. Alternative therapies such as relaxation, massage, yoga, or acupuncture may help (Cherry & Jacob, 2002).

Self-Care Healing Processes

Healing processes involve the healers that facilitate specific practices, individuals or groups receiving or initiating care, and the environment. We can learn from healers about therapies and practices. Many people are participating in classes or groups to learn and practice therapies such as yoga, meditation, and aromatherapy. Learning about complementary and alternative medicine (CAM) therapies requires the guidance of experts. Some types of training take years, and certification indicates a high level of proficiency (Keegan, 2001).

Anyone interested in improving and/or maintaining health must start with self-awareness. We may look outside of ourselves to find answers to stress, fatigue, sleeplessness, and lack of exercise. Accurate self-assessment establishes a baseline of our health status. We may think of holistic health in terms of mind, body, and spirit. Today, we consider the possibility of achieving human potential. Visualize a circle composed of 6 parts: physical, mental, emotional, spiritual, relationships, and choice. All the parts are connected. When one part is inadequate, all parts are affected (Keegan, 2001).

Mary was diagnosed with atrial fibrillation, some tachycardia, and shortness of breath. Her cardiologist recommended waiting and doing nothing, starting on beta blockers, or having surgery. Mary decided to look at alternatives. She began working with a medical professional who understood CAM. It was agreed she would follow a plan that included

- taking specific vitamins and minerals and herbal therapy (antioxidants);

- reducing stress by being selective about activities and time commitments;

- increasing sleep and rest;

- expecting family members to become more independent and self-reliant;

- participating in relaxation and massage therapies;

- allowing time to relax and not do anything;

- changing her diet to reduce sugar, fats, and artificial ingredients and to increase fruits and vegetables.

Her symptoms gradually subsided and she felt stronger. Mary followed her new regimen all summer and by fall was ready to start her teaching job again (Keegan, 2001).

The interest in nontraditional therapies continues to grow. Nurses can be ready to help individuals, families, and groups make the best choices for themselves.

ALTERNATIVE, COMPLEMENTARY, AND INTEGRATIVE HEALING THERAPIES

As you continue to learn about nontraditional therapies, you will see different terms used. The literature frequently combines complimentary and alternative medicine (CAM). The three most common terms are alternative, complementary, and integrative therapies. The terms represent the evolving nature of these therapies. There is an emphasis on holistic healing throughout all of these approaches.

Healing Therapies

Alternative healing therapies are defined as therapies outside the conventional health care system. Complementary healing therapies are used in combination with conventional (allopathic) medicine (Robinson & Kish, 2001). The newest term is integrative therapies. This approach combines different CAMs with allopathic medicine.

A selected therapy may be implemented as an alternative, complementary, and integrative remedy. For example, yoga is practiced by persons who have no medical reason for doing so. Yoga is complementary when used with a medical regimen. For example, a person with arthritis is seeing her physician who recommends anti-inflammatory medications and suggests a mild form of yoga to maintain flexibility.

Yoga is integrative when it is part of standard practice. A physician's standard arthritis regimen may include medications, yoga, stress reduction, and biofeedback. This approach puts a variety of therapies together to treat the whole person.

Healing Traditions

Allopathic (Biomedicine) Medicine

Before discussing therapies, it is useful to understand the origins of CAM. Before the 1800s, people used common remedies to treat illnesses. Homeopathic medicine and natural substances such as plants were commonly used. Modern medicine is based on germ theories, chemical imbalances, genetic defects, and the belief that it is possible to eliminate most diseases and illnesses. We see and experience the benefits of modern medicine in treating illness but some believe other approaches are needed to truly experience health.

Chinese Medicine

For over 3,000 years, Chinese medicine has been practiced. Today, at least 25% of the world's population uses the metaphysical principles of Taoism, Confucianism, and Buddhism. The concept of opposing forces in the body (yin and yang) represents the energy needed to maintain life. Disease is thought to be caused by imbalances of yin and yang due to internal imbalances (Robinson & Kish, 2001).

Ayurvedic Medicine

Ayurvedic medicine is based on philosophy, religion, and science. It was developed over 2,000 years ago as an Indian Hindu system of healing. This is a holistic approach to life. The five elements of fire, earth, air, water, and space are required to balance the three body types (doshas) of thin, muscular, and fat. Imbalance of the doshas causes disease. Unhealthy lifestyles, stressors, emotional upsets, environmental conditions, or toxic materials cause imbalance. The goal is to restore balance (Robinson & Kish, 2001).

Homeopathic Medicine

Homeopathic medicine is based on using small doses of substances that cause the symptoms, representing the belief that "like cures like." The substances or remedies are plant, mineral, and animal materials. The remedies are thought to stimulate a person's own body systems. Patients are interviewed to specifically determine their symptoms. Individual remedies are selected for each illness. Common conditions treated with homeopathic medicine include childhood illnesses, allergies, arthritis, and asthma (Keegan, 2001).

Osteopathic Medicine

Osteopathic medicine started in the 1800s with the philosophy of wellness. All our body systems are intertwined and dependent on each other for health. Osteopathy considers it essential to maintain the integrity of the body structures. Manipulations of the spine and joints are important parts of osteopathic medicine. Today, osteopathic physicians practice similar to allopathic physicians. They prescribe medicines, do surgery, and include complementary therapies into their practices (Keegan, 2001).

Categories of Therapies

There are numerous therapies, so it is important to understand how they are categorized. It is not possible to become an expert in every type of therapy. Nurses do need to have an understanding of CAM, know how to find resources, and help patients make positive choices. Therapies are categorized according to how they are used.

Alternative Healing Therapies

Some therapies are outside the realm of allopathic medicine because they are unproven, dangerous, or not well understood by health care providers. Some therapies are part of ancient cultures such as Chinese, Indian, and Native American. Western cultures have little exposure to them. We value the latest therapies, treatments, and medications. A holistic approach to health care opens the door to CAM. Allopathic medicine alone cannot provide care for body, mind, and spirit.

Therapies that focus on "mind over matter" are often suspect because it is not obvious what is happening. For example, core energetics seeks to break down defense mechanisms. The purpose is to reach our spiritual level. Persons may have cathartic experiences that allow them to be more loving or creative (Keegan, 2001). There is not much known about this therapy. It is almost impossible to conduct objective research. Other therapies, such as Native American, African, or Asian, are not well known outside those communities. Therefore, the therapies are not often used in complementary or integrative treatment plans.

Complementary and Integrative Healing Therapies

Complementary therapies are alternative therapies that are used with conventional, allopathic therapies. Integrative therapies are those that are used as part of allopathic medicine.

Complementary and integrative therapies are commonly included with traditional care. Nurses routinely use several complementary therapies. Table 10-1 lists a selection of therapies.

TABLE 10-1 COMPLEMENTARY THERAPIES USED IN NURSING PRACTICE
Active listening
Humor
Imagery
Journaling
Massage
Meditation
Music and art therapy
Prayer
Presence
Story telling

Adapted from Snyder & Lindquist, 2001.

Classifications of Therapies

At least 1,800 therapies have been identified. Because there are so many, it is helpful to classify them. One way to categorize the wide-range of therapies is as follows:

- Alternative medical systems: acupuncture Ayurvedic medicine, cultural-based health practices, environmental medicine, homeopathy, and naturopathy.

- Mind/body interventions: biofeedback, art, music and dance therapy, yoga, self-help groups, relaxation, meditation, and prayer.

- Biological treatments: specialized diets and herbal therapies.

- Body therapies: chiropractic, various massage approaches, osteopathy, pressure point therapies, and some yoga maneuvers.

- Energy therapies: reiki, therapeutic touch, and bioelectromagnetic-based therapies (Cherry & Jacob, 2002, Keegan, 2001).

Dietary Supplements

Dietary and herbal supplements are used by almost 50% of Americans. Throughout the world, herbs are commonly used. Historically, people did not think dietary supplements were necessary to maintain health. Even if they wanted to use supplements, few were available. They ate simple, home-made foods and were physically active.

Specific foods that contained vitamins C and D were then identified to prevent scurvy and rickets. Essential nutrients were made available as supplements. Today, dietary supplements are recommended because people are not eating enough of the foods that provide the required nutrients. The recommendations change over time because of additional stresses to the body and new knowledge about health needs.

Some people may think "more is better" when taking supplements. Exceeding recommended doses of supplements is harmful. For example, folic acid overdoses may hide vitamin B_{12} deficiency. Excessive calcium may cause kidney stones (Cherry & Jacob, 2002). Consumers and health care providers need information to ensure they include dietary supplements safely and responsibly. Many people take herbal products in addition to dietary supplements.

Herbal Therapies

Herbs are used by 70-90% of the world population. Herbs have been used in most cultures for thousands of years. Herbs are widely used for disease prevention in underdeveloped countries as well as around the world. Common medicines we use today are derived from herbs (atropine, digoxin, ipecac, and reserpine).

There are over 20,000 herbs and related substances available. All plants have biochemical elements that affect our bodies. For example, tomatoes contain vitamins and minerals. Alkaloid compounds are powerful and include caffeine, nicotine, and morphine. Glycosides contain anti-inflamma-

tory and cardioactive properties. Phenols compounds have antiviral and antibacterial properties. Other plants contain oils and scents (Tryens, Coulston, & Tlush, 2003).

Herbs are sold commercially in different forms. Teas, tinctures, tablets, capsules, and freeze-dried extracts are all found in stores. Herbs have different potencies depending on how they are ingested. For example, tea strength varies according to the time it is steeped. Standardized doses are prepared as tablets or capsules. People may believe herbs are harmless and beneficial if taken as directed. Some common herbs are used widely today.

- Ginkgo is an ancient leaf-bearing tree. The Chinese use the seeds and leaves for lung problems. Current studies support its use in treating vascular and neurological diseases. Patients in one study were able increase their ability to walk without pain. Ginkgo may also reduce short-term memory loss. Persons taking anticoagulants should not take ginkgo because of platelet inhibition (Tryens, Coulston, & Tlush, 2003).

- St. John's Wort is widely advertised. It was originally used to keep away evil spirits. Today it has been studied as a substitute for Prozac® or Tofranil® to treat depression. It is also recommended to reduce nerve pain, injury, and sleeplessness. Topical applications reduce muscle aches and pain. It is also used to promote healing for wounds, bruises, and cuts (Tryens, Coulston, & Tlush, 2003).

- Ginseng is an ivy plant that grows for seven years before it is mature enough to use. Its benefits include increasing physical and mental functioning. It also reduces stress and fatigue. It is widely used (Tryens, Coulston, & Tlush, 2003).

- Dandelion is a common weed with many different properties. The flower heads are made into wine, the leaves have a diuretic effect, and the sap is used to treat warts and corns (Tryens, Coulston, & Tlush, 2003).

The examples described above report the properties and benefits of four commonly used herbs. Many herbs have side effects and contraindications. Because there is so much interest in non-traditional therapies nurses must understand consumer safety, legal implications, education needs, and regulatory constraints. It is essential to have knowledge about combining nontraditional therapies with allopathic medicine. Additionally, nurses need access to CAM resources. That helps them keep current and assist consumers to make informed choices.

COMBINING THERAPIES

Approximately 40% of Americans use complementary therapies. In one study, the well-educated respondents indicated they believed in a holistic approach to their health. Many had chronic health issues such as back problems, chronic pain, anxiety, and genitourinary problems.

Another study indicated persons seek CAM when traditional therapies do not reduce their problems. Teenagers are drawn to CAM because the therapies are "natural," and they can make their own choices. Family members often are using the therapies. About 50% of physicians, especially those in primary care practice, make referrals or recommend CAM. The reasons are patient requests, patient interest, and failure to receive help from traditional therapies (Robinson & Kish, 2001).

Safety of Alternative Therapies

The literature and media often address the biggest concern with CAM, safety. Safety is defined as the benefits of a therapy outweighing the risks. The Food and Drug Administration (FDA) has strict guidelines for standardization and quality. Herbs are not regulated by the FDA. Are the products really natural? Do products have the same strength in each bottle? Products may be exposed to pesticides, heavy metals, and other pollutants. There are differences in growing conditions and the preparation of the products (Robinson & Kish, 2001).

The Dietary Supplement Health and Education Act (DSHEA) of 1994 mandated packaging information. The name, quality, and the part of the plant used are required to appear on the label. If there are daily serving requirements, that is also included (Robinson & Kish, 2001). This type of information is helpful, but some products are not to be ingested and may be toxic. For example, some plant oils used for massage may be toxic, especially for persons who are sensitive (Robinson & Kish, 2001).

National Center for Complementary and Alternative Medicine

The National Institutes of Health, as directed by Congress in 1992, established the Office of Alternative Medicine (OAM). It is now called the National Center for Complementary and Alternative Medicine (NCCAM). The purpose was to learn more about CAM. The office first focused on determining the characteristics of the CAM community and the potential difficulties in assessing the therapies. The first report indicated that traditional medicine is very effective in treating infectious diseases and trauma but is less successful in treating complex, chronic conditions.

Modern medicine increasingly focuses on finding a single solution for an illness or condition. Back pain, for example, is not usually cured by surgery. Many chronic conditions require multiple solutions. NCCAM facilitates objective evaluation of CAM therapies that could promote health. They are also responsible for sharing the information with the public and research training (Robinson & Kish, 2001).

Payment for Alternative Therapies

The majority of the costs for alternative therapies are paid for by the persons receiving the treatment. It is estimated that $27 billion was spent in 1997. People are willing to go outside their traditional health care systems to find remedies (Keegan, 2001).

Studies have supported the benefits of some therapies: chiropractic, acupuncture, massage, and others. Some health plans share the cost. There is the usual co-pay, or a fee is negotiated. The rationale for health plans to support CAM is to encourage people to enroll in the plans. Persons with limited or no health insurance must pay themselves. In that sense, CAM is more available for persons with resources.

Some efforts are being made to expand such services. Lincoln Hospital, in New York, began using acupuncture as an alternative to methadone in their drug addiction center. The practice was started in 1974, and today the clinic is the largest medically supervised drug addiction clinic in the United States that does not use drugs in their treatment. The low cost and low-tech nature of CAM make it cost-effective and useful for different settings (Robinson & Kish, 2001).

Legal Dilemmas

One consideration is how to regulate the providers of the services. Some therapies have formal training and certification processes. Others, especially those that dispense remedies, are less organized. There is discussion about licensure or other forms of regulation.

Additional regulation also impacts nurses. In some states, massage therapists must be licensed and nurses cannot provide massage unless they are licensed. It is essential for this issue to be resolved. What therapies fall within nursing practice? Nurses work in settings with different therapists: acupuncturists, homeopaths, and hypnotherapists. Do the therapists supervise the nurses and delegate tasks? Does the nurse coordinate the treatment plan to ensure that the therapies are congruent with the medical diagnoses? Who determines what patients

are within their scope of practice? Who bears liability for unanticipated outcomes? Is liability insurance an option? (Cherry & Jacob, 2002).

NURSING AND COMBINED THERAPIES

Nurses practice from a holistic perspective. Florence Nightingale wrote about creating natural healing environments and supported art therapy. Today, there are questions about alternative therapies that have historically been part of nursing. Should nurses be experts in various therapies? What do nurses need to know? How much should they share with clients and the community in general? Should they be giving advice or guiding people to resources? It is apparent that the diversity of the U.S. population requires nurses and healthcare systems to provide sensitive, culturally competent care (Snyder, 2001).

Snyder & Lindquist (2001) describe how therapies are part of nursing and have been for many years. Nurses are now conducting research on various therapies to understand the scientific basis of therapies and their efficacy. The nursing profession is positioned for a leadership role in the movement to include CAM in mainstream care. Spiritual care is an example of a nursing role that is now considered a complementary therapy.

Spiritual Nursing

Makhija (2002) discusses the debate about including spiritual science with medical sciences. Nursing theorists including Newman, Rogers, and Watson have contributed to knowledge about spirituality being an integral part of nursing care. The emphasis is on caring. Nurses have an obligation to help patients who are in spiritual distress. They may help through listening, sharing prayer, presence, or linking patients with spiritual advisors.

Meeting patients' mind, body, and spiritual needs supports examining CAM. Learning more about nontraditional therapies and helping patients make reasoned choices are part of nursing.

Learning about CAM

Education about CAM is challenging but needed.

- Evaluate resources, select those that present objective information and are not selling products, and start compiling a list.

- Learn how therapies interact with prescribed treatments and medications.

- Gain knowledge about the training and qualifications of providers.

- Find out what services cost and how they are paid for and reimbursed.

- Network with CAM providers to learn more about what they do and the results they achieve (Cherry & Jacob, 2002)

A traditional nursing role is coordinating care. Today, that role includes examining CAM and working with individuals, families, and the community to see that everyone is receiving the best services possible.

Solutions

In the challenge, Brad and Kevin are seeking answers to their questions about complementary therapies. Marsha, the nurse practitioner at the AIDS clinic who meets with them to share their questions about CAM. Up to now they have relied solely on allopathic medicine. Marsha starts a holistic assessment to establish a baseline of their physical, emotional, and spiritual health. The reasons for their interest are identified.

Brad and Kevin both know the modern medical therapies have sustained their lives and improved their quality of life. They are both able to work but have little energy for other activities. They believe they have reached a plateau. They want to explore additional options for increasing their energy and enhancing their well-being.

Marsha develops a plan to get them started on their journey to self-care and healing. She

- discusses the need to carefully review supplements and herbs for their benefit and any potential interactions with their current medication regimen.

- gives them information about Web sites and books related to CAM.

- gathers more detailed information about their health habits, such as diet, activity, stress levels, and quality of life status.

- conducts a complete physical examination, including laboratory work.

- asks them to complete various health-related inventories and write out the goals for enhancing their quality of life.

- schedules a transdisciplinary team meeting to discuss their current health status and the goals. The meeting will include Brad and Kevin, their physician, dietician, social worker, a healer who is knowledgeable about therapies, and the nurse practitioner case manager.

CONCLUSION

Consumers are taking an active part in their health care. Many health problems, such as obesity, require individuals to take responsibility for their dietary, activity, and lifestyle choices. People are looking for answers to their health problems and are turning to alternative therapies. They seek other therapies when their problems have not been solved by allopathic medicine or when they become interested in new options.

Use of alternative therapies is increasing every year. Many of the therapies are not regulated or standardized. The scientific basis of their actions and benefits are not always well established. Research and regulatory efforts are underway. Nurses and other health care professionals have the

opportunity and responsibility to educate themselves and the public about CAM.

EXAM QUESTIONS

CHAPTER 10
Questions 46-50

46. John is interested in making some self-care choices about his health, so he should

    a. experiment with several nontraditional therapies to see what he enjoys.

    b. start taking dietary supplements and herbs to increase his energy.

    c. accurately assess his current health to establish a baseline.

    d. talk with friends to find out what they are doing for their health.

47. Alternative therapy is

    a. outside conventional health care systems and practices.

    b. part of an ancient culture and is still used today.

    c. frequently used even if its benefits are not established.

    d. provided by highly trained persons who are licensed or regulated.

48. Chinese and Ayurvedic medicine have been practiced for thousands of years. The goal of these therapies is to

    a. provide herbal and other restorative therapies.

    b. continue the use of their ancient traditions.

    c. guide people away from allopathic medicine and technology.

    d. restore balance to the body systems and the environment.

49. Biofeedback, relaxation, and self-help groups are examples of therapies classified as

    a. biological treatments

    b. mind/body interventions

    c. body therapies

    d. energy therapies

50. Nurses can actively participate in efforts to gain more knowledge about CAM by

    a. reviewing research on various therapies to establish their scientific basis and efficacy.

    b. watching television programs that commercially endorse specific products.

    c. asking colleagues what they recommend for specific conditions.

    d. trying new products to see if they make a difference in their level of general health.

CHAPTER 11

CULTURAL COMPETENCE AND CARE

CHAPTER OBJECTIVE

After studying this chapter, you will be able to choose strategies that support cultural competence and care.

LEARNING OBJECTIVES

After studying this chapter, you will be able to

1. indicate ways to include knowledge of different values, beliefs, and health practices into culturally competent care.

2. select nursing interventions that respect individual and group cultural practices.

3. discriminate education materials and research in application to nursing practice.

4. choose strategies to continue learning about different cultures.

OVERVIEW

The United States has always had waves of immigrants. They came to this country with a variety of languages, with limited resources, and with their own cultural practices. Today, immigrants are still coming to the United States with the same characteristics. The difference today is that we are concerned about maintaining our cultural identities. Culture influences all aspects of our lives: physical, emotional, and spiritual. Our language, food habits,

and relationships are intertwined with our daily activities. Nurses and other health care providers need an expanded view of the world. What cultural practices impact health seeking behavior and the ability to follow treatment plans? What types of care are essential to meet patient needs? Health care providers and nurses must respond to the cultural needs of a diverse society.

Chapter 10 focused on nontraditional therapies that are becoming accepted choices in modern health care. When we learn about each other, we are more accepting of new ideas and are more willing to have new experiences. Nurses can provide leadership in helping all populations to receive high quality, culturally competent health and nursing care.

CULTURAL COMPETENCE AND CARE

Challenges

Mrs. Singh has come to the OB clinic at Midwestern University Hospital. She is 7 months pregnant, and this is her first visit. She is 37 years old and has two other children. She speaks little English. She nods and smiles when the nurse asks questions. Her husband is with her. He responds to the nurse's questions and asks additional questions. He translates everything for his wife. She does not ask any questions. The nurse makes a notation in the chart that Mrs. Singh has a limited understanding of English. Mrs. Singh will have a cesarean-section because of a previous one. Mr. Singh has planned to accompany his wife to each appointment. After the first visit, he feels comfortable dropping her at the clinic. During this first visit there is no discussion about contraception or sterilization after the delivery. Her next appointment is scheduled in 3 weeks.

Her husband drives her to the clinic for her next visit, drops her off, and plans to come back in an hour. Mrs. Singh is assessed by a different nurse. The nurse shares information with Mrs. Singh about having a tubal ligation after her delivery. The nurse asks if she wants more babies. Mrs. Singh shakes her head, no. The nurse further explains that the paperwork must be submitted, approved, and the procedure scheduled before her delivery. Mrs. Singh nods, smiles, and signs the permission. When she gets home, she puts the paper in a drawer with other family papers.

She has a healthy baby boy and the tubal ligation. A few months later she is cleaning out drawers and is throwing papers away. Her teenage daughter or Mr. Singh read everything before Mrs. Singh throws it away because they are concerned that she will throw away valuable papers. One document that Mrs. Singh is discarding is the permission for the tubal ligation. Her husband is stunned to find out she had the procedure, and Mrs. Singh is unable to explain the significance of it.

Introduction to Cultural Competence and Care

 We may believe that we are culturally sensitive, understand each other, are tolerant of differences, and accept different health practices. We can believe all the right things, but how do we, as nurses, actually put them into practice? We must look at the broad meanings of cultural competence and then explore how to demonstrate it when making patient care decisions.

Elements of cultural competence are

* being sensitive to and showing respect for different values and beliefs;

* learning about and integrating different values and beliefs when working with patients;

* being proactive about challenging negative or prejudicial behaviors demonstrated by others (Cherry & Jacob, 2002).

Demographic Trends

The United States conducts a census every 10 years. The latest census clearly identifies the changes in our population. African-American and Hispanic groups each represent about 15% of the total population. In 2000, about 9% of new nursing graduates were African-American and about 4.6% were Hispanic. The enrollments in schools of nursing are similar (Cherry & Jacob, 2002).

It is easy to identify the major ethnic groups: African-American, Hispanic, Asian/Pacific Islander, and Native American. These are the federally designated minority groups (Cherry & Jacob, 2002). If we look closely, it is evident that differences exist within each group. For example, persons of Hispanic heritage come from different countries with different customs. Asian persons are diverse, with different languages and approaches to health care.

There are other demographic trends of interest to nurses. We know the population is aging. This has major implications for all kinds of resource allocation, especially health. There is interest in minority groups because of health disparities. For example, African-Americans have higher incidences of cancer, cardiovascular disease, diabetes, and other conditions, than Caucasians do (Cherry & Jacob, 2002).

In addition to the groups mentioned, there are other ethnic groups: newly arrived immigrants from Eastern Europe, Russia, Rwanda, and the Middle East. One of the first challenges for immigrants is always finding a job. In this country, many people are unemployed and cannot afford health care. Persons living at poverty levels have poorer health than the general population (Cherry & Jacob, 2002). Low-income groups face unique issues related to attitudes and access to needed services.

Demographics of Violence

Violence is a trend that affects certain populations. Homicides are the leading cause of death among African-American males, ages 15-34. Children, women, and elderly people are vulnerable to becoming victims. Alcohol and drugs also contribute to violent deaths (Cherry & Jacob, 2002).

Negative attitudes and prejudice are manifest in different types of violence. Society is negatively affected in many ways when people exhibit contempt, intolerance, lack of respect, and ignorance. When diverse groups demonstrate tolerance toward each other, there is a decrease in violence.

Respect for differences moves us forward as a society. We begin to gain knowledge about other cultures. We find out what we have in common. The goal is to celebrate our differences and see how our society brings them together so that society is strengthened.

Demographics of Health Care Workers

Patients from different cultures expect and deserve care that is sensitive to their values and beliefs. Nurses are the majority of health care workers. It is crucial that they reflect society. Nurses can learn about different cultures, but it is difficult to understand and truly know what others are feeling.

A major issue is language differences. Americans are not generally bilingual. Nurses who speak English only will have difficulty communicating with non-English speaking patients.

It is also a challenge to provide holistic care. The ideal situation is to have nurses from different cultures in patient care settings. They understand unique needs, communicate, and can work with families to include important cultural aspects of care.

Barriers to Nurses Being Culturally Competent

Kersey-Matusiak (2002) calls for an action plan to increase cultural competence. Some of the barriers she identifies exist nationwide.

About 90% of registered nurses in this country are Caucasian, 4% are African-American, 4% are Asian, and 2% are Hispanic. The nursing population does not mirror society or the persons who seek health care. They practice from an ethnocentric, American perspective.

Nurses in America are educated primarily in the Western medical model and use that framework to make practice decisions. They have little experience with other cultural beliefs.

Racism is an ignorance about other cultures. There is little effort to include policy changes that are culturally sensitive. For example, visiting hours are limited, and translators may be unavailable.

Managed care puts additional burdens on nurses to make quick assessments and decisions (Kersey-Matusiak, 2002).

Recruitment of Minorities to Nursing

In 1908, the National Association of Colored Graduate Nurses (NACGN) made the first effort to recruit African-American students into nursing. During World War II, there was a great need for nurses, and the federal government funded basic nursing education. The Cadet Nurse Corps supported accelerating nursing programs so graduates would be available to meet the needs of wartime. Two African-American nurse recruiters focused on African-American nursing schools. By the end of war, over 2,000 had gone through the Cadet Nurse Corps (Cherry & Jacob, 2002).

Males are another minority group in nursing. Almost half of the U.S. population is male. About 10% of the nursing graduates in 2000 were males.

The percentage is about the same for males in nursing programs (Cherry & Jacob, 2002).

In the 1960s, there were new efforts to assist economically disadvantaged persons. The goal was to increase access to education. Nursing schools participated in some of the efforts.

• Sealantic Fund was supported by the Rockefeller Brothers' Fund. It helped minority students at 10 universities enter nursing school and supported retention activities.

• Breakthrough to Nursing, a project of the National Student Nurses Association, focuses on increasing the recruitment of minorities, including men, into nursing.

• The American Nurses Foundation funded a project in 1997 to determine the most effective ways to increase the numbers of minority students.

• Chi Eta Phi, a national African-American nursing society, provides scholarships, mentoring, and inspiration to nursing students (Cherry & Jacob, 2002).

• The president of the American Nephrology Nurses' Association included diversity and culturally competent objectives and goals during her presidency. She believes nurses need diverse skills to meet patient needs (Nardini, 2000).

Various strategies have been suggested or used to increase the diversity of health care workers, such as

• Scheduling forums to raise the level of awareness and to discuss issues. Understanding communication patterns and health beliefs, for example, are areas of concern.

• Implementing a system of same-culture mentors and students.

• Having nurses who are educated in cross-cultural care serve as role models and consultants to employers, schools of nursing, and the public.

• Heightening awareness and increasing interest through media such as audio-visual materials, Internet resources, and local radio and TV programming (Cherry & Jacob, 2002).

A diverse workforce makes it possible to provide culturally competent care. Nurses in America need an informed perspective on health and health practices across the world.

INTERNATIONAL PERSPECTIVES ON HEALTH

Our first thoughts about international health may focus on infectious diseases entering this country. We are also aware of major food and nutritional problems in many countries. There are concerns about safe water and air pollution. Other international health issues relate to violence (wars and land mines). From a cultural perspective, nurses can contribute to solving some of these issues.

Cultural Values and Beliefs

Across the world, individuals, groups, and governments believe that health is important. The collective values and beliefs define what is acceptable. Health care delivery is affected by

• Political climate – governing bodies, interest groups, laws and regulations.

• Economic conditions – general economy and resources available.

• Physical environment – waste and pollutants, ecological balance, and sanitation.

• Technology development – biotechnology and information systems.

• Population characteristics – demographic trends, health needs, and social morbidity such as drugs, AIDS, injuries, and problem behaviors.

• Social values and culture – ethnic and cultural diversity, social cohesiveness (Shi & Singh, 1998).

There are wide variations across cultures in decision-making about health. Decisions about who will receive services and what type of services offered are based on culture. Some cultures (China and India) value males more than females. Males there have better nutrition and receive more health care than females. Some African tribes distribute scarce medical resources based on cultural values. Immigrants to the United States bring their cultural values with them. The Western values in this country may not be compatible with other culturally based health beliefs (Shi & Singh, 1998).

Many issues related to health policy and nursing issues are international. We are all concerned about communicable diseases, nuclear accidents, family planning, and AIDS. Research helps nurses and policy makers identify the extent of problems and compare outcomes from different policy approaches. One example of a comparative analysis approach is the Milstead model. It is used by researchers as a guide to develop a comparative analysis project. Its main elements are

- selecting an international setting,

- identifying the problem or policy,

- analyzing sociocultural systems,

- clarifying economic and political systems (Milstead, 1999).

The Milstead model is useful for comparing the impact of health-related policy decisions in different countries. An example of using the model is needle exchange programs (NEPs) in Tacoma, Washington; New York City; and several sites in Rotterdam, the Netherlands. Both of these countries are developed democracies. The cities are all large, urban settings. The policy decisions for needle exchange programs are well documented.

Rotterdam, as part of the Netherlands, has national health insurance. The NEP was started in 1986 because of a hepatitis B epidemic. Today, exchange sites are found in community organizations and storefronts (Milstead, 1999).

The Tacoma program was the first in the United States. It was started in 1988 by an individual, using his own money. It was a street program, which was taken over by the city/county government in 1990. Its legality was debated in court and approved in 1991. The exchange is done at a van parked at certain sites. People may also call in and arrange for the van to come to a site. There are about 3,000 IV drug users in the area who receive 35,000 clean needles a month (Milstead, 1999).

New York City has a pervasive drug problem. Whole neighborhoods are unsafe because of drug activity. Drug use there has status. Drugs are available on the street, in schoolyards, and in the workplace and all ages are involved. Over 200,000 persons use IV drugs in New York City. Additionally, at least 350,000 persons use other types of drugs. Frequently, drug users start with one drug and turn to others. The other problem is contracting HIV/AIDS. The NEP began as an underground program in 1988 because it was illegal in New York to have drug equipment. In 1992 a waiver was granted to operate a NEP (Milstead, 1999).

Summary of the Programs

The NEP programs started as grassroots efforts. The originators of the programs shared the evolution from grassroots efforts to recognized legal programs. All along the way, there were political challenges. Sometimes there was support, at other times politicians would not provide any support. Their political positions were often related to reelection and community support. Frequently, there were differences between state and local officials and community activists. In Rotterdam, treatment was reimbursed. The treatment included 6 weeks of inpatient care. Insurance companies would lose money if NEP were to reduce the need for inpatient care (Milstead, 1999). There is a need for continued comparative analysis to determine how policy decisions affect outcomes in different settings.

International Nursing

The International Code for Nurses was adopted by the International Council of Nurses (ICN) in 1973. It is a statement of ethical practice for nurses around the world. It has the following areas:

- Nurses and People,

- Nurses and Practice,

- Nurses and Society,

- Nurses and Coworkers,

- Nurses and the Profession (Cherry & Jacob, 2002, p.201).

Nurses educated in the United States work, teach, and consult all over the world. They are recognized as international leaders. Their expertise is valued. Nurses can make a difference in health matters across the globe. They are involved in developing international projects, planning and implementing educational programs, conducting research, and evaluating projects. In addition to their professional expertise, nurses need an understanding of health and cultural issues in a global society (Nies & McEwen, 2001).

Environmental concerns are now addressed on a global level. In 1972, the United Nations General Assembly recognized the issues with water, waste, and air pollution. A United Nations conference focused on the human environment. The United Nations Environment Program (UNEP) attempts to clean up water supplies, stop deforestation, find solutions to drought, and eliminating the production of ozone-depleting chemicals (Keegan, 2001).

The Earth Summit in 1992 culminated in the signing of the Framework Convention on Climate Change. In 2000, there was an international agreement to limit greenhouse gas emissions by developed countries (Keegan, 2001). Since that time, the United States and other countries have decided it is not willing to abide by the controls outlined in the agreement.

Other international health concerns include noise, pesticides, and living environments.

Noise has negative effects on health. High levels of noise are associated with hearing impairment, increased blood pressure, distracted behavior, fatigue, sleep disturbances, and perhaps birth defects.

Pesticides are commonly used throughout the world. Efforts to increase agricultural yields, especially in developing countries, increases risks to the population.

Personal space is important to everyone. A healthy space is clean and uncluttered, with good ventilation and little noise (Keegan, 2001). However, many people live in crowded conditions that are dirty and noisy. Consider the large cities around the world that have millions of inhabitants.

It is a challenge to sustain desirable environments. Individuals and groups can do something to improve their own environments. Containing trash and litter is a start. The problem remains if there is nowhere else to put it. In some countries people actually live in trash heaps. Efforts to improve environmental conditions need the cooperation of all countries. Nurses have opportunities to work collaboratively with nurses in other countries to improve health.

CARING FOR PERSONS FROM DIFFERENT CULTURES

There are several areas of knowledge and skills that prepare nurses to give care to a diverse population. Griffin (2003) describes a nurse's experience caring for an Iranian man. She started talking to family members gathered around the bedside. When she directed her comments to the wife and daughter, they lowered their eyes and turned away. She finally figured out that she would have to talk to the man in the room. When she told them the visiting hours, the son-in-law said they could not abandon the father and needed to stay with him. A compromise was worked out and the nurse realized that cultural care had many aspects. She had much to learn. One place to start was by completing assessments that include culture.

Cultural Assessment - Nurses

Before assessing other cultural needs, nurses must examine their own values and beliefs about different cultures. How do we interact with persons from other cultures?

Self-assessment questions include

- What do our family and friends say about other races?

- What biases do we have about foreigners and immigrants?

- Do you or your family attend events with people from other cultures?

- Do you associate specific health practices with certain cultures?

- Have you had negative personal or professional experiences with persons from other cultures? (Cherry & Jacob, 2002).

Cultural Competency Staircase Model

The Cultural Competency Staircase Model is one way for nurses to assess their level of competence and track growth over time. Nurses can assess themselves using the model: it has a scale, with 1 being the lowest level and 6 the highest level of competence.

1. Lack of recognition about the importance of culture when planning patient care.

2. Having an awareness of the importance of culture but self-awareness is limited.

3. Developing self-awareness about one or two ethnic groups and beginning to include cultural information when planning care.

4. A strong sense of cultural awareness and a social network that shares information. Nurses consistently include cultural information in planning care.

5. Being highly aware of personal beliefs, accepting cultural practices as part of care, and anticipating potential patient and staff issues.

6. Having a high level of self-awareness and a broad knowledge about other cultures. At this level, a culturally competent nurse solves related problems and coaches other nurses (Kersey-Matusiak, 2002).

An important aspect of cultural sensitivity is to realize that all ethnic groups harbor prejudices. Cultural understanding has to come from all parties. Look for opportunities to bring different cultures together and discuss the different perspectives each group has about others.

Cultural Assessment - Patients

Nurses use assessment techniques in many different aspects of patient care. Aspects of cultural assessment include

- ethnic affiliation,

- religious affiliation,

- family interactions and social patterns,

- food habits and patterns,

- ethnic health care beliefs and values (Cherry & Jacob, 2002).

Cultural Nutrition Assessment

Each culture has unique food preferences, ways of preparing food, and special significance attributed to certain foods. Nurses can determine dietary patterns and call on a dietitian to work out an acceptable, nutritionally sound diet. An important part of assessing diets is to understand that nurses may not be familiar with nutritional foods from other cultures. For example, Asian populations may not use milk products but do use bones and shells that supply calcium. The goal is not to change patients' diets but to help them have nutritional diets with the foods they accept. A major part of culture is our beliefs about what causes illness and what cures them. Chapter 10 addressed reasons why people use non-Western therapies. For many people, it is related to culture.

Communication

Ledger (2002), a British nurse, shares her experience teaching a week-long course in Spain. She spoke limited Spanish and wondered how she would cope if she needed to receive health care. It made her more aware of how non-English-speaking patients at the Royal London Hospital must feel. She recognized that such patients feel isolation, frustration, or anger. The health care team members also feel frustrated if they are unable to make patients understand what is happening or help them comply with treatment regimens. Patients may have to wait for translators, and then the issue of confidentiality arises. Ledger started talking to others and began different strategies to improve communication.

Sickness and Cures

Many cultures identify illnesses that are not classified the same by Western medicine. For example, "evil eye" may cause illness by admiring someone and looking into their face. People may be born with "strong vision" and can harm others just by glancing at them. Many Mexicans believe in "susto" or fright sickness. The body is brushed for several nights to have the bad spirit removed. Chinese patients often do not like diagnostic tests and think physicians should be able to make a diagnosis by examining the body. They may decline surgery that will mutilate their bodies (Cherry & Jacob, 2002). As nurses begin to understand the importance of cultural beliefs and values, they can blend the diverse approaches to increase patient acceptance of treatments.

Nurses and Ethical Conflicts

Nurses who are educated and practice in the United States share common values related to practice. They practice from common frameworks that set out ethical practice, patients' rights, and quality indicators of care. Several areas of cultural difference may cause conflicts.

The majority of cultures base decisions and actions on what is best for the family or group. In the United States, we strongly support individualism. A conflict may arise when women cannot make their own decisions about healthcare. Males make decisions they feel are best for the family as a whole. The American sense of justice and autonomy do not fit with a collective view of society. There may be instances when the ethical principle of "do no harm" is in conflict with a cultural practice such as circumcision, either male or female. Other examples are patients not accepting treatment for themselves or their children.

Solutions

Mr. and Mrs. Singh are struggling with the discovery that she had a tubal ligation after the birth of their son a few months ago. The Singhs talk with friends to determine what to do. They believe the procedure was done without informed consent. They consult an attorney. The issues were outlined.

- Mrs. Singh had little understanding of English.

- Mr. Singh was not present to translate for his wife when she signed the permission.

- The nurse had the ethical and legal obligation to assure no harm was done to the patient.

- A physician had the legal responsibility to obtain consent and make sure the patient understood what she was signing.

- A nurse could sign as a witness.

- The nurse had the obligation to serve as a patient advocate by waiting until the husband was present, giving Mrs. Singh the form to take home to review it, or find a translator.

The attorney reviews the information and agrees to meet with the hospital attorney to discuss the incident. After a great deal of discussion and legal maneuvers, a settlement is reached in favor of the Singhs.

CONCLUSION

The population in the United States is changing with increasing diversity. We are also becoming part of the world outside our borders. The health care needs and expectations of persons from different cultures are of concern to society and health care providers. The majority of American nurses are Caucasian and have little exposure to other cultures. The nursing workforce needs more diversity. Nurses currently in practice require knowledge and skills to meet the unique health issues of diverse populations. It is a challenge, but nurses in all settings can develop action plans to achieve the goal of cultural competency.

EXAM QUESTIONS

CHAPTER 11
Questions 51-55

51. The best example of a nurses' cultural awareness is

    a. collecting a medical history.

    b. determining the best treatment for the patient.

    c. making sure all advance directives are signed.

    d. identifying ethnic food choices that are part of a patient's diet.

52. Joan, a nurse practitioner, is caring for a young child with fever and diarrhea. The mother explains the problems are caused by an evil eye. A nurse demonstrates cultural sensitivity to the mother's perception that fever and diarrhea are caused by an evil eye by

    a. explaining how to take the prescribed medication.

    b. exploring how evil eye is usually treated at home.

    c. asking a Spanish-speaking nurse to explain the treatment.

    d. talking about the importance of accepting modern medicine.

53. The Milstead model uses the comparative analysis research approach to compare the impact of health-related policy decisions in

    a. different age populations.

    b. small towns.

    c. different cultures.

    d. different countries.

54. The examples of needle exchange programs (NEPs) have a common feature

    a. the programs were equally effective in reducing HIV/AIDS.

    b. governmental support for the programs made them successful and accepted.

    c. exchanges were carried out in the same way at each site.

    d. the programs evolved from grassroots efforts to recognized legal programs.

55. The Cultural Competency Staircase Model helps nurses

    a. determine cultural health practices of different populations.

    b. learn about different cultural and ethnic practices from coworkers.

    c. assess their own level of cultural competence and track their personal growth.

    d. assess cultural knowledge of others and help them learn more.

CHAPTER 12

WORKPLACE ISSUES

CHAPTER OBJECTIVE

After studying this chapter, you will be able to recognize significant workplace issues that impact nursing practice.

LEARNING OBJECTIVES

After studying this chapter, you will be able to

1. recognize employee safety issues and find ways to improve workplace safety.

2. differentiate staffing patterns for their impact on nurses, patients, and the organization.

3. recognize behavioral and substance abuse problems among co-workers and choose the appropriate ethical and legal measures.

4. discriminate work environment effects with and without collective bargaining.

OVERVIEW

Americans spend at least half their time in work-related activities. Health care settings may pay more attention to the physical environment and its maintenance than to the quality and safety of work environments for employees. Healthcare workers face many actual and potential hazards, such as

• exposure to contagious diseases,

• contact with contagious materials,

• allergies to products,

• exposure to chemical and radioactive materials and processes,

• threats to the safety and welfare of employees and patients,

• physical injury,

• verbal and sexual harassment (Tappen, Weiss, & Whitehead, 2001).

Workplace issues also include heavy workloads for nurses that contribute to burnout, fatigue, and issues of patient safety. Nurses also face professional and personal issues such as substance abuse, mental or emotional problems, physical disability, and substandard patient care.

One strategy to improve the work environment for nurses is to have collective bargaining. There are conflicting views about collective bargaining. The major issues are presented in this chapter.

Challenges

Connie is a traveling nurse. She has 10 years of experience in cardiac units, both intensive care and step-down. She has accepted a 12-week assignment at a large for-profit hospital in a midwestern metropolitan area. She works 12-hour shifts and rotates between day and night shifts. After working for 6 weeks, she has observed the following nursing behaviors.

• Betty was observed taking patient medication. The nurse manager confronted her, and Betty quit.

- Brian came to work on weekends with signs of having been drinking. In college, he drank every weekend and has continued the habit since graduation. When confronted about his behavior one Sunday, he said he had stayed up late and drinking was not a problem. During that shift, he gave the wrong medications to patients with similar names. He told Connie about his drinking patterns but denied he was an alcoholic. He believed he always controlled his drinking.

- Mary was depressed. She was able to get to work most days but became increasingly isolated from her coworkers. She was late for work and did not complete her work. At first, the other nurses were concerned and helped her. She was later fired and attempted suicide. When she was treated in the emergency department, the information was sent to the board of nursing. She had a hearing and her license was suspended for 2 years.

- Annette had a worsening disc problem with constant pain. She organized her work and did the minimum so that she could get through the day. She often rested. One day a patient coded, and she could not get up to help. The patient died. Her inability to help was reported to the board of nursing, and her license was suspended for 2 years. (Sloan & Vernarec, 2001).

Connie is concerned about all the problems and wonders if each situation was resolved correctly, in the best interests of patients, the profession, and the nurses. She e-mails other nurses, attends a workshop on impaired nurses, and finds information on the Internet.

WORKPLACE SAFETY

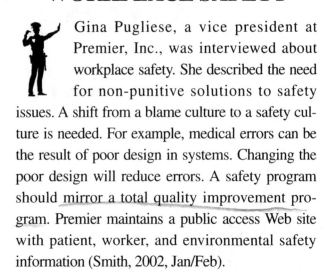

Gina Pugliese, a vice president at Premier, Inc., was interviewed about workplace safety. She described the need for non-punitive solutions to safety issues. A shift from a blame culture to a safety culture is needed. For example, medical errors can be the result of poor design in systems. Changing the poor design will reduce errors. A safety program should mirror a total quality improvement program. Premier maintains a public access Web site with patient, worker, and environmental safety information (Smith, 2002, Jan/Feb).

The Occupational Safety and Health Act of 1970 has been amended over the years to address new safety issues. The Occupational Safety and Health Administration (OSHA) is responsible for implementing the law. Employers must follow the standards for providing a safe, healthy workplace. Records are kept for all occupational illnesses and accidents. Inspection may be conducted periodically. After workplace incidents, there are inspections. Employee complaints may also trigger inspections (Tappen, Weiss, & Whitehead, 2001).

Employee Safety

Nurses work in many different settings. They have contact with many people every day: patients, family members, coworkers, vendors, and delivery persons. When they work in community and home settings, they see and interact with many other people and encounter a number of possibly unsafe situations.

Workplace Violence

Violence in the workplace is not a new issue. The newspapers and other media regularly report incidents. Health care and social services have the highest incidence of workplace violence. Homicide is the second leading cause of workplace death. Health care work settings have about 1,000 murders and 1.5 million assaults each year. Easy access to institutions, long waiting times, high stress situations, violent behaviors by visitors, few staff on a unit, and high risk service areas such as emergency and psychiatric units increase the potential for workplace violence. Incidents may be underreported if there are no policies for reporting or there is a fear that the employee will be blamed (Tappen, Weiss, & Whitehead, 2001).

Trossman (2001) describes the efforts and outcomes of nurses to make their mental health work environment safer after a nurse was injured and suffered a coma. She had been slammed against a metal door by a patient with a known history of violence. Management previously treated violence to employees as "part of the job." Changes in management brought a focus on prevention and zero tolerance for violence. The nurses spoke loudly about the issues. The Illinois Nurses Association and mental health nurses brought the issues before the state legislators. Reforms included the following safety changes:

- Nurses can make the judgment to place violent patients in restraints and administer emergency medications to newly admitted violent patients.

- Patient care monitoring teams review patient information and develop a plan to reduce violence.

- Staff have personal safety alarms, and two-way radios are available to contact security personnel.

- All staff members attend a 2-day workshop on violence and violence prevention.

Additional improvements are being implemented based on the committee and group work of staff. Nurses and other personnel feel safer and there are fewer violent incidents.

The number of persons in nursing homes continues to grow. There are almost 2 million nursing home beds in the country in 17,000 facilities. Certified nursing assistants (CNAs) make up 70-90% of nursing personnel in these settings. CNAs have the least amount of training and education. They provide most of the personal care and

face harassment, threats, and assaults from residents. Violence often occurs during feeding, bathing, dressing, and turning (Gates, Fitzwater, & Meyer, 1999). Registered nurses are in charge of nursing in these settings and have the responsibility to protect everyone.

A study solicited information from CNAs (n=54) and nurse managers (n=6) about workplace violence. All the CNAs participating in the focus group had experienced both physical and verbal assaults. Reporting of incidents was variable. When medical attention was required, a written report was done. Otherwise, there was often just a verbal report. CNAs had concerns about being blamed for incidents. Lack of communication and information about the residents contributed to the violence. The CNAs wanted training to learn how to handle violence, work in teams, understand their rights, and handle stress (Gates, Fitzwater, & Meyer, 1999).

The nurse managers agreed that violence was present in the work settings and that there was not consistent reporting. Lack of reporting was based on acceptance by CNAs that violence was "part of the job," fear of losing their jobs, and drug testing after incidents. The focus in the facilities was on resident and family rights, with few policies, procedures, or discussion of employee rights. They agreed that little or no training was provided during orientation. When asked what would reduce violent episodes, the nurse managers identified education, training, pre-admission screening, family education, decreased admission of mentally ill persons, employee rights policies, improved staffing, and safety committee involvement in the issue.

Workplace violence in nursing homes needs attention and the nurses in those settings can lead the efforts to reduce it (Gates, Fitzwater, & Meyer, 1999). There are effective prevention strategies.

- Be aware of clues that indicate the potential for violence.

- Develop personal relationships with patients

and family members.

- Communicate effectively with patients and family members. Allow them to share their feelings about the situation.

- Recognize and respond to your own feelings about potentially violent situations.

- Know and follow the safety policies and procedures (Tappen, Weiss, & Whitehead, 2001).

Sexual Harassment

Discrimination in the workplace is prohibited by the 5th and 14th Amendments to the U.S. Constitution. The Equal Opportunity Commission (EEOC) has the responsibility for administering and enforcing the laws. It prevents employers from making decisions based on race, color, sex, age, disability, religion, or national origin.

Sexual harassment falls within EEOC responsibilities. There are two forms of sexual harassment: sexual favors being required for job benefits such as advancement or continued employment and hostile environments where offensive conditions exist. Hostile environments include verbal and written comments and behaviors that personally target individuals or groups. Examples are using foul language, making sexually suggestive comments, posting nude pictures, and unwanted touching (Tappen, Weiss, & Whitehead, 2001).

Staying alert and recognizing potential situations may help reduce sexual harassment.

- Present yourself as a professional.

- Discourage personal discussion and comments; keep focused on work-related issues.

- Directly confront harassment as it happens.

- Report incidents.

- Document incidents.

- File a formal complaint and follow institutional policies.

- Seek support from coworkers, family members, friends, and professional organizations

(Tappen, Weiss, & Whitehead, 2001).

Latex Allergy

Health care workers are exposed to many latex products in their work settings. Latex is made from a milky fluid found in rubber trees. About 8-12% of health care workers suffer allergic reactions to latex products. Reactions may be mild (skin drying or blistering), more serious (generalized hives), to most serious (wheezing, swelling, impaired respirations, and anaphylactic shock).

It is virtually impossible to have a completely latex-free environment. Latex is found in emergency equipment, protective apparel, office supplies, and hospital supplies and equipment (Tappen, Weiss, & Whitehead, 2001). Nurses can guard against exposure.

- Be aware of personal risk factors, such as existing allergies and multiple surgeries.

- Evaluate cases of hand dermatitis that may be an early sign of latex allergy.

- Check products that you commonly use for latex.

- Encourage the use of latex-free products on your unit.

- Consider changing work settings to protect your career (Tappen, Weiss, & Whitehead, 2001).

There is more awareness of the problem and alternative products are available.

Needlestick Injuries

Bloodborne diseases are a concern in health care settings. In 1991, OSHA set forth bloodborne pathogen standards. Employers must provide

- free hepatitis B vaccine;

- protective equipment that fits;

- confidential evaluation, treatment, and follow-up;

- institution-wide universal precautions;

- adequate disposal of sharps;

- hazard removal;

- annual employee bloodborne pathogen training

(Tappen, Weiss, & Whitehead, 2001).

Nurses need to protect themselves and be examples to others.

- Always use universal precautions when required.

- Use and dispose of sharps properly.

- Complete a hepatitis B series.

- Follow reporting policies.

- Know the health status of patients.

- Help and support others who are exposed.

- Actively participate in committees that promote workplace safety.

- Educate themselves and others about new equipment and procedures (Tappen, Weiss, & Whitehead, 2001).

Back Injury

Nurses must have stamina and strength to meet the physical demands of patient care. Physical injuries are common. Almost 40% of nurses suffer some type of back injury during their careers. Such injuries may be mild and have no long-term consequences. Others may be so debilitating that nurses can no longer work in some areas.

A study by the National Institute for Occupational Health and Safety found that 98% of patient transfers were done by hooking patients' underarms. This stresses caregivers' backs. Prevention and solutions include the following practices:

- Help write guidelines that reflect current best practices for prevention of injuries.

- Be aware of assistive devices that help move patients and get training on, how to use them.

- Learn and use proper techniques for protecting your back when moving patients.

- Maintain a high level of physical fitness (Tappen, Weiss, & Whitehead, 2001).

Physical Environment

Physical environments impact how we function at work and how we feel about our surroundings. Surroundings that are safe, are environmentally controlled, and have pleasing decors contribute to job satisfaction. The amount of space, placement of workstations, storage for supplies and equipment, cleaning and maintenance services all enhance job satisfaction and efficiency.

The reality is that health care work settings are not optimum environments. Potential violence, overcrowding, poor maintenance, and lack of resources are common (Tappen, Weiss, & Whitehead, 2001). Nurses can work together to improve conditions.

- If collective bargaining is in place, include these issues in contract negotiations.

- Raise community awareness and support for improvements.

- Work with others to develop volunteer programs to support the institution (Tappen, Weiss, & Whitehead, 2001).

STAFFING PATTERNS AND WORK HOURS

Staffing patterns and work hours are issues in nursing because of the current nursing shortage. Staffing relates to having an adequate number of workers to care for patients. There are different ways to achieve that requirement. Work hours are an issue because nurses are working many hours and may have mandatory overtime. The need for nurses will continue to exceed the supply for years to come.

Job opportunities for nurses will continue to increase by 21% through 2006, compared to an overall increase of 14% in all jobs. Today, about 250,000 more registered nurses are needed than are available. The reasons for the shortage are large population increases in some areas. Nurses are aging and retiring. Fewer students are entering the profession than in past years. Nurses with specific skills are in short supply (Tappen, Weiss, & Whitehead, 2001).

Many people are selecting careers other than nursing. Women have many educational and career opportunities today. The number of minority and male nurses is not increasing in spite of increasing diversity in the population (Cherry & Jacob, 2002).

Changes in hospitals and downsizing have reduced the number of bedside nurses. Patients do not recover the same way, there are more complications, and many patients do not have home care. Veteran nurses are leaving. Registered nurses are replaced by assistive personnel with little or no training. Claims that the number of nurses working in hospitals has increased does not take into account what many nurses are doing. Many nurses are not caring for patients but carrying out administrative functions (Gordon, 2000).

The challenge is to make sure there are sufficient nurses, with the specific skills needed, to provide quality care. What impact does the nursing shortage have on nurses as they go to work every day?

- There is a decline in satisfaction as identified by decreases in resources, nurse manager skills, attitudes toward nurses, and lack of empowerment.

- There is concern about an increase in patient care errors when there is minimum staffing (Tappen, Weiss, & Whitehead, 2001).

- An increase in foreign-educated nurses opens the door for abuse by employers, may negatively affect wages, and increases the nursing shortage around the world.

- Nursing salaries have been flat for several years in the face of a shortage. Salary incentives are offered to new hires in the form of bonuses. Agency nurses are hired and travel nurses are

recruited (Cherry & Jacob, 2002).

Work Environment

Work environment is one of the most important factors when recruiting and retaining nurses. Salary is important, but the care environment is more important. Turnover rates are directly tied to workload and staffing patterns. Nurses move to other settings because of unqualified managers and inexperienced staff. Some nurses are recruited to other jobs because of incentives (Cherry & Jacob, 2002).

Safety issues, cited earlier, also contribute to poor work environments. Issues with nurses themselves create problems. Absenteeism, staffing issues, and mandatory overtime are major issues.

Absenteeism

Absenteeism is a problem in hospitals and other centralized organizations because the work environment is difficult. Employee morale is adversely affected, and costs increase. Occupational injury and fatalities in the United States cost $121 billion in 1996. Reasons for absenteeism include

- job dissatisfaction,

- illness,

- caregiving responsibilities,

- work scheduling,

- sick pay benefits,

- injury,

- employer's attitudes about absenteeism.

  Strategies to reduce absenteeism can be effective.

- Creating a culture where excessive absenteeism is not tolerated. Make sure that employees know what is expected, have been informed and sign a statement that they understand. Uniformly and fairly implement the attendance policy and the associated sanctions.

- Shape the organization to the people. Nurses who are satisfied with their jobs are less likely to be absent. Empowering nurses to share in governance and decision-making increases job satisfaction.

- Nurse managers may use reward and coercive power to decrease absenteeism. In some settings, nurses complain that nothing is done to stop excessive absenteeism. Those who come to work as scheduled bear the brunt of increased work. Rewards can include personal recognition, buy-back of unused sick leave, and bonuses for outstanding attendance. For persons who are excessively absent, a disciplinary program can keep increasing sanctions so individuals must improve or be fired.

- Developing a sense of organizational loyalty where values are highlighted is important. Ceremonies to celebrate employee loyalty speak for the organizational values. Long-term employees can socialize and mentor new employees into the culture. Employees who are proud to work for an organization and are loyal will have little absenteeism (Harter, 2001).

Staffing

The two areas of concern in staffing are determining how adequate it is and requiring nurses to work overtime. Managed care has made a significant impact on staffing. Managed care has decentralized services and supported cross-training of personnel. The goal was to cut costs. The mix of personnel has changed from highly educated clinical specialists and registered nurses to include more unlicensed, assistive personnel (Cherry & Jacob, 2002).

Nurses face another staffing issue in addition to shortages. They may be assigned to other units or float between units. Nurses often are not oriented to the other units. They have no experience and with short staffing, they have little support and guidance.

The debate continues today over what is the appropriate staffing mix. While there are continuing questions, there is no agreement on how to determine adequate staffing and what factors contribute to staffing decisions. Obviously, there are wide variations in work settings and patient acuity.

The Joint Commission on Accreditation of Healthcare Organizations (JCAHO) proposes the following solutions to the nursing shortage of more than 126,000 unfilled nursing positions:

- Increase management training for nurses.

- Setting staffing levels based on competency and skill mix related to patient acuity.

- Increase funding for nursing education and creating a standard, post-graduation residency program (2002).

There is increasing concern among professional, governmental, corporate, and community groups about the nursing shortage. Efforts include

- increasing and expanding recruitment efforts,

- providing additional scholarships,

- enhancing recruitment,

- increasing retention (Smith, 2002, Nov/Dec).

While these efforts are useful, the fundamental issues in work environments are not being addressed. The impression is that the shortage is a surprise. It was anticipated but is now a reality that hospitals and other facilities are experiencing. The shortage is a public issue. Many groups are aligning themselves with nursing, and there is increased recognition of the profession. An Internet search resulted in 158,000 matches to the term "nursing shortage." A sampling of these results is as follows:

- The Nurse Reinvestment Act was signed by President Bush but not funded. The provisions include a National Nurse Service Corps, Nurse Education Act, Geriatric Nurse Training Grants, Faculty Loan Repayment Grants, and public service announcements.

- The Robert Wood Johnson Foundation published a report and recommended a national forum to focus on major initiatives. One is to change nursing practice models.

- Johnson & Johnson is supporting a 2-year, $20 million advertising campaign.

- In Iowa, several groups are working to increase the supply of nurses and other personnel by improving work environments and finding ways to increase Medicare and Medicaid reimbursement to fund salaries for staff nurses.

- The Veterans Administration is reviewing utilization and retention efforts.

- Metrowest Community Health Care Foundation in Boston has a Web site that includes information about becoming a nurse, practice settings, and links to specialized nursing sites (Smith, 2002).

Coffman, Seago, and Spetz (2002) describe the effort in California to establish minimum nurse to patient ratios. Nurses generally believe that having fewer patients results in better care. The legislation intends to increase the quality of care. It will also reduce the shortage because nurses would be more willing to practice in hospitals. There are concerns about the increased costs. It is projected that improved patient outcomes and reduced turnover will offset the costs.

Mandatory Overtime

As the shortage continues, facilities have implemented mandatory overtime or mandatory on-call. The practice is common across the country. The U.S. Department of Labor found there was increased absenteeism and injuries along with decreased productivity associated with mandatory overtime. When productivity is reduced, it takes 3 hours to complete 2 hours of work. The long hours required of medical residents is potentially linked to patient deaths (Cherry & Jacob, 2002). There is no evidence that mandatory overtime or floating has harmed patients, but there is concern.

Nurses are negatively motivated by these issues. They believe the staffing crisis today started with earlier concerns about cutting costs. The skill mix was changed, and care delivery models did not support quality staffing levels (Cherry & Jacob, 2002).

Nurses have various ways to cope with unreasonable work hours and poor staffing. They can collectively address the issues on their unit or in their facility. Being actively involved and empowered helps achieve positive outcomes. There are resources to help nurses make decisions.

- *Principles of Nurse Staffing* is a guide to determining staffing. It is free for ANA members by calling 1.800.274.4262. It can be ordered (PNS-1) at http://www.nursesbooks.org.

- Nursing quality indicators, definitions, interpretations, and a guide for implementation can be ordered from 1.800.637.0323 or http://www.nursesbooks.org.

- State nurses associations offer information and support. Find member associations at http://nursingworld.org (Cherry & Jacob, 2002).

When you are interviewing for a new position, consider asking the following questions about staffing:

- Who makes decisions about staffing?

- Is there a shared governance model?

- What is the usual staff mix on different types of units?

- How often do nurses float?

- What is the average length of employment and the turnover rate? (Cherry & Jacob, 2002).

These are just a few of the questions nurses should ask when considering a new job. Networking with others, attending professional meetings, and getting more information about organizations can help in making sound decisions. It is also essential to gain information about an assignment before accepting it.

- Find out specifically about the assignment.

- Determine your expertise, knowledge, and experience.

- Ask if the assignment is temporary or long-term.

- Determine if the type of assignment is common or due to a specific situation (Cherry & Jacob, 2002).

Legislation was passed in California to address such issues as patient-staff ratios and policies for training and orienting nurses to new areas. The bill was passed in 1999, but implementation was delayed until 2001. Federal efforts have been aimed at updating the Fair Labor Standards Act to include limiting nurse's working hours. Additional support for staffing and work issues came from an Institute of Medicine Report (Cherry & Jacob, 2002).

NURSES IN NEED OF CARE

Nurses have the same problems as others in our society. Alcohol, drug abuse, physical/mental impairment, and negative work habits can affect nurses and their coworkers. Impaired nurses in the workplace may have potential negative impact on patients. Care may not be given, and errors may occur.

Additionally, there is potential liability for the employers. Coworkers are concerned about lack of care. They also resent covering for the impaired nurse. Morale may drop. Stress is heightened. Everyone worries about what may happen next.

Nurses must be aware of their professional, legal, and ethical responsibilities when they observe and are involved in situations. It would be ideal if impaired nurses recognized their own predicaments and worked to resolve them. That is rarely the case. Coworkers and patients observe and report the problems.

Common indicators of impairment include

- Actually observing a nurse drinking, taking drugs, or being unprofessional.

- Lack of attention to detail when caring for patients.

- Repeated reports by patients, family members, and coworkers of problems.

- Decline in appearance, abusive language, and displays of anger (Tappen, Weiss, & Whitehead, 2001).

West (2002) conducted a study to investigate early risk factors that lead to substance-related disorders. Impairment is a continuous process, as described by Rogerian theory. There is not one event or cause. Impaired nurses share common characteristics but differ in development, progression, and severity. Personality, heredity, sociocultural situation, and environmental factors all contribute to impairment. If early risk factors are identified, it may be possible to reduce them.

We may think it easy to identify impaired nurses. About 10% of the general population have an addiction. It is estimated that 15% of nurses are or have been impaired. That means if you are working with 10 nurses, one is likely to be impaired or recovering. Addiction is a disease; without treatment, it progresses. After years of not abusing substances, symptoms return during a relapse.

Work environments enable impaired nurses in several ways. Coworkers may not understand addiction. They are concerned about being manipulated, they have a sense of powerlessness when they observe a situation, and they fear legal action. Employers rationalize behaviors, allow poor performance, decrease workloads, and offer excuses.

Impaired nurses are in denial and rationalize their behavior. Education is needed so that nurses can recognize the problem and stop enabling behaviors (Dwyer, Holloran, & Walsh, 2002 and Griffith, 1999). All nurses can support professional efforts to provide help when needed. Without cures, impaired nurses must continue with a program for life. Nurses understand they have the responsibility to report unsafe situations. They may be uncertain about exactly when or how to report.

Disciplinary actions are spelled out in hospitals and other health care settings. Thirty-seven states offer rehabilitation programs. Nurses can voluntarily attend or may be required to attend. Not everyone agrees this is the best approach. Some believe that reporting and self-reporting processes help nurses more. Reporting is done to peer assistance programs, employer assistance programs, state boards of nursing, and state hospital associations (Blair, 2002).

Protecting Whistle-Blowers

When nurses observe problems with staff and patients, they want to report them and feel safe. Some states have passed legislation that protects persons who report information in good faith. Health care organizations cannot retaliate against whistle-blowers. For example, if nurses report unsafe conditions, they cannot be disciplined. One case resulted in an award to a nurse who reported that patients' wishes to stop treatment were ignored (Cherry & Jacob, 2002). Employers usually have policies that support reporting.

The American Nurses Association has developed guidelines for reporting unsafe practice. Each state has a nurse practice act to govern professional behavior. Federal and state regulations address workplace issues. Criminal acts are subject to prosecution. There are also ethical obligations to practice professionally. Lack of knowledge does not protect nurses from the obligation to report substandard practice (Tappen, Weiss, & Whitehead, 2001).

Recovery

Impaired nurses do enter recovery programs. Compassion helps impaired nurses enter and stay in intervention programs. Such programs are cheaper than investigative programs. The cost of participating in a 4-year chemical dependence pro-

gram is one-third the cost of pursuing a traditional investigation for one violation.

Impaired nurses have to be committed to recovery. Two to 5 years of active treatment and monitoring is required. Most states allow nurses to keep their licenses and work in supervised situations.

Returning to work is an incentive for nurses to stay in their program. They must inform the employer they are in a program and a decision is made about an appropriate work assignment. A plan to assure patient safety must be in place and the nurse closely monitored. Nurses must work in an approved setting and cannot work in independent situations.

Nurses can clear their records by completing a program. There is concern about loss of confidentiality. Impaired nurses attend group meetings and report their status to their employers. They are concerned that employers will find ways to fire them. Information regarding the impairment will not be part of licensure records nor will the nurse's information be put in the national database (Sloan & Vernarec, 2001).

Advice to nurses who want to avoid problems and report them include

- Maintain your own health: good nutrition, exercise, adequate rest, and social outlets.

- Be aware of the legal and ethical obligations for professional practice.

- Understand the processes for reporting.

- Share information with coworkers about the resources available for impaired nurses.

- Be supportive of nurses who are seeking help (Tappen, Weiss, & Whitehead, 2001).

Patient Safety

Patient advocacy has always been a part of nursing. In today's health care environment, the role has new meaning. The increasing complexity of healthcare, new technologies, and staffing issues requires nurses to increase their vigilance. There is concern over medication errors and adverse treatment outcomes (Cherry & Jacob, 2002).

As many as 98,000 people die each year in hospitals from errors. Errors occur in all different settings: hospitals, clinics, pharmacies, and home settings. The types of adverse reactions include

- medication and transfusion errors,

- equipment failures,

- surgery errors,

- falls,

- burns,

- mistaken identity (Cherry & Jacob, 2002).

In 1999, the Institute of Medicine (IOM) published a report called *To Err is Human: Building a Safer Health System*. The report acknowledged that adverse events were the result of mistakes rather than incompetence.

Baker, Flynn, Pepper, Bates, & Mikeal (2002) conducted a study of medication errors in 36 randomly selected JCAHO institutions with nursing units that administered at least 50 doses/shift. Medications were administered by nurses on the participating units and observed by a research pharmacist. A total of 3,216 doses were observed. Findings included

- Of the 3,216 doses, 19% (605) of the doses were in error.

- Errors were wrong time (43%), omission (30%), wrong dose (17%), and unauthorized drug (4%).

- Of the errors, 7% had the potential for adverse reactions.

It was evident from this study that the problem of defective medication administration systems varies by cause but is widespread. Effective governmental regulation and adequate nursing staff will help reduce errors.

COLLECTIVE BARGAINING

Generally, discussions related to collective bargaining and labor unions bring out different perspectives and are emotionally charged. These discussions are relatively new in the health care industry. Unions are becoming important, especially with mergers of healthcare systems. Nurses may choose to join coworkers in existing unions or select a separate entity. The American Federation of Labor Congress of Industrial Organizations (AFL-CIO) is a large group that represents mixed unions. The ANA bargaining unit has formalized a relationship with the AFL-CIO and is now called the United American Nurses (UAN). The National Labor Relations Board regulates the number of bargaining units in healthcare systems. Registered nurses are one category (Cherry & Jacob, 2002).

Collective bargaining is aimed at equalizing power between employees and employers. Groups with a common purpose can accomplish more than individuals alone. Large numbers of persons can call attention to issues. Collective bargaining takes advantage of the power of numbers. An effective collective bargaining contract provides considerable protection to employees. The downside is that it may promote conflict rather than cooperation. Nurses become concerned about how strikes affect patients. Most managers and nurses prefer a union-free environment (Tappen, Weiss, & Whitehead, 2001).

Formal Negotiations

Collective bargaining involves formal negotiations governed by labor laws. Groups are represented by designated bargaining agents. A contract defines important workplace issues; economic, management, and practice. The approved contract governs employee-management relations (Tappen, Weiss, & Whitehead, 2001).

Baker, Szudy, and Guerriero (2001) describe an experience that occupational health nurses had when working with labor unions. Occupational health nurses work in unique settings and interface with unions in a variety of ways.

- Providing care to employees who are union members.

- Being a member of a union.

- Being employed by a union in a staff position.

- Representing a governmental agency that is responsible for regulating occupational health and safety.

Nurses must understand the rules and regulations related to contracts and work within that framework. Nurses also need trust relationships with both the unions and management. Workers do not want to feel they are to blame when there are problems. Management wants a safe workplace because accidents and other hazards are expensive and demoralizing for all concerned.

Pros and Cons of Collective Bargaining

Nurses may feel it is unprofessional to belong to a union. When there are shortages, with concerns about mandatory overtime and floating, nurses may consider collective bargaining to formalize resolutions to issues. Collective bargaining could dictate what is needed for quality care. The American Medical Association (AMA) acted to form a bargaining unit in response to managed care issues (Cherry & Jacob, 2002).

It is felt that policies and processes are constricted by the terms of any contract. An issue for nurses is determining who are managers and who is staff. Court decisions have addressed that issue and found that staff nurses, who assume charge duties, are not management. Nurses managers are in the middle because they may be management but they also assume staff nurse duties. Open communication is essential on nursing units, yet nurses involved in bargaining may not cooperate with nurse managers (Cherry & Jacob, 2002).

An advantage of collective bargaining is the protection and right to fair treatment, availability of grievance processes, and ability to work out conflicts and issues (Tappen, Weiss, & Whitehead, 2001). In the future, nurses may realize the potential for collective action to influence corporate and policy decisions. A blend of health care industry goals, public interest, and professional excellence could be possible.

Solutions

Connie is still concerned about the nursing personnel issues she has observed in our challenge situation. Connie has gathered a lot of information about impaired nurse issues. Her conclusion is that the hospital has a punitive approach to dealing with problems. She puts together an information packet for the chief nursing officer and schedules an appointment. Although she is a traveling nurse, she feels she has a professional responsibility to share information. In her meeting, she shares her observations and highlights some of the information she has collected. Connie plans to share the same information in other settings.

CONCLUSION

Workplace issues are numerous. Nurses must pay attention to their own work environments as well as to developing an awareness of what is happening in the profession. Individual and group actions can make big differences. Understanding and keeping informed about current and emerging issues helps nurses prevent problems or address them before there are critical consequences. The outcomes are increased job satisfaction and the ability to maintain quality patient care.

EXAM QUESTIONS

CHAPTER 12

Questions 56-60

56. A proactive safety program should

    a. make sure all safety information is collected.
    b. mirror a total quality improvement plan.
    c. provide education after each incident.
    d. be based on reducing medication errors.

57. One impact of minimum staffing is that nurses are concerned about

    a. how they can have less work.
    b. other nurses on the unit quitting.
    c. having to orient new nurses.
    d. an increase in patient care errors.

58. A major contributing factor to nurses' workplace back injuries is the practice of

    a. transferring patients by hooking under their arms.
    b. two persons lifting and moving heavy patients.
    c. nurses using a primary care delivery model.
    d. transferring patients using mechanical lifts.

59. Impaired nurses in the workplace can have a negative impact on patient care. A common indicator of impairment is

    a. actually observing the nurse drinking, taking drugs, or being unprofessional.
    b. the impaired nurse paying attention to detail when caring for patients.
    c. repeated reports of satisfaction of care by the patients of the impaired nurse.
    d. improvement in the nurses appearance along with a greater level of patience

60. Nurses may be reluctant to join a labor union, but one benefit of membership could be the

    a. ability to greatly increase salaries and benefits.
    b. opportunity to dictate what is needed for quality care.
    c. chance to work with colleagues on important issues.
    d. recognition of the profession and its importance to society.

CHAPTER 13

LEGAL PRACTICE

CHAPTER OBJECTIVE

After studying this chapter, you will be able to recognize legal issues and risk management strategies for professional practice.

LEARNING OBJECTIVES

After studying this chapter, you will be able to

1. recognize potential legal issues and examine ways to avoid them.

2. describe different categories of law as they apply to nursing practice.

3. indicate selected legal issues commonly faced by nurses in their practice settings.

4. discriminate the advance directive processes for their adequacy as currently used in clinical settings.

OVERVIEW

Prevention is always best. Nurses want to stay out of court rather than face legal cases. The public has lost confidence in medicine and health care. There are many reports of medical malpractice, governmental investigations of questionable practices, class action suits, and lawyers who alert the public to malpractice issues.

Nurses must develop an awareness of the different types of law and understand the impact on their practice. It is important to be aware of high risk nursing actions that may trigger legal action. Insight into the types of preventive actions reduces the potential for lawsuits. Nurses have a particular responsibility to serve as patient advocates so their rights and wishes are respected.

Challenges

An elderly patient, Mrs. Batey, is in a nursing home because of post-stroke paralysis, unintelligible speech, swallowing difficulties, and poor nutrition. Mrs. Batey develops decubiti over several months. Nurses and other caregivers follow the clinical pathway for preventing decubiti. When Mrs. Batey develops a fever, the nurse charts it on the clinical pathway but not on the flow sheet. The physician checks the flow sheet but not the critical pathway. No further assessment or treatment is done. Mrs. Batey's condition deteriorates and she dies of septicemia (adapted from Sheehan, 2002).

INTRODUCTION

Traditionally, nurses have not been targets of lawsuits. The reality is that nurses may be sued along with other health care professionals. The public is more aware of health care issues and willing to voice their expectations. One area that triggers negative feelings is health care providers' indifferent and unsupportive attitudes and behaviors. Nurses who demonstrate caring behaviors also portray professional competence (Tappen, Weiss, & Whitehead, 2001). There are different types of laws that serve as the basis for our personal and professional behaviors.

Defining and Creating Laws

 Law is defined as the rules that govern, stipulate, and direct our behavior in social and professional contexts. The U.S. Constitution, local, and state regulations, Congressional statutes, and administrative laws are the basis for legal decisions. There are three ways to create law in the United States.

1. Legislative bodies develop laws that affect the entire population or address specific issues or groups. The Patient Self-Determination Act of 1990 is an example of a federal law that impacts the general public. Nurse practice acts are formulated by state legislators and directly address the practice of nursing.

2. Common law develops as legal decisions are made. Over time, judges will use previous decisions as the basis for making a new decision. Case law is the basis for reviewing previous decisions and determining the legal reasoning that went into forming the legal opinion. As an example, when there is a dispute about property rights, judges review what was decided in the past and use the information to make a new ruling.

3. Administrative law is based on the authority given to governmental agencies. Governmental agencies are charged with the responsibility of administering laws. The Department of Health and Human Services has the responsibility for administering health-related laws. The agency develops rules and regulations that are consistent with the intent of the laws passed by Congress. Boards of nursing have the authority to issue, regulate, and revoke nursing licenses (Tappen, Weiss, & Whitehead, 2001).

Types of Laws

There are two broad categories of laws: criminal and civil.

Criminal laws protect society from harmful actions. The actions may be directed at individuals, groups, or society as a whole. We can think of examples when individuals were assaulted, groups were harmed because of their ethnic or religious affiliation, and terrorist actions threatened an entire society. Crimes are committed against the state, and victims are not compensated from a criminal action.

Crimes are listed by their severity. Felonies are most serious and include murder and some types of nurse practice act violations. Misdemeanors are crimes such a traffic violations and shoplifting. Juvenile crimes are committed by persons under a specified age. Juvenile crime may be as serious as murder but tried under juvenile laws because of the person's age (Tappen, Weiss, & Whitehead, 2001). Nurses may be tried under criminal law for using and distributing controlled drugs or falsifying patient records.

Civil law deals with violations of a person's rights by someone else. There are several categories of civil law. Committing a legal or civil wrong against another person is a tort. Nurses must not harm patients, either intentionally or unintentionally, when providing care. Nurses are legally required to act prudently and reasonably when caring for patients. Negligence is present when there was a duty to care for the patient, there was a breach of the duty, the breach caused harm, and injury resulted. All of these elements must be present for a legal finding of negligence. A nurse may give the wrong medication but if there is no harm, there is no negligence. The standard of care is what a reasonable and prudent nurse would do in that situation. For example, when a nurse gives sleeping medication to a frail elderly patient and does not put the side rails up. If the patient falls and breaks a hip, there is negligence (Tappen, Weiss, & Whitehead, 2001).

Malpractice is professional negligence. Specialized education is required for nurses, and they are professionals. Individual nurses are responsible for their own actions, but employers are also responsible for their employees under the principle of "respondeat superior."

Negligent actions result when harm is caused by not following standards of practice based on

- State, local, and national standards;
- Institutional policies;
- Expert opinions from nurses in specific fields (Tappen, Weiss, & Whitehead, 2001).

Other laws that affect nurses relate to physical care and privacy.

Good Samaritan laws protect physicians and nurses from being sued when they respond to emergency situations and render care. The provider must observe professional standards by providing care that a reasonable and prudent nurse would carry out in a similar situation.

Confidentiality is expected of nurses. If harm comes to a person because a nurse breached confidentiality, the nurse may have been negligent. An example is a nurse sharing information about a patient that causes him to lose his job.

Slander (spoken word) and libel (written word) happen when a nurse, verbally or in writing, makes a false statement and it causes harm to the person. When a nurse tells others and makes a written notation stating a patient has HIV/AIDS even though he is just being tested, there is a potential problem. If the patient is fired from his job based on that information, slander and libel have occurred (Tappen, Weiss, & Whitehead, 2001).

False imprisonment means confining persons against their will. This is a challenging situation for nurses. Some patients may harm themselves, and other patients may harm their caregivers. The key to avoiding this legal issue is to try measures other than restraints first. Try to determine the cause of the behavior and correct it. If that fails, then document the need for restraints, consult the physician, and follow the policies for applying restraints. Psychiatric patient admissions are usually covered by state laws with specific provisions regarding restraints (Tappen, Weiss, & Whitehead, 2001).

Assault (threat to harm) and battery (touching persons without their consent) occurs in hospitals and other care settings. Nurses may threaten patients when they do not cooperate. Nurses also restrain patients who resist treatments. Nurses must remember that in most instances, patients have the right to refuse treatment (Tappen, Weiss, & Whitehead, 2001).

PREVENTIVE PRACTICE

Nurses need to consistently practice competently and within professional and legal standards.

- Stay informed about current practice in your specialty areas. Use standards and evidence as the basis your clinical decisions.
- Make sure your employer has a system for keeping nurses updated on policy and procedure changes and instructions for using new equipment.
- Always follow the institutional standards of care. If nurses should wear gloves when starting IVs, then do so every time.
- Be aware of and follow guidelines for delegating tasks to unlicensed personnel.
- Assess patients for risks such as fall, confusion, or skin breakdown. Implement a prevention plan.
- Be alert to maintaining a safe environment for patients, coworkers, and visitors.
- Document your actions completely and legibly.
- Always report and document adverse incidents and send them to the appropriate persons.

- Observe patients and family members. Exhibiting behaviors such as anger and constant criticism about care may trigger the possibility of a lawsuit. Keep everyone informed, and demonstrate caring and competence in your interactions (Tappen, Weiss, & Whitehead, 2001).

- Serve as patient, family, and community advocates. Educate them about quality care. Become knowledgeable about legislation and participate in professional activities (Greggs-McQuilkin, 2002).

- Sherman (2002) suggests that increased workloads for nurses contribute to increased patient mortality. Nurses have a significant interest in maintaining staffing levels that prevent adverse patient outcomes.

- Follow state laws and institutional policies for reporting violence, abuse, and neglect.

Nurses also have a responsibility to advocate for patients. Persons of all ages face violence, abuse, and neglect. The growing number of elderly persons in the United States raises particular concerns about neglect and abuse. Elderly persons may not be able to manage their financial and personal affairs, and they may be neglected because they live alone or are in poor living situations.

Area Agencies on Aging support and provide various services. Often the agencies contract with legal service organizations to assist elderly persons with life issues. The services are to protect elderly people and their property from harm. Services include preparing documents such as power of attorney, wills, living wills, property issues, family legal issues, and benefits concerns (Hogstel, 2001).

There are also state and local programs to protect elderly people from abuse and neglect. Elderly persons may be victims of theft, money scams, and various types of abuse. States also have ombudsman programs to investigate potential and actual abuse of elderly people at home and in institutional

settings (Hogstel, 2001). Nurses have the ability to make a difference in the lives of people who need protection. An awareness of laws, community resources, and nurses' legal responsibilities are the cornerstone for advocacy and action.

Community education is another prevention strategy. Nurses can work with school, church, and community groups to prevent child abuse. Parents and children need guidelines to prevent abuse and also understand the legal processes to resolve them (Hunt, 2001).

Professional Liability Insurance

Some nurses purchase professional liability insurance as a preventive measure to cover legal contingencies if they occur. There are mixed feelings among nurses about professional liability insurance. Many believe that their employer protects them with umbrella coverage. That may be true for some situations, but if a nurse is sued and damages are awarded, personal property may be lost. Professional liability insurance protects nurses in situations where they are liable for damages (Tappen, Weiss, & Whitehead, 2001).

Another viewpoint is that at the time a malpractice suit is filed everyone involved in the case is named. A patient's attorney may look for the "deep pockets" – person with liability insurance. Nurses and other professionals who have insurance, may be at risk for being sued. Often a lawsuit names groups or entities such as clinics or physician partnerships. Nurses may be included in the suit. If the group decides to settle, an individual nurse's position cannot be addressed or be dropped from the suit (Robinson & Kish, 2001).

Nurses who work in high-risk areas such as obstetrics and advanced practice nurses often elect to have liability insurance. Obstetrics is a high-risk area, and advanced practice nurses work independently with a high level of responsibility for clinical decisions (Robinson & Kish, 2001). When considering purchasing liability insurance, look at the following issues:

- Understand the difference between claims-made and occurrence-based policies.

- Know the risks for your specialty and the type of coverage that fits the risks.

- Be clear about the actions included and the timing of coverage (around the clock).

- Determine specifically what is covered.

- Ask if there are any exclusions in the coverage.

- Find out what the dollar amount is for each incident and each year.

- Ask about who decides on legal counsel.

- Your rights to consenting to a settlement or trial.

- Review different policies for cost and coverage (Robinson & Kish, 2001).

COMMON LITIGATION ISSUES

Nurses discuss among themselves and share experiences about adverse patient outcomes and legal actions taken by patients. Over time, they may recognize patterns or themes of the failures that led to litigation. Nurses can prevent or reduce problems when they

- Properly assess patients.

- Report changes in patient conditions to physicians and nurse managers.

- Document accurately and completely.

- Report coworkers' substandard or negligent care.

- Educate patients and family members about their continuing care.

- Follow internal and external standards of professional nursing practice (Tappen, Weiss, & Whitehead, 2001).

Nurses can increase their awareness of potential problems and use proactive measures to avoid them. Specific problems often have legal consequences.

- Patient falls – identify patients at potential risk and institute fall precautions.

- Equipment injuries – check temperatures, wiring, and functioning.

- Inadequate monitoring – check equipment functioning, take and record body function measurements, monitor lab and other test results.

- Incomplete communication – keep patients and family members informed, thoroughly document, and report changes in patients' conditions.

- Improper medication administration – follow the five rights, assess patients' responses, review medications for interactions (Tappen, Weiss, & Whitehead, 2001).

Documentation of patient care is often an essential part of a legal case. One nurse shared her experience of a patient who used profanity and shouted at her. She charted his exact words because she knew she should document what patients actually said and because she believed it would show his state of mind. The nurse manager objected to the charting and insisted it be re-written with less offensive comments. The nurse manager wanted the nurse to chart the phrase. "The patient used colorful language." The nurse manager was afraid that the charting would offend the survey evaluators who were coming the next week. There was a concern that the original charting would cause problems if the patient took legal action (Anonymous, 2002a).

This issue raises several key points.

- The original notes should not be discarded or altered. Doing that could really hurt someone in court.

- How much offensive language is needed in the chart to create an accurate picture of the patient's behavior? When the language represents a change in behavior or condition, enough examples should be included to convey that sense.

• The nurse manager should focus on the responsibility to protect staff from verbal and physical violence in the workplace (Anonymous, 2002a).

Nurses in England face the same potential legal issues as nurses in the United States. Nazarko (2002) describes the negligent practices that occur in nursing homes. The problems range from failing to provide food and personal cleanliness to physical abuse. The National Health Service is moving from a culture of blame to recognizing that adverse incidents occur in about 10 percent of admissions. The failures have major consequences for the patients. Steps being taken include paying attention to

• organizational structure.

• people management.

• organizational culture.

• lessons learned from errors.

The National Health Service is moving from addressing errors after they happen to preventing them.

RISK MANAGEMENT

There are usually three parts to risk management: system safeguards, interpersonal activities, and damage control. System safeguards focus on policies, procedures, and methods that make sure there is patient follow-up and a process to document the actions. Interpersonal activities are those that promote optimum caregiver and patient relationships: office environments, interpersonal interactions, listening to patient complaints, and correcting negative situations.

Damage control components are needed after an adverse event or a complaint or grievance is noted. Most situations have a resolution, but there are times when there is no solution. When a legal remedy is sought, by patients or family members, all the providers should meet and analyze what happened. This is a good strategy whenever there are problems. It is a time for reflection, sharing of experiences, and planning improvements (Robinson & Kish, 2001).

Medication errors continue to be on the national agenda. Reports of patients' deaths and long-term bad effects raise concerns. Two approaches to analyzing errors have emerged: root cause analysis and failure mode effect analysis.

Root cause analysis (RCA) is used to determine underlying factors that contributed to serious physical or psychological injury or death (sentinel event). The efforts focus on the reasons for the failure or inefficiency of a process. Why did the problem occur? Improvement plans are developed with action items (Wolf, 2002).

The failure mode effect analysis (FMEA) assumes errors are likely to happen. A proactive orientation tries to determine the systems and processes that may cause problems and errors. Checkpoints are set up for each step in a process and evaluated to see the outcomes. Improvement results when everyone involved examines each step and determines if there are weaknesses (Wolf, 2002).

According to Aumiller & Moskowitz (2002) nurses can act as risk managers when they are providing patient care. For example:

• A nurse finds an elderly patient on the floor. The patient is mildly confused. The bed was in the low position, and the side rails were raised. The nurse does a complete assessment and completes the incident report. The physician and nurse manager are notified.

• A nurse notices that the floors in a hallway are wet and slippery but there are no signs posted. She calls housekeeping and stays at the area for a few minutes until signs are placed.

- A nurse participated in a code and charted the facts: completely and promptly, using standard abbreviations. The information given to family members during and after the code was also noted.

Nurses can create safety net strategies to prevent errors. Look at your work environment and find ways to improve the processes in place for patient care and medication administration. How are errors addressed? What are the patterns of errors? Work together to reduce errors, improve patient care, and diminish the risk of legal problems.

Advance Directives

In 1990, the Patient Self Determination Act was passed by Congress because of issues raised in the courts during the 1980s. There were issues about patient and family wishes being ignored. Health care institutions must have policies and procedures to inform patients and their family members about end-of-life decisions. The main requirement is to provide written information about a person's right to make decisions about care and to refuse care. The provider policies must be written. There must be documentation in patients' records indicating whether they have or have not completed advance directives (Hogstel, 2001).

Living Wills

Living wills allow adults to make their wishes known about the types of treatment they want if they cannot participate in making their health care decisions. Situations such as a terminal illness or permanent vegetative state raise issues about treatment. A living will states the patient's preferences. The document is usually filed with the medical record. For a living will to have an effect, physicians, nurses, and family members must respect the patient's wishes and plan care accordingly (Hogstel, 2001).

Durable Power of Attorney for Health Care

The durable power of attorney for health care creates a legal relationship between two persons. A person (the principal) gives another person (the agent) the authority to make personal health care decisions. The principal grants the right to make decisions when there is cognitive incapacitation. This happens in situations when there is trauma, when decisions need to be made during surgery, or during other non-emergency care. An elderly person may have a stroke and be unable to communicate. Decisions about care are needed. Perhaps the greatest problem is finding persons to serve as the agent. It is an enormous responsibility and close relatives or friends may not be available (Hogstel, 2001).

Nurses can contribute to making advance directives effective by

- educating themselves about advance directives;

- educating the public about advance directives;

- developing materials with clear, readable directions;

- recognizing the need for advance directives in all care settings (Hogstel, 2001).

Solutions

Mrs. Batey's family is unhappy about the care she received in the last months of her life. Mrs. They consult an attorney because they are upset about information they received and concerned about the care their mother received. The main issues are presented to both sides.

- The clinical pathway, as it was developed, did not address early and consistent preventive measures that could have prevented the decubiti.

- The nurse, nurse manager, physician, and nursing home corporation were negligent because adequate care was not given to treat her fever and prevent the septicemia.

- The family suffered emotional and psychological harm that required treatment.

The attorneys for the parties involved agreed to a settlement. Administrators and all the parties involved had a series of meetings, using the root cause analysis process. It became clear that family members needed more and consistent information about Mrs. Batey's condition and her prognosis. Her limited food intake made it difficult for her body tissue to remain healthy. The family should have participated in discussions about other methods to provide nutrition.

The nurse should have communicated her concern about Mrs. Batey's fever and continued deterioration. The corporation and nurse manager should have trained staff and had a process in place to share potential and actual patient status changes. The physician should have assessed Mrs. Batey, recognized her condition, and instituted appropriate treatment. The pain and suffering of the family was not documented or apparent.

CONCLUSION

Nurses work in complex settings and must demonstrate clinical competence and caring. These are professional expectations that also protect nurses from litigation. Nurses must proactively protect themselves from hazards in their work settings. Preventive practices are the foundation for maintaining patient safety and avoiding legal problems. The concept and practice of risk management is important in all types of health care environments. Regulatory and approval bodies expect policies and processes to be in place to prevent adverse incidents, and they will review those that have occurred. Nurses, as they carry out their usual duties, are risk managers when they observe and prevent harm.

EXAM QUESTIONS

CHAPTER 13
Questions 61-65

61. If a registered nurse administers the wrong antibiotic to a patient, negligence is present if

    a. there was harm and injury.

    b. an incident report is completed.

    c. the patient's wife complains.

    d. the physician is angry at the nurse.

62. Mary, RN, CNM, just started work in a practice with three physicians and should

    a. not buy liability insurance because she already is covered by the physician group's policy.

    b. buy liability insurance to protect her individual interests.

    c. buy liability insurance because she is a new midwife and not an expert.

    d. not buy liability insurance because she is more likely to be sued.

63. Beverly, an RN, charted a summary of a heated argument that a post-MI patient had with his son in CCU and the effect on the patient's vital signs. The charge nurse asked Beverly to change her charting because the argument was a personal matter. Beverly should

    a. think about changing it to keep everyone happy.

    b. change it so the argument is not included in the chart.

    c. ask her coworkers and do what they agree is right.

    d. leave her charting as she originally completed it.

64. A patient is admitted to a nursing home. One responsibility of the admitting nurse is to provide information about the Patient Self Determination Act. The purpose of the law is to provide

    a. family members with information about the specific plan of care for patients.

    b. information about a the patients' right to privacy.

    c. written information about a patient's right to make decisions about care and to refuse care.

    d. patients with written information about the types and cost of services.

65. In order for nurses to highlight the importance of advance directives with patients, nurses must first

    a. share information with patients.

    b. educate themselves.

    c. teach patients and families.

    d. plan educational programs.

CHAPTER 14

ETHICAL PRACTICE

CHAPTER OBJECTIVE

After studying this chapter, you will be able to choose ethical principles and apply them to nursing practice.

LEARNING OBJECTIVES

After studying this chapter, you will be able to

1. identify selected ethical principles that serve as a basis for decision-making.

2. recognize the functions of ethical frameworks in decision-making.

3. summarize selected ethical issues related to public and health policy, advocacy, and caring.

OVERVIEW

Ethical practice is a core value of nursing. Professional codes and standards give guidance to our practice. The values and beliefs held by society in general also determine the appropriateness of our actions. Ethics is often presented in the context of what nurses ought to do when caring for patients. Because of the increasing complexity of health care and the decisions made at corporate and governmental levels, nurses need an understanding of ethical decision-making in those contexts.

This chapter presents a sketch of the meaning of ethical practice at different levels of decision-making. Nurses must continue to practice according to sound ethical principles and expand their influence in work settings, communities, and society as a whole.

INTRODUCTION

Nurses may not differentiate between legal and ethical responsibilities. Professional guidelines cover a great deal of nursing practice and focus on interventions and tasks. Ethics raise issues about how, or if, nurses should do something. In many situations, it is evident what to do. There are emergencies that require quick actions. Many other situations require nursing care actions that are determined by protocols. Ethical decisions are not always clear-cut. Understanding frameworks for ethical practice is an essential part of nursing practice today and in the future.

Challenges

Nurses on a busy pediatric unit of Good Hope, a large private, urban hospital, feel overworked and frustrated because they are not able to provide the highest quality care. The children on their unit are newly diagnosed with cancer or diabetes, are hospitalized for various surgical procedures, or are being treated for chronic conditions such as cystic fibrosis, sickle cell disease, and orthopedic problems.

The nurses' specific ethical concerns are

- The lack of a team approach to planning care. Physicians make all the decisions and the other disciplines carry out their orders (paternalism, truth, freedom).

- Hospital policies that limit the amount of contact parents, siblings, family members, friends, and others have with the children (equality, human dignity, freedom).

- Nurses have no voice in how care is delivered and are required to work overtime when needed (altruism, equality, justice).

The nurses keep discussing how unhappy they are, how the parents and children are not receiving the care they need, and how tired they are getting from working extra. Finally, a few nurses speak up and identify the need for a plan to address these issues.

THE ETHICS OF PUBLIC AND HEALTH POLICY

We know legislators make new laws every time they are in session. As citizens, we are often not aware of the laws until we are affected in some way. We may go out for dinner and find our bill has a higher tax than previously. We seek help for doing our income tax forms and find out how different the rules are from the previous year. Public policy is developed for the good of society. Different elements of society are connected and impacted by laws made for one purpose. For example, environmental policies impact health-related to air, water, and safety issues. Education policies determine the types of health programs that can be taught in schools and the types of health services available at colleges. Defense department policies set out the types of chemical and biological programs they develop (Milstead, 1999).

The definition of policies is broad. Policies may indicate organizational goals, program proposals, or specific rules. Gag rules sometimes forbid nurses and physicians from sharing information about family planning or giving HMO patients treatment options (Milstead, 1999). Nurses as advocates protect patients' autonomy for decision-making and seek justice so patients have access to care. Public policy affects nurses' ability to practice.

Impaired nurses may face unequal outcomes for substance abuse. Other professionals, such as physicians, may have mandatory treatment without adverse effects on their licenses. Nurses may have their licenses suspended before they are in treatment. Nursing organizations can seek justice by promoting uniform rules for impaired professionals.

Allocation of resources is another ethical policy issue. Politics are an essential part of health care funding decisions. Specific groups may lobby for funding and receive it. For example, persons with end-stage renal disease have medical coverage. Persons needing heart or other types of transplants all must wait for a match. Inmates in prison will receive a transplant without regard to cost. Others, who have money, will be able to have the surgery. Persons with modest incomes and no health insurance will probably not have the surgery. Nurses, individually and collectively, can take political action to pursue justice and equal access to health care.

Other policies prohibit giving out information or providing services related to reproduction. Hospitals may not provide culturally competent care by having translators available so that patients who do not speak English can make informed choices. Governmental agencies decide to use money earmarked for tobacco control for other purposes. In these situations, and many others, nurses can make a difference in their profession and community.

ADVOCACY

Nurses ethical responsibilities include advocacy for patients, colleagues, communities, nations, and the world. Advocates are persons who plead or defend the causes of others. Advocacy may mean seeking just treatment for groups who do not have access to health care. Beneficence may inspire nurses to set up health centers in churches or to participate in international health projects. Nonmaleficence means nurses keep their clinical skills current and develop strategies that support quality outcomes. Fidelity includes remaining faithful to coworkers and patients when seeking solutions to issues.

Professional Advocacy

All nurses can become advocates by using the power based on

- Knowledge and expertise to foster changes in organizational climate.

- Legitimate right and authority to influence the quality of care and support systems.

- Referent power to organize community support for change.

Nurses need leadership skills to be activists in different settings (Hood & Leddy, 2003).

Burnout

Haddad (2002) describes burnout as an ethical issue. Nurses must advocate for each other to prevent or minimize conditions that contribute to it. Burnout includes a combination of emotions, attitudes, and physical symptoms. It causes a loss of concern about patients. Burned-out nurses may be negative toward patients and coworkers.

The ethical issue is responsibility to care for self. When you see coworkers suffering from burnout, you can demonstrate empathy and concern. Advocate for working conditions that reduce the conditions causing burnout. Strategies to sup-

port each other are especially important during the nursing shortage.

Moral Distress

Moral distress is becoming recognized as an ethical concern. Nurses face ethical dilemmas where there are no obvious right actions. Choices must be made according to a specific ethical perspective. Moral distress occurs when nurses know the correct action but cannot carry it out because of workplace, coworker, or personal constraints. External factors that contribute to moral distress are administrative policies, physicians, and the threat of lawsuits. Internal factors are lack of courage, self-doubt, fear of job loss, having been socialized to follow orders, and lack of response to actions in the past. Nurses experience emotional distress in such situations. Feelings of anger and frustration surface (Tiedje, 2000).

One example is perinatal nurses who disagree with early discharge. Mothers and babies go home earlier than some nurses believe is safe. They can do nothing about the policy. In other clinical situations, nurses describe that the focus of practice is on completing tasks. Premature infants may be given formula even when it is possible for mothers to supply breast milk. Nurses see resuscitation performed on persons who do not want it. Nurses with moral objections feel required to fight the system, otherwise feel invisible (Tiedje, 2000).

From Moral Distress to Moral Work

Nurses must first recognize the condition of moral distress. Moral distress is an affective (emotional), cognitive (reflective), and behavioral (action) experience. The reflective aspect allows nurses to consider how much resistance is needed and how actions should be carried out, individually or collectively. Three nurses filed a complaint with the National Labor Relations Board after they were fired for expressing concerns about substandard patient care. A federal judge ruled in their favor.

The nurses used a reflective process to determine that passively accepting substandard care

- places patients at risk,
- demeans nurses professional contributions,
- abandons public trust,
- is negligence (Tiedje, 2000).

An example of collective action is the moral distress of nurses in the Boston area who saw the rate of cesarean deliveries continue to rise. The benefits to maternal and child health were not established. Labor and delivery environments were increasingly high-tech, and low-tech interventions were not used. A non-profit organization developed a series of training and collaborative projects. Twenty-eight providers participated to reduce the rate of cesarean deliveries by changing how labor and delivery was managed. About one-third of the participants could not reduce rates significantly during the project. The reasons were fear of lawsuits, lack of coordination between physicians and nurses, scheduling habits, and myths about managing labor. The moral work in this situation required collective action (Tiedje, 2000).

Moving from Distress to Action

Nurses often feel overworked and worn out by the competing demands of their professional and personal lives. They may think that fighting a system will not make a difference. Nurses must believe they all have the capacity for using their inner strength to make a difference. The following four ways to develop inner strength include:

1. Looking to early and current nursing leaders who made a difference. Recognizing their sense of purpose can inspire nurses today.

2. Story telling has an emancipating power. Nurses use stories to share their moral distress and identify strengths, insights, and strategies for moral action.

3. Realizing that nurses are not powerful can create new visions of practice.

4. Acquiring a coach to provide guidance and support while you learn risk-taking skills and develop a secure base for taking risks (Tiedje, 2000).

Nurses can believe there are great opportunities in health care delivery and nursing to develop the strength and skills needed to act. Margaret Mead, the noted anthropologist, stated, "Never doubt that a small group of thoughtful, committed citizens can change the world; indeed, it's the only thing that ever has" (Tiedje, 2000).

Patient Advocacy

Nurses base ethical decisions on the ANA's Code of Ethics and Patients Bill of Rights. Both of these documents include the expectation of patient advocacy for perioperative nurses. Advocacy has two parts: nurses will support patients' choices and nurses will act on behalf of them. Perioperative nurses are the advocates for surgical patients as they continuously observe and monitor patients' conditions. Surgical patients may experience lack of respect, loss of dignity, actual lies, inadequate informed consent, not following DNR orders, and incompetent caregivers. Patients have no option but to trust nurses during surgery. The quality and continuity of care are areas of concern. Safety issues for surgical patients take different forms

- ensuring that aseptic technique is used,
- verifying patient identity,
- protecting patients from equipment injury (Schroeter, 2002).

Opposing Loyalties

Perioperative nurses work with many different people. They have responsibilities to patients, family members, coworkers, surgeons, technicians, and other OR personnel. When patients make decisions that are unexpected or contrary to usual practice, there is a problem. The closeness of the working relationships and the critical decisions made during surgery create stress.

Nurses coordinate care and must make decisions. For example, when coworkers injure themselves, the circulating nurse must follow through to make sure the worker, patients, and others are protected and policies are followed. Surgeons have a reputation for making unreasonable demands or throwing instruments. The circulating nurse must make critical decisions about what to do in such difficult situations (Schroeter, 2002).

Advocating for Patient Empowerment

Consumers are demanding quality care. They are knowledgeable about health care options. A new model of care that is patient-centered supports patient empowerment. This approach is completely different from traditional, paternalistic health care delivery.

The ethical framework for partnership decision-making fits within a patient empowerment model. There is a different balance of power in the provider/client relationship. Patients gain autonomy and are empowered. The process starts with a dialogue between the parties. Patients need coaching as they learn to be more autonomous in their decision-making (Williams, 2002). The benefits are seen by both patients and providers. They share responsibility for positive outcomes.

Advocating for Specific Age Groups

Nurses who work with parents and children who are having surgery often must explain what is going to happen during the entire process. Even after parents sign the consent form, they have concerns. Nurses can facilitate the communication process by listening and sharing concerns with physicians. Nurses must be objective when giving information, provide a variety of resources, and support parents' decisions. Nurses also have to advocate for children and make sure their interests are being represented. Parental power is not absolute, and others may intervene if a child's interests are not being considered (Schroeter, 2002).

As more elderly persons are having surgery, nurses address the same issues of informed consent, ability to make decisions, differing family views, and necessity for advance directives. Nurses must explain procedures in clear language and make sure family members are informed. Family members may have differing views and needs when they are confronted with making end-of-life decisions for comatose or mentally incompetent loved ones. Address and resolve these issues and concerns before surgery (Schroeter, 2002).

Nurses Advocating for Each Other

Nurses must also advocate for each other. When nurses are in situations that may compromise ethical principles, they need support to make the correct choices. Collective action helps address such situations. For example, unsafe working conditions need action by all nurses. Nurses may not want to participate in certain types of patient care for ethical or religious reasons. They should discuss their limitations when they apply for a position so the restrictions are known. All settings may not be suitable to every nurse (Schroeter, 2002).

Confidentiality and Privacy

The use of technology makes it difficult to maintain privacy and confidentiality in health care situations. Patients need assurance that information they disclose will be confidential. Issues of privacy and autonomy are paramount. Privacy is an issue because of electronic collection, storage, and dissemination of information. There is a Perioperative Nursing Data Set (PNDS) that outlines how to support patient rights during the perioperative process (Schroeter, 2002).

Confidentiality is not absolute because there are situations when information is shared. Perioperative cases may be brought into the legal system. Persons may not want to share their HIV/AIDS status with their spouse or significant other. Patients who are a threat to others must have that information shared. Computer screens are located in public areas such as nursing stations. Family members and other visitors could observe patient information and discuss it with others. Nurses and other workers may seek out information about persons they know or prominent persons in the hospital. When many people have access to patient computer systems, there is loss of privacy (Schroeter, 2002).

Participating in Research

Nurses also advocate for patients who participate in research studies or clinical trials. Ethical research participation issues include

- Subjects should include a cross section of the population.

- Consent must be freely given after subjects truly understand what is involved.

- Institutional approval must be obtained before projects are initiated.

- Any stipends offered cannot affect persons' decisions to participate.

- Subjects must be free to quit the research project whenever they want.

There are Institutional Review Boards (IRBs) which conduct a formal review of proposed research projects. The ethical components of research projects are carefully considered. Nurses serve on IRB committees and advocate for subjects' safety and well-being (Hood & Leddy, 2003).

ETHICAL CARING

What are the ideal ethical characteristics of nurses? How do nurses combine their clinical skills with ethical caring? One description of what it means to be professional goes beyond thinking and acting responsibly. Professionalism and virtue are the desired combination. That combination goes beyond fitting into a work environment. It means becoming a person who is respectful and appreciative of nursing traditions. It is also

being compassionate, wise, competent, and caring. Aristotle, Confucius, and other philosophers, ancient and modern, realized that becoming such a person is a lifetime project. Nurses who are far along on this journey will have a unique approach to addressing ethical dilemmas (Hinderer & Hinderer, 2001).

Nurses consistently try to do what is right. Morality embraces what ought to be done in society. Nursing is equated with caring. Early Indian and Christian nurses demonstrated altruism. The art and science of nursing is centered on caring. Changes in health care delivery make it difficult for nurses to express caring. Some employers view nurses as replaceable technicians who happen to have specialized skills. Developing a close personal relationship with patients requires nurses to focus on ethical responsibilities and obligations. If the nursing profession has a trade relationship with patients, then the ethical focus is on rights. The issue of nurses' rights is manifested in collective bargaining and strikes. The value of caring in that case is diminished (Hood & Leddy, 2003), but it is possible to blend ethics and caring.

Today, examples of caring nurses are found in work settings, the media, professional journals, and patient stories. One story describes how three nurses overcame struggles to become nurses and deeply cared about their roots. Alma MacDougall is employed by the Abegweit First Nation Wellness Center in Canada. She knew the aboriginal people in the region were not receiving the culturally competent care they required. Alma is part of the First Nation community. She demonstrates the ethical principle of altruism; concern for the welfare of others. In the small community of 178 persons, there were 30 suicides in the past year. Residents would not seek help or care for addictions, abuse, or other personal problems. Many had not even seen a family physician. Alma is the first community health nurse, and it is her passion to make sure health services are provided (Hart-Wasekeeikaw,

2003). The stories of the other two nurses are equally compelling and demonstrate ethical caring. The nurses showcased in the article actively follow the ethical principles of altruism, justice, and human dignity.

Solutions

In the challenge situation, the nurses at Good Hope hospital realize they need to be organized to address the ethical problems they face in their work setting.

The unit does not have interdisciplinary care planning meetings. The nurses believe there is a paternalistic approach to patients and their families. Nurses there do not have the freedom to practice according to ethical and professional standards. Parents are given a broad range of options for care. The information given to parents is truthful but may not be the whole truth.

Physicians meet with the parents, tell them what is needed for further treatment or follow-up home care. After the decisions are made, the other disciplines each carry out their responsibilities. The problems are that parents are often confused about what they were told by different persons. There are gaps in determining and organizing home services. Nurses are not sure what discharge information has been given. There may be duplication or gaps in services and information.

The nurse manager, vice president for nursing, and a staff nurse meet with the chief of pediatric services. There is discussion of the issues and information is shared about how interdisciplinary planning works on other units.

The next step is that suggestions for developing interdisciplinary teams will be solicited from everyone who provides care. A group will sort the information and categorize it. Another group will talk to staff on other units with interdisciplinary teams. The third group will review information and summarize it. There are other steps needed to make this approach a reality. The outcome is that an interdisciplinary team approach will be implemented on the pediatric unit.

The visiting hours are from 10 a.m. to 9 p.m. The rule is in place to allow time in the morning for physicians to make rounds and to complete treatments and medications. Another issue is the small and crowded rooms. Having too many people around interferes with providing care. Parents want the option to stay with their children around the clock. When children are in the hospital for several days or weeks, they need to see siblings and friends. Some nurses do allow parents to stay longer or let siblings visit. This causes friction between staff and other parents when some family members are allowed to stay and others are not.

The long-term solution is to lobby the health care system for renovated space. A temporary solution is to allow more visitors during afternoon and early evening hours. One person is allowed to stay around the clock, and a chair or bed is put in each room.

The shortage of nursing staff and mandated overtime are issues for nurses. Primary care is the only model used in this situation. Different models are reviewed to determine how to provide quality, efficient care. A model with a mix of care providers is selected. Training is done. A nurse in charge of a group of patients monitors the quality of care. The new care delivery model reduces the amount of overtime required. Schedules are changed to include options for working more days in a row with more time off or having the work schedule spread out.

CONCLUSION

Traditionally, nursing ethics has focused on caring for patients, telling patients the truth, protecting them from harm, preserving their dignity, supporting their decisions for the care they desire. Today, nurses have to look beyond patients into health care systems, reimbursement rules, governmental policies, and new technologies. Their participation in these areas of influence will make a difference in patient care. How long can new mothers and babies receive hospital and home care? Will there be clinics to provide well baby care at convenient locations? Will funding be shifted from acute and chronic care to primary care?

Nurses face new ethical challenges in their work settings. They may feel a lack of power to improve conditions and be working in less than satisfying environments. Nurses have the ability, individually and collectively, to expand their influence. They are the largest group of health care professionals, are essential to the delivery of care in all settings, and can positively impact health care in the country. Take up the challenge to make a difference. You and other nurses can make ethical choices to improve nursing and health care on many different levels.

EXAM QUESTIONS

CHAPTER 14
Questions 66-70

66. In order for nurses to highlight the importance of advance directives with patients, nurses must

    a. tell patients to seek a second opinion.

    b. not tell patients they have a primary physician.

    c. tell patients to read the information you give to them.

    d. not tell patients about treatment options.

67. Martha, an RN, had her license suspended for 2 years because she took a patient's medication. A surgeon at the same hospital amputated the wrong leg of a diabetic patient. Her license was suspended for 1 year. Martha's coworkers are outraged. They want to do something. An effective action would be to

    a. start a protest and carry signs outside the Board of Nursing office to show their support for Martha.

    b. write to their legislators.

    c. work with licensing boards to have just and uniform rules for all impaired professionals.

    d. collect money to help Martha.

68. An example of beneficence is when

    a. a nurse returns to school to earn a graduate degree.

    b. nurses work as much overtime as needed.

    c. nurses set up a health center in their local church.

    d. nurses cause no harm to patients by following policies.

69. Burnout behavior includes

    a. anger, fatigue, increased absences, loss of concern about patients.

    b. asking coworkers for help to complete patient care assignments.

    c. coming to work looking tired every day.

    d. complaining of allergies and headaches.

70. There are many observations about the essential ethical characteristics of professionals. One philosophical view identifies professionalism as the process of becoming

    a. compassionate, wise, and caring.

    b. competent, skillful, and dependable.

    c. a leader in nursing.

    d. an expert clinician.

CHAPTER 15

LIFELONG LEARNING

CHAPTER OBJECTIVE

After studying this chapter, you will be able to select a variety of educational offerings that support lifelong learning.

LEARNING OBJECTIVES

After studying this chapter, you will be able to

1. describe why nurses are motivated to continue gaining knowledge and skills.

2. identify the variety of educational choices for continuing learning throughout life.

3. analyze creative and innovative approaches to gain access to educational opportunities.

OVERVIEW

Nurses realize that knowledge, information, and technology create changes in practice. Graduation from nursing school and becoming licensed is just the beginning of nursing education. Clinical skills, new equipment, new methods to carry out procedures, meeting continuing education (CE) requirements, and updating competencies are all part of lifelong learning. Nurses work hard, often for long hours because of overtime, and have busy personal lives. It is a challenge just to meet the minimum requirements for education. There are many different types of learning programs and a variety of ways to access programs. Today, learn-ing is an adventure because nurses have so many choices and can select approaches that are right for their lifestyles, educational needs, and learning preferences.

Challenges

Roberta, Janice, and Christine work together on the night shift in a busy emergency department. They are always busy at work and have extremely busy personal lives. They do attend a few professional meetings, complete the required staff development activities, and read professional journals. They want to do more but have not made any definite plans.

Roberta wants to become certified. Janice wants to earn a BSN degree. Christine has a BSN degree and is ready for a master's degree program. One night they have time to talk again. They agree they need a plan to get started. They decide to work together so each can find out how to get started.

FORMAL AND INFORMAL EDUCATION

 Nurses have a desire and obligation to maintain their professional expertise. This can be done through:

- Active participation in interdisciplinary team conferences and patient-centered conferences.

- Attending continuing education offerings related to your area of expertise.

- Attending local, regional, and national conferences sponsored by professional groups.

- Reading journals and books.

- Seeking information on the Internet.

- Participating in research projects.

- Participating in discussion groups on your unit and in your facility.

- Observing and working with experienced nurses.

- Sharing expertise with colleagues by publishing and presenting information (Tappen, Weiss, & Whitehead, 2001).

Today, nurses have many opportunities to continue learning. The reasons they need and to want to keep learning are varied. Because there are so many options, nurses have to carefully plan their own professional development. Selecting the options that meet both professional and personal goals is essential. Some nurses become involved in many different educational endeavors over several years, then they end up with a collection of CE hours, certification, and degrees without achieving their goals.

Nurses are extremely busy and must make wise choices for spending their time. Balancing personal and professional lives is always a challenge because of competing demands. Developing a plan can accommodate both. For example, a goal to earn an advanced degree may mean postponing a family or waiting until children are in school. Becoming certified in a specific area may mean attending sessions or workshops away from home. Maintaining an RN license may require completing a certain number of CE courses.

Nurses are motivated to keep learning for a number of reasons. Licensure required meeting mandatory continuing education standards. California was the first state to implement mandatory CE for licensure. A number of states have added that requirement. The CE requirements must be met within a certain timeframe. Some states designate required content, such as AIDS, STDs, and family violence. Other states do not identify content. A CE provider or professional organization may keep track of CE hours. Periodically, a sampling of nurses is required to produce documentation (Cherry & Jacob, 2002).

Certification may be required to work in specific areas. The American Nurses Credentialing Center identifies the broad areas, including specialist, clinical specialist, nursing administration, and nurse practitioner. Certification recognizes excellence in practice and brings recognition personally and professionally. Employers expect nurses to be current, and certification goes beyond minimal levels. If there are clinical ladders or levels of compensation, then certification may bring a career to a new level.

Some nurses are curious, enjoy learning, and like to explore options. Nurses who are truly lifelong learners seek out and take advantage of all types of opportunities. They read journals, find information on the Internet, attend CE courses, participate in professional organizations, and earn additional degrees. They may have a career plan that includes new positions requiring graduate education. The motivation and achievements of these nurses, often in leadership positions, inspire other nurses.

People who want a nursing career may start at a lower level than they actually aspire to achieve. Reasons include limited finances, lack of role models/mentors, and complicated personal lives. Their first job may be as a CNA because they like working with patients in a health care environment. They may move to an LPN level, then on to an RN level, perhaps because their employers help with tuition. They also see role models and may have encouragement and mentoring. Many nurses have gone through several career stages. They contribute their expanding knowledge and skills to patient care. They also serve as role models for others who are starting their careers.

Some nurses are part of a family or school environment that encourages or expects academic achievement. They know that earning their initial degree is only the beginning. Earning additional degrees broadens their career options and provides a personal sense of satisfaction.

When nurses complete an academic degree, there may not be an immediate salary increase. A higher level of education positions nurses for career advancement and new opportunities. Mee (2001) describes her experience with returning to school for a master's degree. She had been out of school for 10 years and did not have a specific career goal in mind. She and a friend started the program together. She became enthused about nursing again, enjoyed learning new information, and found new friends. There were obstacles, but her advice is to find ways to overcome them. For example, if your employer does not offer tuition reimbursement, find out why and suggest they do it as a retention strategy. Today, Mee is a nurse-editor. She never dreamed of having that type of position but earning her master's degree opened the door. She advises, "Go for the gold."

Nursing is highly specialized, and there is overlap of educational offerings among different specialty organizations. There is also an option to jointly address common needs. One example is a consortium of 11 nursing organizations that was formed to develop a series of annual conferences. The organizations represented all different practice settings. Conferences have emphasized leadership development. This is an efficient and effective way to provide professional development. Additionally, nurses from different areas of practice share their issues and common themes (Redding & Anglin, 2001).

Nurses are motivated to seek educational opportunities throughout their careers. The reasons vary but the outcome is nurses who are well-educated, clinically competent leaders that have achieved their personal and professional goals.

CONTINUOUS, LIFELONG LEARNING

Professional, educational, and hospital agencies provide education opportunities. Certification recognizes excellence in practice. It is voluntary, and individuals apply for it, based on their education, completion of CE activities, and excellence in a specialty area. Nurse anesthetists were the first group to certify nurses.

READINESS TO LEARN

Nurses have already been through one or more educational programs. Planning for additional education requires some thought. Any type of educational endeavor requires socialization into a student role. Socialization requires

- learning new role expectations,

- changing behaviors to function in new roles,

- internalizing new role expectations (Hood & Leddy, 2003).

Social influences impact how people go through behavior changes. Three processes have been identified: compliance, identification, and internalization.

Compliance arises when individuals have not accepted the new values or influences but will behave in a way that is expected. Some nurses attend required staff training but will not actually carry out the new procedures.

Identification is when individuals selectively adopt certain behaviors that preserve or develop new relationships. Performance evaluations may include serving as a mentor or willingness to work overtime. Those behaviors are important to the nurse manager. A nurse may take on those behaviors to please the nurse manager and receive a positive evaluation.

Internalization is when individuals accept the norms and values of the new behaviors. They take on the new values (Hood & Leddy, 2003).

The progression from compliance to internalization is presented in the following example. A nurse attends an educational activity that demonstrates the use of a new IV pump. At first, the nurse uses the pump only when an old one is not available. In fact, she tries to "reserve" one when she starts her shift in case she needs to have a new patient on an IV. After a few months she is more comfortable with the new pumps, sees the advantages, and will not use an old one.

Stein (2001) describes a qualitative study that examined behavior changes among members of a chapter of the American Association of Critical Care Nurses. The goal of educating members is probably the most important activity of voluntary professional organizations. These organizations focus on learning, change, and empowerment. Informal learning occurs outside of formal settings and includes learning by: doing, experiencing, observing, and mentoring. In this study, informal learning included mentoring, coaching, networking, and experiencing. Positive feedback encouraged members to learn more.

The study found its members reported a number of behavior changes, including

- how to use equipment for presentations,
- the skills needed to arrange meetings and conferences,
- complex communication skills to speak in public, lead groups, and present CE programs,
- transfer of new behaviors to other settings.

Increased confidence, commitment to the profession, and leadership skills were identified as themes. The nurses also got new jobs and promotions, earned higher degrees, changed career paths, earned certification, and were elected to offices. Active participation in a professional organization is one path to lifelong learning and professional development (Stein, 2001).

Emotional Readiness

Anyone wanting to undertake an educational activity should determine how emotionally prepared they are for the activity. Short activities may not affect emotions as much as longer activities. Some of the concerns are: anxiety, support, motivation, risks, and frame of mind.

Anxiety Level — When we are very anxious, our ability to perform cognitive activities (taking a test) or psychomotor skills (giving an injection) are affected. High or low anxiety may result in not doing much. Moderate anxiety can motivate or drive us to act and complete what is needed. Fear is often what causes anxiety. For example, a nursing student may fear patients will be harmed while moving them from a bed to a chair. They may fall. The student does not get a patient out of bed because of anxiety. Patients may be in denial about their condition because of fear (Bastable, 2003). They may be anxious and not really understand the discharge instructions or be unable to give their own insulin correctly.

Support System — Having support systems in place helps establish emotional readiness. Nurses frequently go to training and educational sessions together. Sometimes, a group of nurses decide to go to school together or study for the same certification examination. Nurses know that emotional support given to patients helps them to be ready to learn what they need to know to manage their health (Bastable, 2003). With Internet and online education, both patients and nurses find support systems in people they may never meet, but come to know. Chat rooms and online nursing programs encourage sharing and provide support for meeting learning goals.

Motivation — We sometimes make judgements about a person's motivation. A patient may be categorized as not being motivated to learn how to take medications. Nurses may not be motivated to handle any more than their job and personal responsibilities. Motivation means that we really have the desire and intention to complete an activity. A person's past experiences with learning, both negative and positive, affect the level of motivation for a new educational activity. Past success builds confidence to try something new. Past failure makes a person fearful about failing again, so anxiety increases and motivation decreases.

Risk Taking — Some people are risk takers; they want to learn something new or have new experiences. Others are happy with a set routine. To take risks, nurses need to make the decision and then determine how to reduce the risk (Bastable, 2003). It may be a great risk to try to complete a graduate program or earn critical care certification. Once the decision is made to do it, how can the risks be reduced? Making sure there is family and employer support, organizing financial resources, and planning time management strategies are just a few examples.

Frame of Mind — People have different needs that affect their ability to learn. If an individual is struggling to survive, it is impossible to think about becoming involved in educational activities. Nurses who are self-actualized are more ready to learn (Bastable, 2003).

Registered nurses who return to school for a BSN degree have experienced the "returning-to-school-syndrome." The honeymoon is the first stage and is positive. Nurses can make the connection between past experiences and the new experience. Once they are into the first courses, the honeymoon is over. In the second stage, nurses may start to feel inadequate about meeting the new expectations. They have to begin thinking about meeting new expectations by changing their behavior.

During the third stage, there is conflict. The roles the nurses were comfortable with no longer seem to work. They are not comfortable with new roles. They may feel depressed, angry, or helpless. They may have academic problems.

As they reintegrate, they may reject the BSN program and be hostile. Students who do not get through the syndrome remain hostile or may act as if they accept the program so they can finish. In either case, nurses who finish the BSN program and do not integrate, will continue to defend their nursing practice and devalue their education. These behaviors can have a negative effect.

Nurses who integrate the old and new cultures have a positive resolution. They are able to function at a different level. They have a different sense of what nursing is and can be (Hood & Leddy, 2003).

Experiential Readiness

Experiential readiness is defined as learners' previous learning. Nurses may not feel prepared for certain types of learning experiences. For example, a course may require computer skills, providing a CD-ROM rather than printed material. Even CPR courses are more automated than in the past. Nurses may want to change from working in an ICU to an OB unit. They feel anxious because their previous experience is different from what is expected in the new area. If they can find commonalities, such as using the nursing process and carrying out assessments, they may realize they have some useful experience (Bastable, 2003).

Level of Aspiration — We all have different levels of aspiration. Our past experiences and current expectations may raise or lower our aspirations. Other factors such as health status, personal responsibilities, and financial resources make a difference. A nurse may aspire to become certified in a specialty area but with three teenage children, full-time work, and caring for her mother who lives alone, her level of aspiration may shift (Bastable, 2003).

Orientation — Orientation is described as parochial or cosmopolitan. Persons with a parochial orientation have limited life experiences, are closed to many new ideas, and trust traditional approaches. Someone with a cosmopolitan orientation has wide life experiences, is receptive to new ideas, and stays interested in learning new things to use in practice and life (Bastable, 2003).

Knowledge Readiness

What we know about a subject or topic is our knowledge base. We are ready to learn if we know something about what will be taught. For example, if you know medical terminology, you will feel comfortable about attending a medically oriented workshop. If you are starting a new job and have completed an online review of pharmacology, you have current knowledge. You feel ready to pass the required course at your new job. Another nurse may not have worked in a setting with many IVs and would not feel ready to take a test that included that information. When you are investigating an educational opportunity, you should determine the type and level of information so you can feel comfortable and get the most out of the program (Bastable, 2003).

Cognitive Ability — Information must be processed so it is understood. Cognitive ability is individual. Nurses have a high level of cognitive ability, which is demonstrated by the decisions they make everyday in their work. When looking at options, some programs are highly scientific. You may find this in sharing research findings. If your goal is to learn about a specific skill related to your clinical practice, you would not select that type of program (Bastable, 2003).

EDUCATIONAL DESIGNS AND DELIVERY

All nurses have experienced traditional education. They have been in large lecture rooms and small face-to-face groups, taken part in skills labs, and had clinical experiences. Depending on when they completed their education, such traditional experiences may be all they had. Nurses who graduated in the last few years and nurses who have completed CE courses or other educational programs probably have had new types of experiences. Not only are delivery approaches different today, but the organization and presentation of information is different.

Educational Material Design

The changes in delivery of education require change in how materials are designed. For example, the material shared at a CE program may be interesting because it is colorful, has bullets with summarized information, and there is a PowerPoint presentation. Nursing journals have graphics and color with a variety of "brief" information categories.

Material is designed to fit on CD-ROMs, videos, and disks. Pictures and graphs are included in educational materials. It is important to use several criteria to evaluate materials you receive, develop, and use for patient education. Areas of evaluation are

- Accurate & Current — Consider the source of the information. Is it evidence based or opinion? Is it written in a popular magazine, consumer journal, or a professional journal? We respond to information based on the source. For example, patients pay more attention to something from a professional source than a friend. When you share educational materials, you must check everything. You want accurate and current cancer information when sharing it for patient education. With so many new research findings, new drugs, and updated techniques, it is difficult to keep current. Nursing and other health-related books have a long publishing cycle. The books may have been started at least 2 years before they are published. If they were published 4 years ago, information is actually 6 years old.

- Organized — When you are trying to learn something or teaching others, the organization of information makes a great difference in learning outcomes. Think about an experience you had when learning a new procedure. The information filled several pages. The pictures did not fit the material or help explain it. You became frustrated. You took your own notes so you could understand it and listed the steps as they made sense to you. When preparing materials for patients, break down the information into small steps in a logical order. Organizing material in a question and answer format is useful. The audience may have common questions that can be answered. It saves repeating the same information (Bastable, 2003).

- Language — Nurses know medical terminology but common language often is sufficient. Do not complicate material. Use scientific and medical terms when appropriate. It is especially important to consider literacy levels when preparing patient education materials. Written materials are not the only ways to share information. Using other methods such as videos is also helpful. Understand the literacy levels of the general population and the populations you serve. Diverse populations often have English as a second language. Patient materials need translations and plain language (Bastable, 2003). For example, a Centers for Disease Control and Prevention polio immunization pamphlet went through a series of redesigns. The original pamphlet had 16 pages at a 10th grade level. A later version had 391 words (a double spaced page has about 250 words), in a Q & A format with a 6th grade reading level (Andrus and Roth, 2002).

Nurses are not only continuing to learn but also are teaching and sharing educational materials with patients and community groups. Evaluating materials when you attend a presentation or complete a course gives feedback for improvement. When you are responsible for staff development or patient teaching, critically examine the materials. Commercially prepared materials usually have instructional design elements included. It may be more cost-effective to prepare simple, effective materials. Color printing makes it easy to prepare quality materials that get the message across. Be creative as well as focused on the desired outcomes. Have confidence in your ability to critique and develop educational materials.

Educational Delivery Options

We have gone from classrooms and attending face-to-face meetings to a variety of innovative methods of education.

- Internet online programs, CE offerings, information sharing, and communication with colleagues.

- CD-ROMs that store print, graphic, and animated information.

- Online examinations for classes, CE courses, licensure, and certification.

- Teleconferencing with audio and visual components.

- Virtual settings and simulations that mirror the "real" experiences. For example, listening to heart and respiratory sounds on a Web site rather than listening to a real person's chest.

Kozlowski (2002) presents an introduction to distance education. Students and instructors may never meet; they are in different locations. Learning may be synchronous (when faculty and students meet at the same time in the distance classroom) or asynchronous (when faculty and students do not have set times to meet but post and share information in the distant classroom).

Asynchronous learning is the most common because it is flexible for students living in different time zones and allows students to participate when they have time. Adult learning principles recognize adults' ability to learn independently. The students are given learning activities, access to sources of information, instructor guidance, and evaluation feedback. Searching for a program includes the following steps:

- Beginning to look at Web sites that have listings of different schools so you can make comparisons between programs.

- Paying attention to the state approval and accreditation status of each school.

- Comparing costs for credits or courses. Is financial aid available? Will your employer provide tuition reimbursement for a distance program?

- Determining if there is an orientation course and the type of continuing and technical support.

- Understanding the computer hardware and software requirements to function in the program (Kozlowski, 2002).

It is always helpful if you know someone in the program or a graduate. Going through a distance education program with a friend provides a lot of support.

Schardt, Garrison, & Kochi (2002) compared the learning outcomes of students who completed a traditional classroom course, CE Evidence-Based Medicine, with students who completed the same course online. They wanted to determine which group retained more knowledge. The classroom students completed the course in 8 hours with mostly lectures and some small group activities. The faculty interacted with the students only in the classroom. The online students had 6 weeks to complete the course.

The post-course questionnaire indicated the online students retained twice as much knowledge

as the classroom students. The authors attributed the better performance and retention of the online students to

- more time to read course materials, practice skills, and apply the information to work settings

- more interaction between faculty and students (The faculty spent about 4 hours a week with the online students, both individually and in groups.)

- more personal motivation of the students (They had to be organized and take an active part in their learning.)

Further research is needed to discover other factors that influence performance. Distance CE education, for some topics, may be a more effective teaching strategy than traditional classroom instruction.

Solutions

In the challenge, Roberta, Janice, and Christine have been working on their plan to learn more about educational opportunities. They are ready to move forward. The three nurses decide on a "divide and conquer" approach to getting information. All three use the computer for Internet activities but Janice has excellent skills. She will look at Web sites and send Roberta and Christine Web addresses that fit their goals. Roberta finds out the employer tuition plan for all three types of educational activities. Christine finds some articles that give information about selecting educational and professional programs. All of them talk to other nurses they know who have completed learning activities.

They meet outside of work to discuss and share their information. They will continue to meet until each person is ready to start an educational program. They will mentor and coach each other until they realize their goals.

CONCLUSION

Nurses participate in lifelong learning activities. A first step is to identify a career path for learning activities. What is required to maintain an RN license? What is required by the state for continuing licensure? What do employers require for staff development? Beyond requirements, nurses can make choices about developing additional clinical expertise, becoming certified, earning additional degrees, and learning to satisfy their curiosity. Learning is formal and informal. Taking advantage of both types of learning enhances professional and personal development.

EXAM QUESTIONS

CHAPTER 15
Questions 71-75

71. One required reason nurses are motivated to continue learning is to

    a. meet mandatory, continuing education requirements for licensure.

    b. satisfy the demands of employers to earn additional degrees.

    c. have time to do extra activities and learn.

    d. meet their own needs to increase their self-confidence.

72. Asynchronous learning is a creative solution for busy nurses because

    a. nurses can take a lot of courses when they are ready.

    b. students can go to class in the evening.

    c. nurses can go to classes when they have a lunch break.

    d. students can log on to the computer when they have time.

73. Compliance is a socially influenced learning behavior defined as

    a. doing what is expected by the instructor.

    b. observing what others do and copying it.

    c. behaving as expected but not accepting new values.

    d. behaving as expected and accepting new values.

74. A demonstration of social support for a nurse anxious about attending an out-of-town conference would be

    a. having a friend agree to attend the conference also.

    b. taking anti-anxiety medication prescribed by a physician.

    c. friends having a send-off party.

    d. family members telling her to stay home if she is anxious.

75. One criterion to use when reviewing material to include in a professional presentation is

    a. how interesting it looks.

    b. that it is written by someone you know.

    c. whether it is based on evidence rather than opinion.

    d. that it is a recommendation from a friend.

CHAPTER 16

MANAGING YOUR CAREER

CHAPTER OBJECTIVE

After studying this chapter, you will be able to indicate choices that support career management and development for nurses.

LEARNING OBJECTIVES

After studying this chapter, you will be able to

1. evaluate the status of your professional career.

2. identify ways to plan for your preferred future in nursing.

3. specify career and self-development tools to reach your goals.

OVERVIEW

In the past, nursing careers generally involved bedside nursing in settings where patients stayed for several days, months, or years. There were a few supervisors and charge nurses. Some nurses worked in public health and other community settings. Instructors staffed schools of nursing. Today, if you were to list the different nursing careers and roles, it would be extremely long. Changes came about because health care expanded, specialization increased, sites for providing care moved beyond traditional settings, training and education requirements became greater than before, and approval, accreditation, and governmental regulations increased.

All the changes mean nurses are needed in new roles. They must plan how to survive and thrive in nursing, no matter what jobs they have at a specific time. Search in a variety of places. For example, you may not have thought about being a traveling nurse or working overseas. Become certified in a specialty area of interest. Additional education, especially related to technology, is useful. Oral and written communication skills are needed for almost any position. Employers value employees who have the ability to work with others, display good work habits, and possess critical thinking skills.

Career management is also needed because nurses are mobile and often work in new situations. The days of working for one employer for an entire career are rare. Nurses have so many options that some effort is required to learn what is possible. Part of developing a career means self-development. Personal characteristics impact how nurses are viewed by others. This chapter helps nurses examine where they are and where they want to be.

WHERE YOU ARE TODAY

Challenges

Amy, Wilma, and Robert work together at Orchard Haven nursing home. The nursing home is part of an expanding system that is acquiring assisted living facilities and adult day care centers. The nurses believe there will be new career opportunities as the company expands. They are highly skilled in their current jobs and have focused their professional development on geriatric and long-term care issues. Amy is the evening supervisor. Wilma is responsible for quality assurance and related areas. Robert assists with staff development. They talk about options and decide to meet with the nurse administrator.

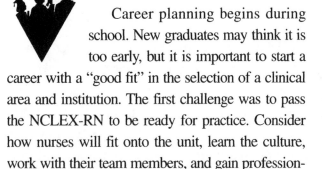

The Beginning

Career planning begins during school. New graduates may think it is too early, but it is important to start a career with a "good fit" in the selection of a clinical area and institution. The first challenge was to pass the NCLEX-RN to be ready for practice. Consider how nurses will fit onto the unit, learn the culture, work with their team members, and gain professional confidence (Tappen, Weiss, & Whitehead, 2001).

A nurse's first position is the beginning of a career. Think about where you want to be in 5 years, 10 years, and later. What experiences, education, and certification will help you get there? When looking for a position, you may focus on becoming employed to get experience before moving on to what you really want to do. If possible, think about what you really want to do and gain experience in that area or a related one (Tappen, Weiss, & Whitehead, 2001).

At the Crossroads

We all face crossroads in our lives regarding decisions about our immediate future or long-range plans. Career changes may be motivated by life changes: a move, health issues, increased family obligations, or personal situations. Career changes are also motivated by the career itself and possible problems with stagnation, frustration, stress, dissatisfaction, and boredom (Manion, 2002).

Work experience provides the opportunity to appreciate different types of environments and discover personal preferences. When making a decision about your first job or a new one, analyze your own strengths and weaknesses as well as those of potential employers and the job market. Address the opportunities and threats that may affect your decision. Look at your financial obligations and make decisions about that security (Tappen, Weiss, & Whitehead, 2001).

Work environments can encourage or discourage professional development. The quality of work expected and environments encouraging critical thinking, supporting new ideas and projects, and rewarding professional growth are indicators. The availability of educational programs and financial support contribute to participation. Nurse managers can inform staff of professional development events. Organizations can recognize achievements through career ladder plans. Advancement can be based on a variety of criteria such as education, specialty certification, and experience (Tappen, Weiss, & Whitehead, 2001).

Manion (2002) recommends a first step when making a decision about change; stop and think honestly about your career. She recommends 6 key questions to answer.

- What is the quality of the interpersonal relationships in my workplace? Researchers have found that an employee's level of organizational commitment is affected by relationships. Nurses will stay with a job because of the people they work with or leave a job for the same reason.

- Is the work I am doing important to me? Nurses do flourish in settings where the work is meaningful to the patients and society. In some cases, the work may be meaningful but so much time is spent on other tasks that it is not rewarding.

- How much freedom and autonomy do I have at work? Studies of intrinsic motivation confirm that people enjoy their work most when the level of autonomy matches their knowledge and skill levels. Consider how nurses are included in decision-making, the governance model used, and the processes for problem-solving.

- Are there opportunities for growth and development? Evaluate how your work stimulates and challenges you. Identify the resources for continued growth and development as well as option for introducing innovations.

- Do I see that there is progress as a result of my work? Nurses who work at the bedside with patients everyday can usually answer, "Yes!" Nurses who work in departmental or organizational positions find it a difficult question to answer. This leads to frustration, and nurses tend to leave such situations (Manion, 2002).

The results of your answers may reflect how important some aspects of work are to you. Others may attach different values to the questions. For example, the hours you work and the short travel time may be more important to you than the level of autonomy or the importance of the work. You may decide you do not need a change. You are ready to start planning your future if you are interested in exploring the possibility or are ready to actually make a change.

PLANNING FOR YOUR FUTURE

You have already answered some questions about what is important to you. Self-assessment focuses directly on your strengths and weaknesses. This type of information provides a focal point for moving forward in planning your future. The U.S. Department of Labor identified universal job skills for all types of work.

- Leadership and persuasion.

- Problem-solving and creativity.

- Working as part of a team.

- Manual dexterity.

- Helping and instructing others.

- Initiative.

- Frequent contact with the public.

- Physical stamina (Hood & Leddy, 2003).

Not all jobs will require all the skills but they certainly apply to nursing. Your self-assessment will include those areas.

Self-Assessment

A SWOT analysis is an approach used in the business world to consider new ventures. When you use this approach, you can look at yourself and at work environments on the basis of strengths, weaknesses, opportunities, and threats.

*S*trengths — Assess your accomplishments. Include work experience, education, certification, interpersonal skills, and special skills such as computer ability.

*W*eaknesses — These are the opposite of strengths. You may have no interest in further education or training, do not adapt to change easily, or cannot understand health care as a business.

*O*pportunities — Consider new markets, applications of technology to practice areas, and increasingly vulnerable populations needing care.

*T*hreats — Look at changes in health care, the economy, world events, and governmental regulations. For example, changes in funding for health care may affect who is eligible for care and how much funding is provided (Tappen, Weiss, & Whitehead, 2001).

Rojak (2000) outlines a number of questions for a self-assessment.

- Am I prepared to start a job search or seek advancement?

- Do I have the personal and professional tools to change my career?

- Do I have transferable skills that are valued?

- Does my current résumé completely represent me?

Once you complete your self-assessment, you have information to take some initial steps to move your career forward.

- Develop a global perspective so you are aware of broad changes that could affect nurses. Look at different levels of organization: local, state, and national. For example, new federal legislation provides support for nursing education options.

- Learn self-promotion and raise your professional visibility.

- Practice networking to make new contacts and gather information.

- Have a positive attitude so it is evident that you will do your best.

- Build your skills by taking CE classes, completing certification courses, or volunteering for special projects. Having excellent computer skills is a plus.

- Have a résumé that reflects all your accomplishments and professionally presents them (Rojak, 2000).

CAREER DEVELOPMENT

Nurses may not keep a complete record of all their accomplishments, but it is important. For example, when it is time for your performance evaluation, do you find it difficult to recall everything you did the past year? When you need to document your eligibility for certification, do you have to collect the information? How do you keep track of your CE and staff development activities?

Professional Portfolio

There are many ways to organize your professional accomplishments. People probably have different images of a portfolio. Nurses are familiar with résumés, but a portfolio may be a new idea. Bell (2001) describes how portfolios have different elements, based on nursing roles. Portfolios go

beyond career changes, additional education, and expanded community service activities. Faculty members submit a "book" when they apply for promotion or tenure. A nurse researcher will track proposals, funding received, publications, and presentations. A nurse who works as an independent contractor uses a portfolio to track the work completed as well as business aspects of the work.

Purposes of a portfolio are to

- provide a repository for all the previous career information;

- project a professional image with all the information organized;

- communicate accomplishments (Bell, 2001).

Portfolio Sections

The first part is a current résumé. Update your resume on a regular schedule. Waiting an entire year to update allows information to be forgotten or lost. One strategy is to have a folder where all notes are kept until you update your résumé and portfolio. You may want to review everything three or four times a year.

Establish a yearly career growth plan. What do you want to accomplish? A growth plan helps identify the types of experiences you need to achieve your goals. You can also determine the resources and time needed. Perhaps you need a particular CE course or a mentor to help you figure out what you should do to achieve a long-term goal. If you decide you want a nurse manager position, then you need to review a position description and find experiences to prepare you. You may not have any experience with budgets but could take a CE course or gain experience by doing a course practicum in that area.

Copies of your yearly performance evaluations, and any other supporting documents about your performance, should be in one section of your portfolio. Perhaps colleagues or patients wrote letters of appreciation or an instructor wrote an evaluation of your performance; these should be included.

- Keep reference letters, a list of contacts at agencies and organizations, and business cards from your contacts. You can also request letters that highlight your service. For example, if you chaired a committee in a professional organization that planned a major conference, you should ask for a letter describing your contributions. People are happy to do that if you are specific about why you want it and what they should include (Bell, 2001).

- Keep copies of health related documentation in your portfolio so you know where to find proof of your TB test, hepatitis series, and other immunizations.

- Keep copies of nursing licenses, certification certificates, and at least one original transcript of all completed courses and degrees.

Your portfolio has the documentation you will need for your performance evaluations, for enrolling in school, and for seeking a new job.

Résumés

Writing résumés is both an art and a science. It represents you as a professional. You want it to highlight your accomplishments, but it must be brief, clearly written, and to the point. Think about how your résumé would stand out from all the others. Nurses may mistakenly include personal information about the number of children, marital status, or church affiliation. Employers cannot ask those questions, and it is unprofessional to include them. When you interview for a position, you may bring up your religious affiliation if it impacts your ability to work on certain days.

Writing a résumés

- Use high quality paper and printing. Print several originals, or have quality copies made at a printing business.

- Keep it short and to the point. The information should match the specific job you are seeking. For example, if you want a manager position, then highlight those types of experiences. Two pages are enough space to include your essential information.

- Formatting gives an overall impression. Leave a lot of white space on each page. Use readable type (12-14 point), include headings, and have at least 1-inch margins all around.

- Focus on what you can contribute to the organization. Match your background to a specific position.

- Include specific descriptions about your education, experience, credentials, professional development, committee and project experiences, community service, and awards or special recognition.

- Often a job objective is included, such as "Position as an evening charge nurse in a trauma center."

- It is essential to use correct spelling, grammar, and standard English. Avoid slang and abbreviations. Look up words or use a word processing spell check. Such programs will also check grammar.

- Have a professional look to the finished product; no pictures, personal information, fancy paper, or scent (Tappen, Weiss, & Whitehead, 2001).

Ask family members and friends to critique it. Consider their comments because they can offer a different perspective.

Interviewing

Spending some time to learn about potential employers' expectations can help you make a choice. You may know people who work there. Family or friends may have been patients. Check out quality indicators such as rankings, approvals, and recognition.

Write a cover letter that is personalized. You may need to call and get the name of a person to direct it to. If no one is available, then use a memo format rather than a letter. Many times organizations start with faxed or computer-based information. Then applicants are selected for interviews.

Preparing for an interview is stressful. You wonder what to wear, worry about arriving on time, and stress over what will be asked. Preparation makes it less stressful.

- Get advice on appearance.

- Do a practice drive to the site and check out parking so you can allow enough time to actually get to the office where the interview is held.

- Do a mock interview with a friend.

- Know something about the organization.

- Anticipate the types of questions that may be asked: why do you want to work here, what can you contribute to our organization, and what are your career goals?

- Be prepared, with written notes, to cover what you want to know. Do not be afraid to ask about salary, benefits, orientation, and work schedules. The interviewer should provide that information but might not cover it during the interview.

- Hand write a thank-you note and mail it the next day.

- If you accept a position, write a letter that includes what you are accepting (Tappen, Weiss, & Whitehead, 2001).

STRATEGIES FOR SELF-DEVELOPMENT

Nurses are responsible for becoming the people they want to be, as confirmed by their values, beliefs, personal qualities, and perspectives on life. These characteristics are translated into how they practice nursing. Think about the person that you were 10 years ago and the person you are today. What characteristics do you like about yourself and what do you want to change? We all think of making changes.

Personal habits and behaviors carry over to our professional lives. Self is developed through our conscious and unconscious perceptions of our experiences, accomplishments, failures, conflicts, and humiliations. The self receives feedback from life experiences. Significant persons in our life send messages that are positive, neutral, or negative. Positive messages strengthen that part of the self (Hood & Leddy, 2003).

Personal Self-Development

Our behaviors and habits reflect our unique personality. How we respond to difficult situations is also individual. Our lifestyles reflect our level of self-development. Consider how you meet minimum expectations for managing your health. Do you

- Get adequate rest?

- Eat regular meals?

- Maintain a near-average weight?

- Participate in recreational activities?

- Exercise on a regular basis?

- Use little or no alcohol?

- Abstain from smoking?

- Practice spiritual values?

- Find ways to control stress?

- Maintain positive interactions with family members and friends? (Hood & Leddy, 2003).

Self-assessment of your personal life is the first step in determining how to develop into the person you want to become. Identify the areas that need attention

- Physical health – eating habits, weight issues, complying with treatment regimens, using preventive health measures, and stress reduction.

- Emotional health – building positive relationships, increasing self-esteem and confidence, improving communication, practicing anger control, and changing attitudes.

- Spiritual – recognizing and living according to values and beliefs and developing support systems (Hood & Leddy, 2003).

There are numerous programs, self-help groups, educational materials, and information about changing our lifestyles. Nurses are part of society and face the same issues found in the general population. Nurses have the responsibility to be role models for family members, patients, communities, and society. It is incongruent for nurses to smoke, be obese, and not participate in health screening, and have other health risks. Nurses, individually and collectively, must pay attention to health issues.

Professional Self-Development

Issues in our personal lives are carried into our work settings. Many nurses exhibit job and other stress in negative ways.

- Tiredness

- Anger and frustration

- Lack of physical stamina to meet the demands of their job

- Impairment due to alcohol and substance abuse

- Lack of confidence to advocate for themselves and their patients

- Burnout.

Finding support to change the work environment is essential. Nurses' voices must be heard so the conditions that cause the problems can be minimized.

Nurses also will benefit from protecting and improving their image. Physical appearance is one issue. How nurses dress and identify themselves is extremely important. The days of starch white uniforms, white stockings, nursing shoes, and caps are gone. When nurses dressed in that way, they were accepted as having authority and gained attention. Patients and family members recognized nurses. Nurses have marginalized the profession by not maintaining a professional image (Cherry & Jacob, 2002).

The public prefers that nurses dress in a traditional manner. One nurse commented on the attire of nurses in an emergency department. They wore T shirts with logos, stretch pants, mismatched jogging suits, stained and wrinkled clothes, and tennis shoes. When patients are admitted, what kind of image will they have of nurses who are dressed for play rather than work? Patients and families cannot figure out who is a nurse and who is a housekeeper. One suggestion is for nurses to wear conservative scrubs and a white lab coat with the name and credentials monogrammed (Cherry and Jacob, 2002).

Roberts (2000) describes nurses as being an oppressed group with little control over their destiny. Nurses are not empowered because they have poor individual and group self-esteem and identity. Positive identity requires an understanding of the cycle.

- Pre-encounter is the part of the cycle when people accept and are comfortable with their oppressed status.

- Encounter is an event that changes people's view of life and causes them to think in new ways.

- Immersion-Emersion is a time of separation from the dominant group and wanting to be with others who understand the new reality.

- Internalization is the sense of self-confidence from being part of a group that has the same goals.

- Commitment involves moving to action and improving conditions for the group.

The development of the profession requires nurses to change and challenge their image and work. How nurses feel about their profession and about themselves as professionals influences how they think and act in professional relationships (Hood & Leddy, 2003).

Solutions

The nurses at Orchard Haven are ready to meet with Kay, the nurse administrator. Amy, Wilma, and Robert want to explore career options and learn more about trends and changes in the system. Kay, the nurse administrator, arranges a luncheon meeting. She shares information about the system changes on the horizon and what they mean. The changing roles of nurses are discussed. Kay suggests some strategies to prepare for the future.

• Decide on a career path. If they want to stay in the gerontology field, they need to focus on a specific area such as practitioner, administrator, gerontology nurse, patient/staff trainer, or risk manager.

• Earn a graduate degree in a specialty area.

• Achieve certification.

• Find a mentor to help with career development.

• Become active in a professional group to begin networking.

Kay agrees to meet on a regular basis to share information and mentor their efforts to develop their careers.

CONCLUSION

Nursing and health care is extremely complex, and change is constant. Change usually brings opportunities. Nurses need to prepare themselves for this environment. So much time is spent caring for others that nurses do not take the time to manage their own careers. Preparation starts with self-knowledge. Start with self-assessment to determine your strengths and weakness, then look at options for developing new areas of expertise. Planning is essential for making choices that sup-

port your goals. Personal and professional development is crucial for achieving lifetime career goals.

EXAM QUESTIONS

CHAPTER 16
Questions 76-80

76. Researchers have found that an employee's level of organizational commitment is affected by the

    a. quality of interpersonal relationships.
    b. quality of patient care and the physical environment.
    c. physician and nurse relationships.
    d. friendliness of an employee's supervisor.

77. One aspect of a job nurses can review when they are considering staying or leaving is

    a. the time they spend driving to and from work.
    b. opportunities for growth and development.
    c. continued salary increases and benefits.
    d. how much the patients appreciate what nurses do.

78. SWOT analysis is borrowed from the business world and helps nurses

    a. learn about new career options.
    b. learn how to apply to graduate school.
    c. look at themselves and at their work environments.
    d. perform a peer review.

79. Carrie has just completed graduate school. She has been a registered nurse for 7 years. She has a new position in a staff development of a large hospital. She knows she needs a professional portfolio to

    a. organize all her information to project a professional image.
    b. be ready if she wants to start a new job in the future.
    c. organize her life by putting all her information in one place.
    d. be ready if her supervisor wants to see her accomplishments.

80. Nurses who work in difficult environments and are overworked and frustrated can change conditions by

    a. gaining support from physicians and other disciplines.
    b. threatening to strike or slow down until there is change.
    c. supporting each other and having their voices heard.
    d. bringing their complaints to administration.

CHAPTER 17

CHANGING ROLES AND OPPORTUNITIES IN NURSING

CHAPTER OBJECTIVE

After studying this chapter, you will be able to identify how nursing roles are changing and choose new career options.

LEARNING OBJECTIVES

After studying this chapter, you will be able to

1. recognize traditional and emerging roles for nurses.

2. identify ways to manage changing roles.

3. explore new career opportunities found in diverse settings.

4. select resources to compare and contrast information about new career options.

OVERVIEW

Nurses in the past had traditional roles and career opportunities. Depending on the historical time frame, they were working in homes as private duty nurses or in public health settings. For many years, the majority of nurses worked in hospitals as staff or bedside nurses or supervisors. The changing health care environment, the complexity of treatments, and regulatory mandates have not only expanded nursing roles but also increased the number and types of careers. Nurses can examine expanded roles and emerging career opportunities to become prepared for new careers.

TRADITIONAL AND EMERGING NURSING ROLES

Nursing, along with other professional health care roles, are changing and will continue to change. An example is hospital pharmacists. Pharmacists are now found on patient care units collaborating with physicians and nurses. They no longer just dispense drugs from the hospital pharmacy. The reasons for changes include a focus on managed care, redesign of positions, and the elimination of some positions. Nurses are faced with fitting into expanded roles. There are external forces such as collective bargaining, decreased reimbursement, and the bottom line for health care business that impact nurses' decisions to stay in traditional settings (Lewis & Kruckenberg-Scofer, 2000).

Challenges

Kimberley works in a busy intensive care unit (ICU). She started 10 years ago as a staff nurse. For the last 3 years, she has been responsible for staff orientation and development. She was also on the group that planned the new ICU unit. She selected the equipment and worked with designers on the physical layout. She completed training to learn how to use the new equipment. It took a year to train all the nurses and get settled in the new unit. Now Kimberley feels she is not challenged. She knows her job very well. She loved all the activity of developing the new unit and interacting with the vendors. Kimberley is thinking about a career change but does not know exactly what she wants to do.

Nursing Roles

Apker (2001) describes roles as particular behaviors associated with identified positions. Cherry & Jacob (2003) define nursing roles as the traditional duties and responsibilities of professional nurses without regard to practice setting. The concept of a role is to identify the universal activities of nurses. Roles are derived from the historical development of the profession, societal expectations, legal and ethical obligations, and practice standards.

The categories of identified roles remain the same but continue to expand. For example, the educator role has changed from primarily providing individual teaching when patients were discharged from the hospital to extended monitoring and providing health education in different settings. There are seven major roles.

1. Care Provider — This is the fundamental role of nurses. The nursing process is used to establish patient needs and set up the relationship. Nurses also actively coordinate patient care in collaboration with health care professionals. Caring is the essence of this role and is demonstrated every time nurses are providing care (Cherry & Jacob, 2002).

2. Educator and Counselor — The emphasis on health promotion, discharge planning, self-management of chronic illnesses, and care at home highlights the need for this role. Formal education at all levels, staff development, and continuing education are required activities. The counselor role has expanded in recent years as patients gain more information and choices. Nurses help them sort out the options and serve as resource persons (Cherry & Jacob, 2002).

3. Patient Advocate — Nurses seek to promote the welfare and interests of patients. This includes making sure their needs are met in any setting where they receive care. It also means supporting their rights and helping them become empowered (Cherry & Jacob, 2002).

4. Change Agent — This role has taken on new meaning since it was first conceptualized. What would nurses change? This role is increasingly important as new ways to provide care, system redesigns, and new technology require adaptation in how work is done and how patients respond. Considering new approaches and determining desired outcomes will require change (Cherry & Jacob, 2002).

5. Manager and Leader — The management of care goes beyond the bedside. Nurses have a responsibility to care for families, groups, and communities. Leadership requires vision and the commitment to improving patient and professional outcomes (Cherry & Jacob, 2002).

6. Researcher — Nurse researchers have made significant contributions to the development of nursing science and the improvement of patient care. They also work on interdisciplinary projects to look at health issues from a holistic perspective. Nurses in clinical settings everywhere are participating in research by collecting information and applying the findings to practice (Cherry & Jacob, 2002).

7. Coordinator of a Transdisciplinary Health Care Team — Patients often receive care in different settings, over long periods of time, and have complex treatment needs, a group of professionals collaborate on care. Coordination is the key to assure patients are receiving cost-effective, appropriate care. Nurses spend more time with patients than other disciplines. All aspects of care are addressed by nurses, who have the knowledge and skills to coordinate the different services (Cherry & Jacob, 2002).

Managing Changing Roles

Nurses are generally not prepared for change. Change is often unpredictable, intense, and fast.

Changing environments are described as chaotic. There are quick decisions that may not be the best. Time and resources are spent without obvious positive outcomes. A positive way to look at change is to identify opportunities. Nurses who are alert to changes are ready to adapt to change. Find your own unique characteristics. What are your abilities that help you expand and build a new career? (Lewis & Kruckenberg-Scofer, 2000).

Apker (2001) investigated how nurses in a managed care environment made sense of their changing roles. She focused on the communications behaviors that nurses used to function. The hospital had a patient-focused model in which the services were organized to focus on meeting patient needs. Communication across disciplines and among all staff was essential. The units are arranged in pods with the same staff regularly assigned. Supplies and support services are also pod-based. A summary of staff responses covers how they described their roles.

- Communication and support, especially from nurses managers, helped with role development. Nurses managers differed on how they approached certain areas. Some nurse managers were not implementing the shared governance program because they could not relieve nurses from patient care. Other managers thought it was important, and the nurses supported participation. They were willing to take on the extra burden so they could be represented.

- Nurses actively contributed to discussions. All disciplines understood the patient-focused model and supported shared communication and decision-making.

- Role development was difficult due to financial and time constraints. Nurses attended off-site meetings and shared the information with their coworkers. Others nurses engaged in informal role development. They took on roles such as pod coordinator, nurse preceptor, and wound care specialist.

- Nurses had to create time for role expansion. Some nurses felt their educator role was so important that they worked with patients for as long as needed to make sure they understood how to use a therapy such as an inhaler.

- Roles were not clearly understood because nurses had little or no training or information about managed care. If they collaborated and communicated with other nurses, their sense of role was clarified.

- The nurses received many different messages from others about their roles. Administration expected nurses to do "busy work," such as housekeeping, ordering and stocking supplies, and answering the phone. They felt rushed with their patient care activities.

Communication was essential for the nurses as they learned new roles, understood their expanding roles, and adapted to change in existing roles (Apker, 2001).

Nurses throughout the world are facing similar challenges in managing their roles. In England, the complexity of preparing nurses and health visitors for their roles was discussed at a conference. There is a need to move from traditional roles. Changes in nursing education are needed to respond to the health needs of society. Three areas need attention in professional education.

- Preparation for a career with changing roles, lifelong learning, and continuing professional development.

- Including principles of efficiency, effectiveness, integration, and flexibility.

- Developing alliances, collaboration, and communication with other health care providers (Hayward & Porter, 2001).

New Roles

Schenk & Hartley (2002) describe coaching as a new role. Nurses in this role work with patients to help them change behaviors. The focus is on the patient rather than the illness. A structure and approach is designed to fit the patient's needs and reach behavior changes that are sustainable over time.

In one survey, nurses who were changing or expanding roles generally selected consulting or independent roles. The skills they brought to their new or expanded roles included analytical skills, collaborative experiences, and facilitation abilities. They also had clinical expertise, were effective communicators, and had marketing experience. Resources needed for new roles are general skills, knowledge, and personal characteristics that transfer to the new situation. Computer skills were essential in new roles as well as business skills and budgeting (Lewis & Kruckenberg-Scofer, 2000).

When considering a role change, keep the needs of the new situation in mind.

* Be open, flexible, and committed to change.

* Take risks and have backup resources.

* Set your goals and priorities.

* Get ready for change by improving computer and other skills.

* Follow your passion and stay committed to quality.

* Step into nontraditional roles and keep doors open (Lewis & Kruckenberg-Scofer, 2000).

CAREER OPPORTUNITIES: WHERE ARE NURSES WORKING AND WHAT ARE THEY DOING?

Nurses work in many different sites, and the sites have changed in the last 2 decades. Hospitals, public and community health settings, ambulatory care settings, and nursing homes or extended care settings are the major employers. There are an estimated 2.2 million registered nurses in the United States. Public health, community, and ambulatory care settings have experienced the

greatest growth in the last 10 years. In 1980, about 66% of nurses worked in hospitals, compared to 59.1% in the year 2000 (Table 17-1) (Bureau of Health Professions, Division of Nursing, 2000).

TABLE 17-1 EMPLOYMENT SETTINGS	
Settings	2000
Hospitals	59.1%
Public/Community Health	18.3%
Ambulatory Care	9.5%
Nursing Home/Extended Care	6.9%
Other	3.6%
Nursing Education	2.1%
Bureau of Health Professions, Division of Nursing, 2000.	

The national survey of nurses identifies the six major employment settings and one "other." It does not give information about emerging career opportunities.

Nontraditional and Emerging Nursing Careers

Nurses are probably aware of different careers but may not have explored them. *NurseWeek* lists 46 nursing careers on its Web site. Some are traditional, but many are not. We will explore some nontraditional, emerging roles.

Ambulatory Care Settings

Almost 10% of nurses work in ambulatory care settings. Outpatient surgical centers have expanded in the last 20 years. Nurses in these settings carry out traditional roles and care for patients who are there for the day. They provide care during all phases of the surgery. They may be on call and check on patients the day after the procedures (Hood & Leddy, 2003).

Special Care Centers

Hospitals and health care systems have expanded services to centers that address the needs of special groups. Some centers are national in scope and specialize in one type of service. For example, women's health care centers provide a range of related services. Cardiac rehabilitation services are found at centers in hospitals, physician offices, and fitness centers. The goal is to provide expert care to persons with specific health problems such as diabetes, heart disease, and cancer (Hood & Leddy, 2003).

Community Nursing Centers

These centers provide primary care to patients who do not have access to private care. The center may receive funding from different governmental and community groups. Colleges of nursing have nurse-managed clinics, and others are supported by community groups or churches. The focus of centers is on health promotion and changing lifestyles (Hood & Leddy, 2003).

Community Education

Health education and screening has moved into the community. Nurses are prepared to share their skills to teach in community settings. Nurses who work in a community setting often extend their services to the wider community (Hood & Leddy, 2003).

For example, school nurses organize community health events. This is an area that nurses can develop into a business because of the great need for health education.

Forensic Nursing

Nurses in this field provide care to victims of violent crimes. They most frequently work in emergency settings but may go to other sites where there are victims. Forensic nurses are skilled in counseling and knowledgeable about community resources. The main goal is to ensure that the injuries are documented and that evidence (body fluids, hair, tissue) is collected and preserved for future trials. Nurses often testify at trials. Another part of their role is community education (Hood & Leddy, 2003).

Murphy (2002) describes working in the field. She is a forensic investigator (FI) and goes to crime scenes. She examines the victims and communi-

cates with the medical examiner to determine the next steps, coordinates moving the victim, and completes documentation.

Telehealth

There are many nursing positions that are not direct patient care but provide service at different levels. Telehealth is an approach to providing health care and sharing information by technology. Poison control centers are perhaps the earliest example. Today, telehealth has expanded to include transmission of patient information, diagnostic results, monitoring patient health, and storing information. For example, a person's pacemaker is monitored by sending information by telephone. ECGs and x-rays are read by specialists who are not on site. Individuals with specific conditions may access education sites and talk with providers. NASA and the U.S. military make the most use of telehealth. It is projected that money is saved by sharing provider expertise, decreasing provider and patient travel time, increasing access to education, and supporting early access to care.

Nurses have opportunities to participate in telehealth by caring for patients at a distance, developing education programs, and contributing to nursing research (Cherry and Jacob, 2002).

Business/Corporate Nursing Careers

Nurses work in business and corporate settings and use their nursing expertise to improve patient safety, make policy, and to develop new markets for products and services.

Insurance and Managed Care Companies

Nurses in these settings may evaluate the care given to patients. In managed care, nurses make decisions to approve services. They also work on business-related activities: auditing medical records, evaluating quality, ensuring customer satisfaction, and making recommendations for policy changes (Hood & Leddy, 2003).

Telephone Triage and Health Care Advice Lines

Managed care companies, clinics, and health care systems often use nurses to respond to patient questions, provide information, and determine the urgency of care needed. This area started as a marketing technique, but it was soon apparent that it had a positive impact on managing the use of health services, especially emergency departments (Hood & Leddy, 2003). Nurses follow protocols when talking with patients. They clearly state their role is to assess symptoms and give advice for follow-up care. The protocols give information about prioritizing the severity of symptoms to determine what type or level of care is needed (Lafferty & Baird, 2001).

Sales Representative

Nurses are found in all types of medical sales positions: equipment, devices, pharmaceuticals, and business services. It is only in the last several years that more nurses have been entering the business field. Nurses learn how to use new equipment and provide support and follow-up. Usually staff training is done. Nurses understand the health care environment and can be successful in a sales position (Hood & Leddy, 2003).

Workers' Compensation and Occupational Health

Nurses may work for companies that provide health services for their employees. In those settings, nurses treat injuries, screen for hazards, provide educational programs, monitor the work environment for unsafe conditions, and keep records of their activities. Nurses also work for insurance companies to monitor the progress of workers who are off the job due to injury. The insurance companies are paying workers' compensation and want to get employees back to work. Nurses assess workers' status, determine that they are getting the appropriate services, and design individual plans so employees can return to work in some other capacity if needed (Hood & Leddy, 2003).

Consulting

Companies and institutions are seeking outside sources for specific services and projects. It is cost-effective when the tasks are short term and the organization lacks employees with the needed expertise. Services may include preparing accreditation and regulatory reports, providing education and training, developing new systems and programs, and other special services (Hood & Leddy, 2003).

Nurse Entrepreneurs

Nurses often begin to think about starting a business after some distressing event or because they saw a need. Identifying a trend or an unfilled need is a start. There are many resources to help people start a business. Nurses often start their businesses on a part-time basis. Others are ready to make a new start and take the required risks. Personality characteristics needed include self-confidence, determination, perseverance, resiliency, and a need for achievement (Hood & Leddy, 2003).

Advanced Practice Nursing

Advanced practice nurses are usually identified by their graduate preparation in a specialty area. The traditional preparation has been clinical specialist, nurse practitioners, midwives, nurse anesthetists, nursing administration, and nursing education. A minimum of a master's degree is required, and certification is required for clinical practice. Advanced practice nurses work in many different settings, often independently, and are professional leaders (Hood & Leddy, 2003).

Informatics Nurse Specialist

This career combines nursing science with information management and computer science. It is possible to become certified in this area. Nurses participate in all activities related to organizing, analyzing, and evaluating data and information (Cherry & Jacob, 2002). This is a new career and nurses can help shape how information technology is used to benefit patients, nurses, and society.

Case Managers

Case management includes all the steps in the nursing process, with an emphasis on coordination. Coordination of care is needed for frail elderly patients, transplant patients, and persons with co-morbidities. These patients need services over a long time. Skills needed include being flexible, adaptable, and having knowledge of community resources. Certification is available (Zurlinden, 2002).

Quality Manager

A career as a quality manager is available in both inpatient and outpatient settings. These nurses improve processes, implement changes, and measure outcomes. They review findings and look for ways to improve care. This focus is especially needed because of the emphasis on cost effectiveness and quality patient outcomes (Cherry & Jacob, 2002).

Flight Nurse

Flight nurses have critical care experience and are usually certified. They work in trauma centers and the military. They have independence as they make quick decisions. The settings are located where patients have accidents or serious illnesses (Cherry & Jacob, 2002).

Solutions

Kimberley has been thinking about a new career. Sharon, one of the vendors she worked with on the ICU project, invited her to lunch. Kimberley was surprised when Sharon told her the company was looking for a nurse to help hospitals plan new ICU units, select equipment, and do training. Sharon was impressed with Kimberley's organizational abilities and ICU knowledge. They discussed details about the position. Kimberley decided to take a week's vacation and spend it at the company. She would continue to explore other options and get more information. After the time she spends at the company, she believes she can make an informed career choice.

CONCLUSION

Nurses continue to fulfill traditional nursing roles. While the roles expand, nurses are exploring and entering new careers. There are other careers such as parish nursing and traveling nursing. Nurses try new careers for different reasons: burnout, downsizing, boredom, physical problems, additional education or certification, and being asked by a colleague to consider a new career. Use the many different resources available to compare the different requirements for careers as well as the advantages and disadvantages. It is helpful to network and have a mentor when looking for a new career. You should spend time talking with nurses in the careers you are considering. Do your own research. Do a self-assessment, build on your strengths, plan ahead to learn new skills. You will be prepared to continue the traditional nursing roles as well as move to a new career.

EXAM QUESTIONS

CHAPTER 17
Questions 81-85

81. Nurses carry out the traditional roles that have been part of the profession for years but today those roles have

    a. changed and confuse nurses as they work in different practice settings.

    b. contracted as nursing becomes more specialized.

    c. remained the same but nurses have much heavier work loads.

    d. expanded to include more responsibilities.

82. When facing changes from a corporate takeover, a healthy way to stay positive is to

    a. find a new job.

    b. take a vacation during the time when the new owners take over.

    c. focus on the new opportunities the takeover will bring.

    d. take early retirement.

83. One group of nurses adapted to their changing roles by

    a. reorganizing the physical layout of their unit into work-friendly pods.

    b. writing a list of what they needed to help them during the transition.

    c. transferring to other units that were not changing until later.

    d. keeping everything the same, as much as possible.

84. Forensic nursing is a new career whose main goal is to

    a. counsel and reassure victims so they begin to feel better.

    b. be prepared to testify at trials.

    c. share community resources with victims.

    d. document injuries and preserve evidence.

85. A nurse who no longer feels challenged in her position, and is unsure of what changes to make, would do best to

    a. network and find a mentor.

    b. talk with her coworkers.

    c. ask family members what they think.

    d. look at job ads in the newspaper.

CHAPTER 18

STRESS REDUCTION

CHAPTER OBJECTIVE

After studying this chapter, you will be able to recognize stress reduction approaches to improve individual lifestyles.

LEARNING OBJECTIVES

After studying this chapter, you will be able to

1. indicate selected stress reduction management strategies.

2. recognize signs and symptom of work-related stress problems.

3. select stress-reducing actions for daily life.

OVERVIEW

Americans are stressed out. We know that because our lives are so hectic. We never have enough time. The media bombards us with messages that we are stressed and must need all the advertised products and medicines. Over two-thirds of visits to physician offices are stress-related (Keegan, 2001). Nurses experience work-related stress but must also deal with coworkers, patients, and family members who are stressed. It is imperative that nurses learn as much as possible about stress reduction. They can include these measures in their own lives, be role models for patients, and carry out their educator role. This chapter explores the many facets of stress and stress reduction.

STRESS

Challenges

Bertha has been a nurse for 15 years. For the last 6 years, she has worked on a cardiac step-down unit. The turnover rate is high, and nurses have had very small salary increases in the last 3 years. Bertha has been trying to stop smoking for over a year. She has no time or energy to participate in an exercise program. Her children are in college and her husband works rotating shifts. With her rotation schedule, they may not have time together for several days. She does not cook because she would be the only one eating. She has little social life but does have support from her extended family. She feels her life is a mess and wonders how she can change it. She sees a flyer about a stress reduction workshop being conducted by the local chapter of the nurses association. She decides to attend.

Stressed Out

 Americans are highly aware of stress and face it every day in their personal and work lives. Nurses work in high stress areas. Common sources of workplace stress are

- changing technology, job requirements, processes, and interactions;

- conflicts between home, work, and other environments;

- family care responsibilities;

- violence and abuse in the workplace;

- legal and regulatory actions related to work (Tappen, Weiss, & Whitehead, 2001).

New graduates may feel that going to school was the biggest challenge they will face. Then they start to practice. Just learning what they need to function in their work setting is stressful, at least for the first several months. Fitting into the work environment, adjusting to a new work schedule, differences in school and work expectations, and the high demands of the work setting are realities. Choices they face include giving up professional values, examining ideals, and cutting corners in order to complete assignments (Tappen, Weiss, & Whitehead, 2001).

Bryant, Fairbrother, & Fenton (2000) conducted a survey of Australian nurses to determine if there was a relationship between personal characteristics and workplace stress. They found

- Nurses who participated in physical exercise had lower stress levels at work than nurses who did not exercise.

- The greatest stressors were heavy workloads and poor staffing.

- Nurses did not perceive that patients and family members contributed to workplace stress.

The authors concluded that the nurses liked their profession and planned to continue working. Their most pressing concern was workload.

Defining Stress

Stress is a complex set of physical and psychological responses. We look at a situation and decide if it will have positive, negative, or neutral outcomes. Our previous experience serves as a guide. Stressors are circumstances or encounters that challenge us physically and psychologically. Stressors are usually thought of as negative influences but they can also be positive. For example, building a new house is stressful but positive. Taking on a new job is the same; if the change is something you want for your career you will adapt to the stress (Alters & Schiff, 2001).

Hans Selye first described the stress response. We go through alarm, resistance, and exhaustion. Our bodies can only respond and stay in a stress mode for a period of time. There are both physical and emotional responses. Symptoms include

- increased cardiac and respiratory rates,

- weakness and dizziness,

- GI upsets,

- fatigue and sleeplessness,

- headaches,

- substance abuse,

- absenteeism,

- low concentration,

- anxiety (Tappen, Weiss, & Whitehead, 2001).

The stress reaction allows humans to immediately respond to threats. These physical and psychological changes make it possible for us to react to and survive life-threatening situations. Low levels of stress can positively affect performance by increasing efforts to perform and focus attention. The key is to manage stress so it is positive or the negative reactions are minimized (Alters & Schiff, 2001).

Mind and Body Interactions

The links between many physical conditions and psychological conditions are established. Stress exacerbates such conditions as asthma, rheumatoid arthritis, and migraine headaches. Persons with irritable bowel syndrome (IBS) have bouts of cramping, constipation, or diarrhea. Psychoneuroimmunology studies the relationship between the immune and nervous systems. This new field addresses the mind-body connection (Alters & Schiff, 2001).

Personality, Disease, and Stress

We observe how patients and family members have different reactions to stress. People who generally view life from a negative perspective may encounter a challenging situation and not have the resources to overcome it. Another person, who has a positive outlook, has a personality that acts as a buffer. Stress-resistant individuals may view events as potentially positive. They will find ways to overcome the problem. Children learn how to handle their stress from family, relatives, and teachers. We have heard about type A and type B personalities and how they react to stressful situations. Historically it was thought that there was an increased risk of heart disease with type A personality traits. However, in the 1980s, it was recognized that many people with type A personalities did not develop heart disease. Current thinking supports the notion that people with negative thinking, anger, and hostility are more likely to develop heart disease than persons without those behaviors (Alters & Schiff, 2001).

Measuring Your Stress

People express their levels of stress in subjective terms: "I am so stressed because I had a flat tire," "It really doesn't bother me that my girlfriend moved out," "I feel I am coping OK with my mother's death." We may have feelings of not being in control of our lives, having too many obligations, or not enough time to accomplish all we need to do.

Stress levels are sometimes classified according to several measures.

• Length of time under stress — Experiencing stress for long periods increases the chance of physical and psychological problems.

• Frequency of the stress — Some triggers for stress are occasional, while others are continuous. If spouses argue every day, there is more stress than if it happens on a yearly vacation.

• Degree of stress — Individual reactions determine the degree of stress. The death of a child is highly stressful, but the cumulative effect of earning low grades in school, over many years, is also highly stressful.

Stress has a greater impact on individuals when there is a sense of being unable to control the life events that produce stress (Keegan, 2001).

Measuring stress provides some objective information to compare to your feelings. An Assess Your Stress, 10-question scale is quick to use and explains the scoring and results. The medical information on the scale is from the Cleveland Clinic.

The Social Readjustment Rating Scale was developed by two psychiatrists in the 1960s. It is also known as the Holmes-Rahe scale. It has 53 items and focuses on life events. Each item indicates the maximum points that respondents can assign. The respondents decide how many points to give each item. There is an explanation of the results.

Both scales are available on the WebMD site listed at the end of the book. There are many other scales to measure stress. The usefulness of completing a scale is that you can match it to your subjective feelings. It may help to understand that just being busy is not really stress, or you may consider lifestyle changes if you have a lot of stress. Once we recognize the stressors in our lives, we can consider stress-reducing options.

STRESS-REDUCING OPTIONS

Keegan (2001) describes stress as a "false alarm." The alarm goes off, as if there is a fire. There is a physiologic response. The body is charged up and ready to fight or flee. Most of the time, there is no danger. The fire alarm is going off but there is no fire. The challenge is to turn off the alarm system and, more importantly, do not turn it on in the first place. There is a great deal of advice available about reducing stress (Keegan, 2001).

Relaxation Techniques

Relaxation techniques are easy to use in almost any situation. Persons of any physical ability can do them.

- Deep breathing is slow, measured breaths that help shut off the danger alarm.

- Muscular relaxation is tensing and relaxing different muscle groups. This is especially helpful for necks and shoulders that get tense. It only takes a few minutes.

- Visualization is imagining a peaceful landscape. Use all your senses to put yourself in that place. You will feel like you are actually there. In a short time, you feel relaxed and rested.

- Taking notes helps keep track of different methods that work for you. Then you can focus on one, or a combination of approaches, that makes a difference for you (Keegan, 2001).

Chambers-Clark (2002b) suggests the following options:

- Having a relaxing cup of herbal tea. Herbal teas do not contain caffeine.

- Thought stopping requires you to stop your own thoughts that cause you stress. Think about a red light and mentally say, "Stop."

- Learning biofeedback to control autonomic nervous system functions. Biofeedback has been used to treat many stress-related symptoms such as migraines, spastic colon, hypertension, and phobic reactions.

Individuals must change their lifestyles to reduce stress.

LIFESTYLE CHANGES

There are two elements to a healthy lifestyle. We first need to protect our health and then promote it. Health protecting behaviors are what we do every day. We eat enough, take supplemental vitamins, wear seat belts, dress appropriately for the weather, and stay away from people who have colds or flu. The next part, promoting our health, is difficult.

Most Americans realize they need to make lifestyle changes to improve health, lose weight, and reduce stress. The changes are not drastic but require sustained commitment. We are always open to trying new approaches to achieve these goals. Starting and stopping is a common pattern. Improving our lifestyles decreases illness and lengthens life. Consider the following changes: are you living a healthy life or do you plan to make changes?

- Getting adequate sleep.

- Eating regular meals, reducing fat and salt intake.

- Doing regular, at least moderate exercise.

- Using little or no alcohol.

- Maintaining weight within a normal range.

- Eating a balanced breakfast each day (Hood & Leddy, 2003).

Health promotion is driven by the desire to increase health and well-being and become self-actualized. Why are some people able to make positive changes? Some significant reasons are:

- knowledge of benefits,

- lack of major barriers,

- positive reinforcement,

- supportive relationships (Hood & Leddy, 2003).

Strategies for Lifestyle Changes

Well-established habits are difficult to change. We resist change because it may mean:

- giving up pleasure,

- adding stress,

- straining relationships,

- altering our self-image (Hood & Leddy, 2003).

We all need to accept responsibility for our health. Modern therapies and medical technology cannot maintain or improve our health if we do not follow simple health practices. Everyone can become empowered to make sound health choices (Hood & Leddy, 2003).

DEVELOPING COPING STRATEGIES

Individuals tolerate stress differently. How strong we are, when faced with stress, makes a difference. Some people will work through the stressful event, others become ill, and others just give up. Personality and habits make a difference in stress tolerance.

- Recognizing stress before it really starts is best. Use stress-reducing methods right away.

- Avoiding stress is another approach.

- Getting rid of or minimizing stress is a common strategy.

- Converting a stressor to something that is not so stressful by reconsidering its meaning.

- Experiencing the same stressor repeatedly may desensitize it. On the other hand, it may also weaken tolerance to it and make it worse.

- Differing capacities to handle stress are important in determining how much tolerance a person has to stressors (Keegan, 2001).

Individuals can increase their stress capacity. Situations that once were interpreted as stressful do not trigger a stress response when the capacity is increased. A nurse who is always stressed out because she is behind in charting every day could decide she will always be behind, until the end of the shift, and not be stressed about it. Her capacity for tolerating stress is increased. The ideal solution is to find a way to fit charting into her routines throughout the day.

Increasing Stress Tolerance

We can examine ways to increase our capacity to tolerate stress.

- Take routine work breaks.

- Evaluate relationships and commitments.

- Make a concern list to recast stressors.

- Reflect on your career, life, and financial plans.

- Communicate with family and friends about problems, goals, and visions.

Coping Statements

One way to get started managing behaviors is to develop coping statements. Whenever you feel upset, anxious, or angry, a coping statement can help you step back and see what is happening. Reflect on your thoughts and then decide on options for dealing with the problems. Actually write out the statements on paper. This is an ongoing process. Keep trying alternatives until you find the ones that work for you (Keegan, 2001).

LIVING WITH STRESS

Nurses face stressful situations in their work environments. The reasons are well known. Nurses who try to maintain high standards feel stressed the most. Nurses either lower their standards or try to give their best. At some point, conscientious nurses experience burnout. They are in situations where the demands exceed resources. Energies are exhausted. Stress in nurses is seen as

- sleep disturbances,

- fatigue,

- loss of appetite,

- inability to concentrate,

- being late to work or frequent absences,

- mood swings,

- resenting patients and coworkers (Hood and Leddy, 2001).

Burnout is described as the progressive decline in work and other performance because of high levels of stress and the inability to keep coping with it. Burnout is related to personal factors that include parenting and family care giving responsibilities, personal activities such as school, community, and church.

Work environments contribute to burnout in various ways.

- Strict boundaries and bureaucratic organizational structures.

- Ambiguity, autonomy, flexibility.

- Staff shortages, lack of resources.

- Lack of responsiveness by management.

- Working in environments with poor patient outcomes.

- Hostility and indifference among colleagues.

- Little opportunity for advancement.

- Poor job status, recognition, pay, benefits, or working conditions.

- Introduction of technology without staff input or training.

- Lack of balance in personal life (Tappen, Weiss, & Whitehead, 2001).

Burnout has financial, physical, emotional, and social consequences. To reduce burnout

- increase personal control to reduce powerlessness;

- increase commitment to work and life activities;

- manage your stress;

- develop an awareness of your responses to stress;

- believe that you can change your approach to life and your behaviors;

- develop specific actions to reduce conflicts that cause stress (Tappen, Weiss, & Whitehead, 2001).

Mee (2002) describes a time when she worked as a float nurse. She worked overtime so she and her husband could buy a home. She worked long hours in settings with patients who were hooked to machines. She felt like a robot. Burnout comes on slowly. She did not connect with other nurses and

was isolated. Her advice is to let off steam, share experiences, use problem-solving, and reduce stressors.

A proactive approach for nurses is to think about the possibility of burnout before it happens. Nurses can empower themselves and make changes.

- Improving work environments to have control over decisions.

- Supporting and helping each other.

- Leaving work behind when we go home.

- Taking vacations and breaks from work.

- Learning how to center, the ability to relax during stressful situations. Regaining physical, mental, and emotional balance and refocusing on the immediate situation (Hood and Leddy, 2001).

Cosentino (2002) shares strategies for helping a coworker who is stressed. Offer specific assistance such as sharing work. Often the persons you help will begin to share feelings. This shows you care. Listen but do not try to offer solutions. Another approach is directly addressing your observations that the person seems stressed out. Do it in a way that is not confrontational but identifies changes in behavior. When several nurses are stressed out, it is imperative that nurse managers address the causes and seek to minimize them. As always, prevention is best.

Lowden (2001) describes the situations of nurses who have taken a new job or new responsibilities. They feel overwhelmed instead of having a positive experience. She advises the following actions:

- Talk to the supervisor and find out what the goals are for the position. You can focus on what is important to the supervisor and the organization.

- Find a mentor, a person with a similar position, whose work you respect, and with whom you can communicate.

- Look to professional organizations for support, empowerment, and current information.

These strategies will help nurses live with the stress of their jobs.

Franko (2002) describes a stressful situation in a perioperative setting. The needs of patients, family members, and staff all have to be met for positive outcomes. The shortage of perioperative nurses increases stress in an already high-stress area. The key to reducing stress in this environment was communication. It took hard, continuing work to maintain open communication. The result was that stress was reduced because problems were prevented or minimized.

Solutions

Bertha attended the stress reduction workshop and is ready to make changes. She found that attending the workshop motivated her. She realizes that the challenge is to sustain any changes she plans to make in her lifestyle. Her plan is to

- Join a support group to quit smoking. She knows this will help her over the long term.

- Explore non-hospital job opportunities with a goal of changing jobs within 6 months.

- She will start walking 1 mile at least 3 days a week. She believes she can fit that into her schedule. Her husband will also walk with her when he is home.

Bertha understands there are several other lifestyle changes that would benefit her but wants to start with manageable changes. If she can sustain these for several months, she will be ready to make additional changes.

CONCLUSION

The work environments for nurses are going to continue to change. The result is continuing or increasing stress. Nurses can help themselves, and each other, by understanding how stress affects them. Measuring the amount of stress we have makes it possible to identify the need for stress reducing options. Changing our lifestyles is one strategy that can have positive results. Most people have habits they need to change or want to find new ways to protect their health. Increasing our coping abilities and looking at concerns from a different perspective helps reduce stress. A combination of lifestyle changes and increased coping strategies are keys to healthy living in spite of the stress we face.

EXAM QUESTIONS

CHAPTER 18
Questions 86-90

86. Nurses feel the impact of job-related stress primarily caused by

    a. disliking the nursing profession.

    b. changing patient acuity, difficult family members, and too much paperwork.

    c. changing technology, job requirements, processes, and interactions.

    d. disliking their coworkers and the organization.

87. The Australian nurses who responded to a survey about work-related stress identified the greatest stressors as

    a. heavy workloads and poor staffing.

    b. patients and family members.

    c. physicians and other staff members.

    d. poor salaries and rotation schedules.

88. Stress-induced illness is most likely in people who also have

    a. mental illnesses that require treatment.

    b. negative thinking, anger, and hostility.

    c. other physical illnesses.

    d. a family history of such illnesses.

89. Judith, a nurse on a recovery unit, is stressed out every day because nurses have to move the patients out of recovery quickly. She can increase her capacity for stress by

    a. taking a yoga class twice a week.

    b. socializing with friends at least 1 day a week.

    c. converting the issue and focusing on caring for the patients until they are ready to move.

    d. complaining about the unrealistic expectations to the nurse manager and her coworkers.

90. Robert, an ICU nurse, uses stress-reducing strategy as a way to

    a. take more time off and enjoy life.

    b. increase personal control and reduce powerlessness.

    c. call in sick when he feels really stressed out.

    d. increase self-confidence and reduce organizational conflicts.

CHAPTER 19

HUMOR

CHAPTER OBJECTIVE

After studying this chapter, you will be able to specify the role of humor and its value in healing.

LEARNING OBJECTIVES

After studying this chapter, you will be able to

1. indicate the value of humor and laughter in our lives.

2. recognize positive humor.

3. integrate positive humor as a healing technique in nursing practice.

OVERVIEW

Humor and laughter are part of the human makeup. Making jokes, laughing, and smiling are human characteristics. Humor is used in positive and negative ways. Positive humor often mirrors our everyday lives with a twist that makes it funny. Negative humor can end with someone feeling hurt or degraded. We have all heard a person state, "I was just trying to be funny" or "It was a joke." Humor adds fun and joy to life, makes us appreciate a lighter side of our existence, and can actually help us physically and emotionally.

Nurses usually interact with patients and family members in serious situations. Patients may

want to interject humor into a serious situation. It may be a way to cope. Nurses can have a positive and cheerful disposition even when workloads are heavy and they feel stressed. Nurses and patients will benefit from such a demeanor. This chapter examines humor in our personal lives and professional roles.

Challenges

Roberta is the new nurse manager on a rehabilitation unit for persons with spinal cord injuries. The average age of the patients is 25 years with a range from 12 to 50 years. The patients stay at least 1 month, often longer. The unit is their home.

Roberta is excited about her job. She uses humor both personally and professionally. Looking at the lighter side of life has helped her through some difficult personal situations. Her previous experience in rehabilitation settings has given her insight into how nurses and patients use humor.

In her new situation, she observes the environment is regimented and has a military approach to staff/patient interactions. The work of rehabilitation is taken seriously. Roberta is interested in changing the environment by creating a more home-like atmosphere that includes humor when appropriate.

VALUE OF HUMOR AND LAUGHTER

Job stress is becoming the number one reason workers receive compensation. Employee workers' compensation averages $12,000 a year per person. U.S. workers take about 15 tons of aspirin a day. Twenty-five percent suffer from anxiety-related illnesses. Taking ourselves too seriously may result in terrible side effects (Buxman, 2002).

Christian Hageseth (1988), a psychiatrist, wrote a book about the art and psychology of positive humor in love and adversity. It was written 15 years ago and describes humor in a nutshell.

- Humor is a broad concept that embraces a way of looking at life and behavior that fits with our perceptions.

- Humor is an innate human quality. The potential for humor is always present. It is an essential part of life.

- Our life experiences change our perspective on humor. It is possible to improve our humor and become more skillful.

- The original form of humor is loving rather than aggressive. We can learn to cultivate positive humor.

- Positive humor contributes to physical and mental health.

- Positive humor can reduce stress and improve communication.

- Humor is a balance between being appropriate and excessive.

Many Americans are living longer than persons in past generations. Several factors contribute to long life. Finding joy and laughter in life is important. There are references in religious writings to a cheerful heart being good medicine but a crushed spirit drying up the bones (Eliopoulos, 2001).

POSITIVE HUMOR

Humor is a difficult concept to measure and define. It is believed the word, humor, was derived from the Greek references to the four principal fluids of the body; blood, phlegm, yellow bile, and black bile. A balance of the four is needed to maintain "good humor." An imbalance causes "ill humor." Plato and Aristotle viewed humor as enjoying the misfortunes of others. Comedy portrayed men at their worst. Freud's work included an exploration of the similarities between dreams and jokes. He divided jokes into four categories; sexual, aggressive/hostile, blasphemous, and skeptical (Mooney, 2000).

The relationship between health and humor has been observed for many years. Humor impacts almost all body systems, causing increases in respirations, muscular activity, heart rate, and catecholamines. Laughter is an aerobic experience. The pituitary gland produces endorphins, a natural opiate. Using our senses of smell, sight, touch, and movement increases the production of endorphins (Mooney, 2000).

Emotion-focused strategies can reduce stress. This approach alters the appraisal of a potentially threatening encounter. Humor, in such situations, can serve as a buffer. It helps to form constructive views and strategies to deal with the stress (Alters, & Schiff, 2001).

The following guidelines are useful for determining if humor is positive, rather than negative:

- Anxiety is reduced for everyone who is interacting.

- People are brought closer together both physically and psychologically.

- Communication is enhanced.

- People accept new ideas and information.

- Listeners gain a new perspective.

- People are invited in to share the experience.

- People are moved toward good health.

- Positive humor is free and friendly (Hageseth, 1988).

HEALING THROUGH HUMOR

The experience of Norman Cousins who described his unique experience with using humor while suffering from ankylosing spondylitis is well known. He watched funny movies, laughed, and was pain-free for several hours. He also laughed and used humor while recovering from a heart attack. He believed that positive emotions influenced health (Mooney, 2000).

Jech (2003) shares examples of research studies that support the role of laughter in

- decreasing stress hormones,

- improving moods,

- enhancing creativity,

- reducing pain,

- reducing blood pressure,

- stimulating the body's immune system,

- clearing the respiratory tract,

- relaxing the skeletal muscles in the arms and legs.

In one study, orthopedic patients who watched funny videos required fewer pain medications than those who watched drama videos. It is also believed that humor can serve as a distraction so patients' pain tolerance is increased (Jech, 2003).

You may be wondering at this point if positive humor is truly beneficial. Using humor in every stage of an illness helps people get through the process. During an early stage of an illness, individuals may use humor to help them rationalize going to a physician. When people are being diagnosed and treated, they may use humor to make the waiting time pass more quickly and to laugh at the procedures they go through. Humor creates a bond

between patients and caregivers. After the experience, humor is used to look back, to forget the pain, and regain a positive perspective on life (Hageseth, 1988).

ROLE OF HUMOR IN NURSING PRACTICE

Nurses face many difficult situations in their work. Patient outcomes are not always positive and humor may not fit the situation. How can humor help nurses? "Patient has chest pain if she lies on her left side for over a year." "On the second day the knee was better and on the third day it had completely disappeared." Jech (2003) shares two examples of humorous entries in patient records. We have all seen such entries and chuckled over them. Humor is beneficial for nurses and patients.

Benefits of Humor for Nurses

O'Grady (2000) describes how laughter lightens our load. Every day, in nursing, there are many opportunities for humor. We should not be afraid to find them. Nurses should enjoy the funny and sometimes, ridiculous experiences. Share humor with other nurses and patients. Laughing requires the same energy as crying.

New nurses need many skills when they start a new position. Maintaining a sense of humor helps. Not taking yourself too seriously is one way to adjust to new situations (Marquis & Huston, 2003).

Nurses who teach students, staff, patients, and community members can add humor to their presentations. Humor increases the audience's attention and helps establish rapport. Humor can reduce audience anxiety and creates a positive atmosphere. Using humor to describe an event that others have experienced sets a positive tone for the interactions (Bastable, 2003).

Stress is toxic to our well-being. Humor helps nurses survive psychologically. Nurses often feel powerless in their work situations and feel they lack control. Nurses who completed a 6-hour course, using humor with coworkers and patients, were helped to realize they do have control by the choices they make. The use of humor can reduce conflict and break the ice when situations are tense. A designated area in work settings, such as bulletin boards, is ideal for humorous material (Jech, 2003).

Buxman (2002) offers tips for nurses managers to help lighten staffs' hearts and workloads.

- Set the tone to help staff realize they have your permission to have responsible fun at work.

- Set the environment so it reflects humor; posters, signs, and having light-hearted activities.

- Set the pace by using humor on a regular basis.

The result should be happier and healthier staff members.

Benefits of Humor for Patients

Brassil (2002) asks, "Do you use humor with your patients?" Most people appreciate some humor. In therapeutic situations, nurses must first establish trust before including humor. This approach is not appropriate in all situations. Elements to consider are timing, environment, and the physical/emotional states of patients. When you wonder if humor is appropriate in a situation, use a smile as an alternative; "a smile is the whisper of a laugh."

In the last 20 years, there has been increased concern about children's responses to stress and their ways of coping. Humor is one way children cope. There are many ways pediatric nurses can include humor when caring for their patients.

- Include humorous approaches in assessments or tasks; "I am using a light to look in your mouth because your mouth does not have a window."

- Share jokes, riddles, songs, poems, and stories.

- Use word games to include humor.

- Have a humor basket or cart with a variety of humorous materials: books, videotapes, puz-

zles, magic tricks, bubble pipes, and other items.

Nurses are interested in measuring patient outcomes related to the use of humor. Studies are being done to answer questions about the therapeutic value of humor (Dowling, 2002).

Nurses who view the aging process as a developmental stage can sustain a sense of delight and determination in that group. Aging is an opportunity to continue to grow and have satisfaction with life (Eliopoulos, 2001). Humor is an integral part of the process.

Local scout troops and school groups can gather riddles and jokes to place on patient trays or in the dining room to start conversation and reduce isolation. Persons with cognitive impairment, such as Alzheimer's disease, can be included in humor. They may recognize facial gestures when someone is sharing a joke or remember humorous stories after they have lost memory and communication (Jech, 2003).

Humor has been included in the care of depressed and suicidal patients. Patients may be able to laugh at things that frighten them and use humor as a way to communicate. When patients are in acute crises, humor is not helpful. Humor can distract patients when they have pain, but nurses need to do complete assessments to assure the most therapeutic pain relief measures are used (Jech, 2003). Nurses can find additional ways to include humor in their practice.

Solutions

Roberta realizes that changing the environment of the rehabilitation unit and including humor is a major undertaking. She is anxious to make changes but realizes she needs to assess the environment, involve patients and staff, and fit within the overall organizational goals. She also realizes that an interdisciplinary approach must be used. She decides to fit her goals within the existing environment and use previously collected information as a starting point. Her initial plan is to review

- patient satisfaction surveys from the last two years,

- patient outcomes compared to national data,

- interdisciplinary staff suggestions for changing the environment,

- accreditation and other external reports,

- organizational goals and expected outcomes.

Based on the results of all the reviews, Roberta will

- compile the information into a S (strengths), W (weaknesses), O (opportunities), T (threats) format;

- begin sharing information with various individuals and groups for their feedback and input;

- include the new information into a revised SWOT plan;

- convene a group to work on an action plan, with priorities and target dates.

Roberta is committed to using an inclusive process to make improvements on her unit. She knows it will take many additional steps to see the results.

CONCLUSION

Positive humor brings people together, strengthens communication, and helps people gain new perspectives on situations. Being sensitive to individual and cultural perspectives about humor is essential to avoid offending anyone. The value of humor in healing is documented in many studies and in anecdotal accounts from individuals. Because nurses work in stressful environments, they need to find ways to reduce stress. Humor is one way. Find ways to look at situations in a positive, cheery way. Humor, in our personal and professional lives, will lighten our load and lift our hearts.

EXAM QUESTIONS

CHAPTER 19
Questions 91-95

91. A pediatric nurse uses humor when interacting with patients because he/she

    a. is good at making jokes and entertaining people.

    b. enjoys watching comedies on TV and sharing them with others.

    c. wants to attract attention and increase her self-esteem.

    d. has learned through life experience that humor helps sick children.

92. Jennifer decides to add some humor to her clinical presentation at a conference because she wants to

    a. increase the audiences attention and help establish rapport.

    b. encourage the audience to laugh and not be so serious.

    c. become known as an excellent speaker.

    d. distract the audience.

93. Research has shown that positive emotions influence health. Laughter is found to

    a. increase stress hormones.

    b. increase pain.

    c. reduce blood pressure.

    d. tighten skeletal muscles in the arms and legs.

94. When patients are in pain a funny TV program can serve as a(n)

    a. time to relax.

    b. enhancement.

    c. way to forget troubles.

    d. distraction.

95. Nurses in a busy ambulatory care center may use humor to

    a. make themselves feel better about their work.

    b. share funny stories that they all enjoy.

    c. reduce conflict and break the ice when situations are tense.

    d. joke about their patients.

CHAPTER 20

BALANCING YOUR LIFE — A HOLISTIC PERSPECTIVE

CHAPTER OBJECTIVE

After studying this chapter, you will be able to indicate approaches to achieving a balanced life — based on a holistic perspective.

LEARNING OBJECTIVES

After studying this chapter, you will be able to

1. identify factors in the realm of whole person wellness.

2. distinguish the concept of mind/body communication.

3. select ways to maintain a high level of physical, emotional, and psychological wellness.

OVERVIEW

There is great interest in exploring our health from all different perspectives. Nurses take care of people with physical and psychological problems. Sometimes there is an obvious connection. A person with advanced Alzheimer's disease has many physical problems. Depressed persons may not eat or take care of themselves. Most people know the importance of maintaining or improving physical health. Nurses need to start with themselves. They are in high-stress work environments, juggle many different responsibilities, and have a variety of professional demands. Learning more about balancing all aspects of our lives will lead to making choices that help us achieve and maintain physical, emotional, and environmental health and wellness.

Challenges

Susan is a school nurse with responsibility for three different schools. She originally worked on a pediatric unit for 10 years. She has a BSN degree and is certified as a school nurse. She likes her job because it fits with her family life. Her three children are in school, and she is on the same schedule. She is extremely busy while school is in session. Her family depends on her to do everything at home. Her husband works long hours and comes home exhausted. He is too tired to do much around the house. They both attend the children's activities. Susan started having bad headaches this year and has tried different medications but they do not help that much. She feels stressed and really does not have time for herself. She talks with other school nurses at a staff meeting. They talk about alternative therapies to reduce stress. Barbara has read a little about different therapies and decides to find out more about them.

WHOLE PERSON WELLNESS

The predominant approach to health in the United States focuses on the diagnosis and treatment of illness. It is really a paradox that many persons are exercising, trying to eat better, and using weight reduction products while at the same time more than half of the population is overweight. A whole person model does not focus on selected disease entities. Whole person wellness aims for optimum health, nothing less. That goal is different for each of us. There are categories to identify the related concepts: physiological, mental, emotional, social, spiritual, and environmental elements of individuals, groups, and communities. Wellness is not a place or state that we reach but it is a continuing, dynamic process.

People often use the terms health and wellness interchangeably. The concepts are related. Being healthy allows us to function independently. Wellness means we are functioning at our highest possible level. Having both health and wellness makes it possible to achieve our goals and live life as we like. Health is a continuum, and we move forward and backward, depending on internal and external changes in our environments. Strategies for self-care that promote whole person wellness include

- Caring for yourself in order to care for others – Nurses put patient needs above their own but must realize the need for a balance. For example, you have been working an extra 12-hour shift, each week, for several months. You are scheduled to take a 2-week vacation. Your nurse manager asks you to take only 1 week of vacation because the unit will be short-staffed. You know the unit is always short-staffed. You really need a vacation. Your response is that you need to care for yourself and will take 2 weeks off. Cymerman (2002) challenges nurses to nurture themselves. We are not indispensable; others can step in. Self-nurturing is not self-centered but is about caring for ourselves. It is a proactive choice and can bring joy and health to our lives. Women have many different roles, and nurses face a particularly demanding work role. She offers advice about creating the life you

want: unclutter your life, figure out what is really important, look at quality not quantity when making life choices, and include self-nurturing activities in your life.

- Physical health – Persons are in good physical health when their body systems are functioning at an optimum level. They are able to do whatever they feel like, based on their abilities. For example, a person confined to a wheelchair may have the ability to compete in athletic events. Blind persons care for themselves by learning to use other senses, such as touch.

- Psychological health – This area of health means accepting responsibility for our behavior, the ability to cope with challenges, being comfortable with our emotions, feeling good about ourselves, and having a positive outlook on life.

- Spiritual health – Human beings have beliefs that provide direction or purpose to life. We have a sense of hope, can live through times of crisis, and have meaning to our lives every day. Nurses' beliefs about love, forgiveness, and acceptance stem from their inner beings. Having a high level of spiritual awareness contributes to nurses' ability to maintain a healthy outlook.

- Intellectual health – We need the ability to solve problems and use higher order thinking skills to function at a high level. Nurses use such skills to determine alternative courses of actions, make judgments, and effectively process complex information.

- Social health – Being able to form relationships that are supportive and intellectually rewarding, identifying with social groups, and belonging to social and community groups are all evidence of social health.

- Environmental health – This area of health has a major impact on our daily lives. Basic contributors to health are clean water and air, waste management, control of social problems such as crime and violence, and safe and adequate housing (Alters & Schiff, 2001).

Wellness Programs

Employee sponsored wellness programs were started in the 1980s. Employers knew the average cost for health care, for each employee, was around $3,000 a year and $225,000 over a lifetime. Hospitals recognize that health care environments are stressful. Many are developing wellness programs. Programs have different features.

- Onsite exercise areas and other wellness programs such as weight reduction.

- Bringing in commercial programs such as Weight Watchers at Work.

- Offering cash to spend on wellness programs.

- Informal programs such as walking groups stated by coworkers.

- Offering rewards such as reduced health insurance rates for participation.

- Changing to healthier food offered in the cafeterias.

- Setting up walking trails inside and outside a hospital.

Nurses cannot help patients to be healthy if we are not healthy ourselves (Domrose, 2002).

Principles of Whole Person Wellness

Individuals who aspire to become healers in alternative/complementary therapies are guided by a set of principles. They train themselves to be in touch with the self. These same principles are helpful for anyone who is determined to understand whole person wellness.

The separation of the whole person into mind, body, and spirit is a concept that does not fully explain the connections. Mind, body, and spirit are unified and there is an interdependence. Mind, body, and spirit share the same consciousness.

Attitudes, beliefs, and values play a major role in health and disease. Empowerment of self provides the opportunity to create and maintain wellness. Change, through experiential learning, is essential to achieving wellness (Keegan, 2001).

One approach to exploring whole person wellness is understanding how the mind and body influence each other.

MIND-BODY CONNECTION

The mind-body connection was first described in the 1800s when Freud and Jung wrote about the complexities between the mind and body. It is helpful to understand how the two entities are connected. One type of therapy is Gestalt, the German word for whole. The journey to a holistic perspective on life requires becoming fully aware of feelings, perceptions, and behaviors. The focus is on the here and now.

Birx (2003) describes healing as the process of becoming fully aware of others and ourselves. Healing requires that the whole person be involved. We become aware by being fully present when providing care. Being present brings mind and body together.

Nurses provide care from a holistic framework. A holistic practice requires nurses to bring their authentic self to the patient relationship. It is the art of nursing. This approach is based on harmony within mind, body, and spirit. When we are able to experience our real self, there is a high degree of health. Becoming the persons we want to be (self-actualized) creates an environment for individuals to reach their full potential (Cumbie, 2001).

ACHIEVING A HEALTHY ENVIRONMENT

We are aware of the impact of environment on our health and our ability to maintain wellness. The concern and evidence of the negative impact humans have on the environment is becoming more visible. The Industrial Revolution, throughout the 19th and 20th centuries, started major environmental destructive forces. Natural resources such as minerals and wood were used for manufacturing and building. Water and air were polluted from the manufacturing processes. People crowded into cities to work in factories. There was large-scale migration of people from Europe to the United States and from rural to urban areas. The health of groups and communities was negatively impacted (Keegan, 2001).

The United Nations organized a conference in 1972 on the human environment. In 1992, an Earth Summit was held in Brazil. Over 30,000 people and leaders, from around the world, attended. There was some agreement on climate change issues with a goal of reducing greenhouse gas emissions (Keegan, 2001).

We are aware of many actual and potential environmental issues

- pesticides,

- food irradiation,

- water pollution,

- indoor and outdoor air pollution.

People around the world face many environmental problems that negatively impact their health and welfare (Alters & Schiff, 2001). Nurses and patients face poor environmental conditions every day.

Acute care settings have been described as toxic work environments. Nurses are expected to give quality care when they experience understaffed and poorly equipped situations. Nurses are exposed to chemicals, radiation, infectious diseases, violence, stress, and physical injury (Hood & Leddy, 2003). A few environmental problems are presented in the next section.

Noise Pollution

High levels of noise are common in many work settings. More than 20 million workers in the United States are exposed to hazardous noise, often

in white-collar environments. Studies have demonstrated that high noise levels reduce pulse and respiration rates. An increase of fat being released into the bloodstream has also been observed. People who are exposed to noise levels of about 70dB (decibels) throughout the day become irritable or tense. Hearing loss may occur from long-term exposure. There are reports of increased blood pressure, sleep problems, and a drop in school performance. A major concern is the impact of noise on patients. Patients get very little rest in some settings. The phenomenon of intensive care psychosis is well documented (Keegan, 2001).

Think about your own work setting. There are always several people in the environment. Open spaces, such as emergency, intensive care, and recovery areas, generate a great deal of noise from interactions and equipment. Closed spaces such a private patient rooms may generate noise from the equipment and have several people in the room.

Joint Work Space

Shared workspace is found in most health care settings. Inpatient settings have many common areas that are noisy and distracting because of the number of people. In outpatient settings, space may be inadequate to assess patients. Comfortable places to sit while talking with patients may be unavailable. The ergonomics of work settings related to furniture and tasks including reaching, bending, lifting, and stretching are areas to consider when determining the effects of workspace environment on health.

Achieving wellness in your environment takes effort. Collaborate with others to have a voice in making decisions about it.

- The physical layout of your work setting is important. Reorganize or improve it to reduce noise, crowding, and comfort.

- Schedule patient care activities to allow for periods of rest.

• Carefully evaluate the ergonomics of furniture and equipment use.

MAINTAINING TOTAL WELLNESS

People who appreciate the importance of making healthy choices and following them are on the path to maintaining total wellness. We know friends and family members who understand what they need to do to maintain their health but do not follow through. What accounts for the differences in people's health behavior?

• Motivation is the strength or urge that makes people act. Motivation is based on our past experiences, perceived needs, personal values, external influences, and personal choices.

• Efficacy is the belief that we are able to change our behavior. Barriers to realizing that include poor education, lack of support, or lifestyle.

• Vulnerability refers to threats to our health. If there is a great threat and changing our behavior will make a difference, we are more motivated (Alters & Schiff, 2001).

When we are motivated and are managing our health, it means we are making choices.

Decision-Making Model

Using a systematic process to make health related choices increases the probability the decisions are sound. When people make impulsive decisions, based on advertising, emotions, and attitudes, the choices may not be the best. A decision-making model helps sort out health information and make reasoned decisions.

• Information is received from many sources.

• Consider your own attitudes and beliefs.

• Recognize the need to change.

• Accept the value of change.

• Evaluate your options.

• Consider the positive and negative aspects of options.

• Make a decision.

• Analyze the outcomes.

• Review benefits and harms.

• Continue with your choice if the benefits are sufficient (Alters & Schiff, 2001).

The work sheet will help you use the decision-making model (Table 20-1).

Analysis Model

We are bombarded with vast amounts of health-related information. We need some way to

TABLE 20-1: DECISION-MAKING MODEL WORK SHEET						
	Physical	Psychological	Spiritual	Intellectual	Social	Environment
Information						
Attitudes & beliefs						
Need to change						
Value of change						
+ & - of choices						
Make decision						
Analyze outcomes						
Review + & -						
Continue choice						

make sense out of it and determine if it is useful. An analysis model is useful when trying to sort out information. An analysis model identifies a few questions to ask when reviewing health-related information.

- What statements can you verify, and what cannot be verified?

- Is the source reliable?

- What is the rationale for sharing the information?

- Are there biases in the information?

- What is the main point of the information?

- Does the information attack the credibility of scientists or medical authorities? (Alters & Schiff, 2001).

Using the analysis model may seem cumbersome, but when people are making decisions to maintain total wellness, they need the best information.

In addition to media and print information, many people use the Internet to find health information. It is possible to use the analysis model for information from that source. The source of the information is identified on each site. It is important to distinguish between advertisements, commercially sponsored sites, and sites sponsored by governmental or professional groups. You can usually determine site sponsors by the last three letters of the web addresses: com are commercial, gov are governments, org are nonprofit organizations, and edu are educational institutions (Alters & Schiff, 2001). Nurses can use this information and share it with patients, family members, and community groups.

Maintaining Total Wellness in Work Settings

Ufema (2002) challenges nurse managers to be proactive in helping staff maintain total wellness. She shares strategies she used to improve staff morale and wellness.

- Found a person to offer guided imagery to staff.

- Provided massage sessions for staff.

- Arranged for patients' pets to come on the unit for visits.

There are many other creative ways to help staff maintain a high level of wellness and share their own wellbeing with patients.

Solutions

Barbara, the school nurse, spent time looking at alternative therapies to help reduce her stress and headaches. Barbara realizes her life is stressful. She has too much to do, has little help from her family, and is beginning to have health problems. She knows she cannot spend a lot of time doing some activity but does want to start something. She is going to take yoga classes at the local YMCA for a month and then supplement the group sessions with a videotape at home. When school is out, she will try to do more for herself. She will also continue to read and find information about alternative therapies. She knows there are other changes she needs to make to reduce stress and to improve her health.

CONCLUSION

Being really healthy means managing stress by accessing our levels of creativity to solve problems, interacting with others on a daily basis, enjoying close relationships with significant others, being connected to family, friends, and community (Keegan, 2001).

The components of whole person wellness are nutrition, exercise, stress reduction, relaxation, introspection, a sense of purpose, and being connected to others (Keegan, 2001). We all have the responsibility to reach an optimum level of health and to encourage and support others to do the same.

EXAM QUESTIONS

CHAPTER 20

Questions 96-100

96. The concept of whole body wellness is

    a   a focus on selected disease entities.

    b. to aim for a minimum level of functioning.

    c. a continuing dynamic process.

    d. a place or state that we reach.

97. A nurse whose nurse manager and some of her coworkers ask her not to take time off because they will be short-staffed must remember that self-nurturing

    a. means being committed to being an excellent nurse.

    b. means being committed to caring for herself.

    c. is mostly focused on meeting patient needs.

    d. means putting patients first and personal activities second.

98. The best way to address two common employee health problems in a wellness program is to start with

    a. support groups and educational programs.

    b. an onsite psychotherapy program and social times after work.

    c. massages and aromatherapy.

    d. an onsite exercise area and a weight reduction program.

99. Birx describes the art of nursing as

    a. bringing our authentic self to the patient relationship.

    b. maintaining whole person wellness to optimize patient care.

    c. being open to new ways of meeting patient needs.

    d. bringing compassion and care to the patient relationship.

100. Acute care settings have been described as toxic work environments because

    a. ventilation is poor and temperatures are not controlled.

    b. there are chemicals, noise, and potential for physical injury.

    c. there are soiled bandages, drainage bags, and used needles.

    d. floors are slippery, faucets leak, and paint is peeling.

This concludes the final examination. An answer key will be sent with your certificate so that you can determine which of your answers were correct and incorrect.

RESOURCES

ORGANIZATIONS

American Academy of Nurse Practitioners
Capital Station, PO Box 12846
Austin, TX 78711
1.512.442.4262

American Association of Nurse Anesthetists
222 South Prospect Avenue
Park Ridge, IL 60068
1.847.692.7050

American College of Nurse-Midwives
818 Connecticut Avenue NW, Suite 900
Washington, DC 20006
1.202.728.9860

American Holistic Nurses Association
P O Box 2130
Flagstaff, AZ 86003
1.800.278.2462

American Nurses Association
600 Maryland Avenue SW, Suite 100 West
Washington, DC 20024
1.800.274.4262

National Association of Hispanic Nurses
1501 16th Street NW
Washington, DC 20036
1.202.483.2477

National Black Nurses Association
8630 Fenton Street, Suite 330
Silver Springs, MD 20910
1.202.589.3200

WEB SITES

Chapter 1

Tips for time management
http://add.miningco.com
http://www.mindtools.com

Chapter 2

Suggestions for dealing with complex situations
http://www.mindtools.com

Several articles on change
http://www.drucker.org
Look under Articles, then Articles by Author Index

Chapter 3

University of Arizona Communication Department site with extensive information
http://www.ic.arizona.edu

Chapter 4

Article: *How the Internet will change our health system.*
http://www.healthfutures.net

Project HOPE: The People to People Foundation, Inc.
http://www.benton.org

Networking for Better Care: Healthcare for the Information Age.

Report from the Benton Foundation

Chapter 5

Understanding organizational culture and increasing productivity
http://www.nadona.org

Information about Magnet status (the highest recognition awarded to nursing services by the American Nurses Credentialing Center)
http://www.nursingworld.org

Chapter 6

Decision-making
http://www.mindtools.com

Test your ability to manage change quiz
http://www.maknaus.com

Chapter 7

Information about managed care and HMOs
http://www.ana.org

Case Management Resource Guide
http://www.cmrg.com

National Association of School Nurses
Information about school nursing, roles, education, and certification
http://www.nasn.org/

Chapter 8

Look under studies for quality benchmarks
http://www.100TopHospitals.com

Public Sector Continuous Improvement Site
Large site with many links, library, reading list, organization links and more.
Quality Improvement Information
http://deming.eng.clemson.edu/pub/psci/

Nursing-Sensitive Quality Indicators for Acute Care Settings and ANA's Safety & Quality Initiative
Staffing and Quality
http://www.ana.org

Chapter 9

Interdisciplinary education and practice
http://www.aacn.nche.edu

Chapter 10

American Holistic Nurses Association
http://www.ahna.org

American Association of Oriental Medicine
http://www.aaom.org

American Botanical Council
http://www.herbalgram.org

American Herbalists Guild
http://www.healthy.net

Herb Research Foundation
http://www.herbs.org

Chapter 11

The Center for Cross-Cultural Health offers excellent information and resources for culturally competent medical and nursing care.
http://www.crosshealth.com

Ethnomed site is supported by the University of Washington and offers information on selected African and Southeast Asian cultures.
http://ethnomed.org

Chapter 12

United American Nurses – AFL-CIO
Information about unions and collective bargaining
http://www.uannurse.org

JCAHO strategies for relieving the nursing shortage
http://www.jcaho.org

Johnson & Johnson advertising campaign,
Discover Nursing
http://www.discovernursing.com

Nurse Power initiative is an illustrated site with
versions in three languages. It describes nursing
careers and the exciting career opportunities.
http://www.nursepower.net

Premier, Inc. is a one-stop resource for safety,
resources, tool kits, and templates for safety planning.
http://www.premierinc.com

Texas Peer Assistance Program for Nurses is an
example of how an assistance program works.
http://www.texasnurses.org

U.S. Department of Labor, OSHA site with guidelines for preventing workplace violence for healthcare and social service workers.
http://www.osha.gov

Chapter 13 Web Sites

American Association of Nurse Anesthetists
Legal briefs section
http://www.AANA.com/legal

Legislative information for nurse practitioners and
other interested nurses
http://www.npcentral.net/leg/

Chapter 14

The Center for Applied Ethics and Professional
Practice designs, implements, and evaluates solutions to health and community problems.
http://www.edc.org/CAE/

The Nursing Ethics Network (NEN) is a nonprofit
organization of professional nurses committed to
the advancement of nursing ethics in clinical practice through research, education, and consultation.
http://www.nursingethicsnetwork.org/

Ethical Issues in Research Involving Human
Participants
http://www.nlm.nih.gov/

Bioethics: Strengthening Nursing's Role by
Maureen Habel, MA, RN, an online CE article
from *NurseWeek*.
http://www.nurseweek.com

Chapter 15

Western Schools specializes in the publishing of
high quality, value-priced continuing education
courses for all types of nurses.
http://www.westernschools.com

American Nurses Association Site – includes
Online Journal of Nursing Issues
http://nursingworld.org

Chapter 16

Résumé Rehab tutorials and resources with links to
many other sites
http://www.zzpixel.com/resume-rehab

American Nurses Association site — offers current
news, certification information, and much more to
develop your career.
http://nursingworld.org/

Sigma Theta Tau, International Honor Society for Nursing
http://www.nursingsociety.org

Chapter 17 Web Sites

American Academy of Nurse Practitioners
http://www.aanp.org

American College of Nurse-Midwives
http://www.midwife.org

American Forensic Nurses
http://www.amrn.com/aboutus.htm

American Nursing, Informatics Association
http://www.ania.org

National Association of Clinical Nurse Specialists
http://www.nacns.org

Quality Management
http://www.ncqa.org and http://www.nahq.org

Flight Nursing
http://www.seaox.com/wannabe.html

Chapter 18

Site for information about biofeedback —
Biofeedback Network
http://www.biofeedback.net/index.html

Academy for Guided Imagery
http://www.healthy.net/agi

Dealing with stress
http://www.mindtools.com

Quizzes and information about all aspects of managing stress
http://my.webmd.com/search

Chapter 19

Patty Wooten, RN, BSN, has tips on developing and improving a sense of humor. Site has articles and information about the therapeutic use of humor.
http://www.jesthealth.com

Humor-related Web sites:
Melodie Chenevert, RN
http://www.pronurse.com

Karyn Buxman, RN
http://www.humorx.com

Site with jokes and humor
http://www.humormatters.com

American Association for Therapeutic Humor
http://www.aath.org

Chapter 20 Web Sites

Center for Mind-Body Medicine
http://www.cmbm.org

Resource about workplace distress or violence
http://nurseadvocate.org

American Nurses Association
Information on work-related issues
http://www.nursingworld.org

Nurses' Health Study, a 25-year longitudinal study of nurses — The goal of the study was to identify factors that contribute to health across the life span. The study is often cited and has raised public awareness about the commitment of these nurses to maintain and preserve health.
http://www.channing.harvard.edu/nhs/index.html

Health Care Without Harm
http://www.noharm.org

Nightingale Institute for Health and Environment
http://www.nihe.org

GLOSSARY

administrative law: Governmental agencies develop administrative law based on the authority given to them by legislative bodies.

advocacy: Pleading or defending the causes of others.

allopathic (biomedicine) medicine: Scientific medicine practiced in the United States today.

alternative healing therapies: Outside the realm of allopathic, scientific therapies.

alternative positioning: A negotiation principle that examines conflict on the merits of a situation.

analysis model: Identifies questions to ask when reviewing health-related information.

asynchronous learning: Independent learning that allows students to access classroom and services according to their own time schedule.

ayurvedic medicine: A Hindu system of healing that is holistic and based on balancing elements of the environment with body elements.

bedside or point of care systems: Permits documentation to be performed where the patient is at different times.

browser: A software program that reads information written in programming language.

burnout: Combination of emotions, attitudes, and physical symptoms that contribute to lack of concern for patients and for nursing.

chain of command: Centralized power in organizations characterized by layers of authority.

change: Processes to adjust organizations and environments to make improvements.

care provider: Meeting the needs of patients and coordinating care.

case management: Method to balance quality and costs.

certification: Process for voluntary recognition of expertise in a specific area of nursing.

change agent: Helping others adapt to changing healthcare systems and processes.

chaos: Theory that looks for order in disorganized systems.

Chinese medicine: Based on maintaining a balance between opposing body forces.

civil law: Deals with violations of a person's rights by another.

classification systems: Method for organizing related information.

clinical decision-making: A process of selecting interventions and actions to help clients reach desired outcomes.

clinical pathways: Guide to providing services efficiently to reach expected outcomes in a set timeframe.

collaboration: Working together on joint assignments.

collective bargaining: Actions taken by organized groups of workers to equalize power between employees and employers.

common law: Developed from previous legal decisions to serve as the basis for new decisions.

communication: Transmitting information and influencing others.

communication processes: The elements of communication that explain sending, receiving, and understanding messages.

community-based practice: Defined as people, location, and social systems.

compassionate communication: Based on caring, trust, truth-telling, and maintaining confidentiality.

complementary healing therapies: Alternative therapies that are used with conventional, allopathic therapies. Integrative therapies are those that are used as part of allopathic medicine.

complex, adaptive system: Responds to change by sharing information, uses innovation and creativity, encourages learning, adaptability, and risk-taking.

computer-based patient records (CPR): Description of 12 important features of electronic patient records.

confidentiality: Keeping information private and disclosing only to persons who have a need to know.

conflict: Result of two incompatible events that come together.

coordinator of a transdisciplinary health care team: Organizer of the care that patients receive from several disciplines.

coping strategies: Efforts to reduce situations and events that trigger stress.

cost efficiency: Benefits received are greater than the cost of the service.

criminal law: Protects society from harmful actions.

critical self-assessment: Reviewing how you spend your time.

critical thinking: Discipline of thinking that looks at information and situations fairly and objectively.

cultural assessment of nurses: Examining our own values and beliefs about different cultures.

cultural assessment of patients: Collecting information related to a patient's cultural preferences.

cultural competence: Showing respect and being sensitive to different beliefs and values.

cultural competency staircase model: A self-assessment model for nurses to measure degree of cultural competence.

databases: Collections of files with different types of information, such as text, images, and voice.

decision-making model: Systematic process to make health-related choices.

demographics: Information collected to describe populations (such as age, gender, and ethnic background).

dietary supplements: Vitamin and mineral additions to diets.

documentation: Recording of information in some type of record.

Donabedian model: One approach to defining and measuring healthcare quality.

durable power of attorney for health care: Document that gives another person the legal right to make health care decisions when the other person is incapable of doing so.

early adopters: Persons who are the first to accept innovations.

early majority adopters: Persons who wait to see the impact of innovation.

educational delivery options: Variety of methods used to bring education to learners.

educational material design: Appearance and presentation of information so it is accurate, current, organized, and esthetically pleasing, with appropriate language.

effective communication: When messages are received and understood.

effective leadership qualities: Include integrity, courage, initiative, energy, optimism, perseverance, balance, self-assurance, and the ability to handle stress.

electronic health records (EHRs): Store all a person's health information in a computer-based format that is accessible to other providers.

ethical conflicts: Values and beliefs related to making nursing decisions.

evidence-based practice: Decisions based on both expert clinical decision-making and optimum external evidence.

experiential readiness: Person's previous learning.

failure mode effect analysis: Assumes errors will occur and uses a proactive process to prevent them.

false imprisonment: Confining persons against their will.

formal negotiations: Discussions, governed by labor laws, to reach contract agreements.

good Samaritan laws: Protect health care professionals from being sued when they give aid in emergency situations.

group decision-making: Requires negotiation, consensus, and collaboration for success.

health literacy: Ability to read, understand, and carry out health instructions.

herbal therapies: Plant products used to prevent illness and improve health.

home health care classification: A system used to measure outcomes and effectiveness of health services in the patient's home.

homeopathic medicine: Uses small doses of substances that cause symptoms to stimulate body systems.

humor: Positive way of looking at life and enjoying interactions.

implementing chaos theory: The three phases identified include accepting the challenge, knowledge, and persuasion.

innovation: Introduction of new ideas, processes, and products into our lives.

institutional quality of life: For residents in institutional settings, it means cleanliness, safety, noise control, odor control, autonomy, and freedom to voice concerns.

integrative healing therapies: Therapies used as part of allopathic medicine.

Internet: A worldwide network of computers that ties systems together.

Internet service provider (ISP): Service that provides access to the Internet.

knowledge readiness: Person's previous level of education in a particular area.

laggards: Persons who are the last to accept innovations.

late majority adopters: Persons who wait until there is peer pressure to adopt innovation.

leadership: Ability to influence others.

legislative laws: Regulations passed by legislative bodies at the local state, and federal levels.

libel: Written utterances that are not true and cause harm.

litigation: Legal processes to seek solutions to issues.

living will: Document that makes the wishes of individuals known regarding the type of treatment they want when they are not capable of participating in the decisions.

malpractice: Negligence or malfeasance by members of groups who are professionals, have specialized education, and are responsible for their own actions.

management: Activities that involve coordinating people, time, and supplies.

manager and leader: Organizer of all types of care to improve patient and professional outcomes.

mandatory continuing education: A specified number of educational hours and content required for continuing licensure.

Milstead model: Used to compare the impact of health-related policy decisions in different countries.

mind and body connections/interactions: Link between psychological and physical responses.

modular nursing: Nurses working in a particular geographic area of a facility.

moral distress: Occurs when nurses know what they ought to do but cannot because of administrative policies, physicians, or the threat of legal action.

national health care programs: Provide universal coverage for everyone.

negligence: causing harm to persons you had a duty to protect.

North American Nursing Diagnosis Association (NANDA): Association that categorizes and computerizes patient information specifically for the discipline of nursing.

nursing care delivery models: Approaches to organizing and dispensing care.

nursing informatics: Process of find and using information, computers, and related technology.

Nursing Interventions Classification (NIC) and Nursing Outcomes Classification (NOC): Two systems to classify nursing interventions and nursing outcomes.

Omaha system: Describes and measures patient care categories, primarily for non-institutional settings.

optically scanned records: Paper records scanned by an optical scanner and stored electronically.

organizational climate: Defines how others perceive and feel about an organization.

organizational culture: Combination of beliefs, role of authority, and employee controls and rewards.

osteopathic medicine: Based on a philosophy of wellness and maintaining the integrity of the whole body.

outcome measures: Determine the effectiveness of an institution or system.

partnership model: Co-primary care is a nurse paired with an LVN or CNA who work together consistently.

patient advocate: Promoting the welfare and interests of patients.

primary health care: Focuses on preventing disease or injury.

problem-solver: Uses analytical skills to resolve issues.

professional change: Processes to improve self and the profession.

professional liability insurance: Protects nurses in situations where they are liable for damages.

professional portfolio: Organized way to present the documentation of your professional accomplishments.

professional practice standards: Guidelines, rules, and regulations to govern practice.

proprietary hospitals: Operate as businesses.

public and health policy: Indicate organizational goals, program proposals, and specific rules.

quality assessment: Measuring quality by using standards.

quality assurance: Commitment to carry out quality activities continuously.

quality indicators: Use of professional standards and health services to increase the chance of positive outcomes.

quality report cards: Quality indicators to review when selecting a managed care provider.

redesigning health care: Focuses on who does what jobs and getting work done more efficiently.

reengineering health care: Processes changed to accomplish tasks more efficiently and effectively.

researcher: Develops nursing science to improve patient care and advance the knowledge base of nursing.

respectful communication: Listening attentively, acknowledging what has been said, and showing appreciation for contributions.

résumé: Document that contains professional information and accomplishments.

returning to school syndrome: Phases individuals go through as they fit into a student role.

risk management: Focuses on preventing harmful events in clinical practice and facilities management.

role model: Behaviors that promote positive changes, by being an example to others.

root cause analysis: Used to determine underlying factors that contributed to serious injury.

self-assessment: Process of reviewing your strengths and weaknesses.

self-care choices: Individuals selecting options for their care.

self-contracting: Plan that determines how you will allocate your time.

self-development: Activities that enhance our lives, personally and professionally.

sexual harassment: Sexual favors required for job benefits and hostile environment with sexual references.

shared leadership: Includes shared self-directed teams and shared governance.

slander: Verbal utterances that are not true and cause harm.

social systems: Economic, educational, religious, welfare, political, safety, and other entities.

socialization: Process of fitting into a new role that requires learning expectations, changing behavior, and internalizing new expectations.

spiritual nursing: Acknowledging spiritual distress by listening, sharing prayer, presence, or linking patients to spiritual advisors.

staffing patterns: Actions to ensure there are adequate numbers of health care team members to care for patients.

standardized language: Common terminology shared across disciplines to exchange information.

SWOT: Approach to evaluating Strengths, Weaknesses, Opportunities, and Threats when considering new ventures.

synergy model: Emphasizes how patient care is organized through interdepartmental challenges; supports infrastructures for patient assessments, career advancement, and interdepartmental collaboration.

stress: Physical and psychological responses to alarming situations and events.

stress capacity: Level of stress individuals tolerate before feeling stressed.

team building: Following the principles of dignity, respect, trust, and respect for coworkers to benefit patient care.

time awareness: Paying close attention to time and its relationship to schedules.

time tools: Creative approaches to organizing time.

time wasters: Tasks that have few benefits and satisfaction.

total quality management (TQM): Management philosophy to transform organizations, improve profits, and decrease costs.

transdisciplinary health care: Includes collaboration, redesign, discharge planning, and patient-focused care.

Unified Nursing Language System (UNLS): Common system to evaluate quality and effectiveness of care.

values and beliefs: Criterion we use to judge ourselves, also what we think about the criterion.

verbal conflict: When two or more persons disagree and verbally share opinions.

voluntary hospitals: Have a single mission and are community based.

whistle-blower: Person who reports workplace issues or violations in good faith.

whole person wellness: Caring for self in order to care for others.

workplace violence: Aggression and harmful behaviors at work sites.

World Wide Web (WWW): A worldwide system of databases within the Internet for people to communicate from different sites.

BIBLIOGRAPHY

Activity logs: Finding how you really spend your time. (n.d.). Retrieved November 11, 2002, from http://www.mindtools.com/pages/article/newHTE_03.htm

Allen, S., & Spera, P. (2000). The Nurses in Washington Internship program allows nurses to learn about the legislative process. *AORN Journal, 72*(3):516-521.

Almost, J., & Spence-Laschinger, H. K. (2002). Workplace empowerment, collaborative work relationships, and job strain in nurse practitioners. *Journal of the American Academy of Nurse Practitioners, 14*(9):408-419.

Alters, S., & Schiff, W. *Essential concepts for healthy living, 3rd ed.* Boston: Jones and Bartlett Publishers, 2003.

American Nurses Association. (1980). *Nursing: A Social Policy Statement.* Washington, DC: American Nurses Association Publishing.

American Nurses Association. (1994). The scope of practice for nursing informatics. Washington, DC: American Nurses Publishing.

American Nurses Association. (1995a). *Nursing's Social Policy Statement.* Washington, DC: American Nurses Publishing.

American Nurses Association. (1995b). *Nursing Data Systems: The Emerging Framework.* Washington, DC: American Nurses Publishing.

American Nurses Association. (1995c). American Nurses Association bylaws as amended July 2, 1995. Washington, DC: American Nurses Publishing.

Andrus, M. R., & Roth, M. T. (2002). Health literacy: a review. *Pharmacotherapy, 22*(3):282-302.

Anonymous. (2002a). Expletive deleted. *Nursing, 32*(6):20+.

Anonymous. (2002b). Nurse shortage causes chaos. *Australian Nursing Journal, 10*:(3), 13.

Apker, J. (2001). Role development in the managed care era: a case of hospital-based nursing. *Journal of Applied Communication Research, 29*(2):117-136.

Ash, J. S., Anderson, J. G., Gorman, P. N., Zielstorff, R. D., Norcross, N., Pettit, J., & Yao, P. (2000). Managing change: analysis of a hypothetical case. *The Journal of the American Medical Informatics Association, 7*(2):123-134.

Aumiller, L., & Moskowitz, M. (2002). The staff nurse as risk manager. *Nursing Spectrum,* Retrieved November 21, 2002, from http://nsweb.nursingspectrum.com

Baker, R., Szudy, B., & Guerriero, J. (2000). Working with labor unions. *AAOHN Journal, 48*(12):563+.

Baker, K. N., Flynn, E. A., Pepper, G. A., Bates, D. W., & Mikeal, R. I. (2002). Medication errors observed in 36 health care facilities. *Archives of Internal Medicine, 162*(16):1897+.

Barr, B. J. (2002). Managing change during information systems transition. *AORN Journal, 75*(6):1085-1092.

Bastable, S. B. (2003). *Nurse as Educator: Principles of Teaching and Learning for Nursing Practice.* Boston: Jones and Bartlett Publishers.

Bell, S. K. (2001). Professional nurse's portfolio. *Nursing Administration Quarterly, 25*(2):69-73.

Birx, E. (2003). Nurse, heal thyself. *RN, 66*(1):46-49.

Blair, P. D. (2002). Report impaired practice-stat. *Nursing Management, 33*(1):24-25.

Bowers, B. J., Lauring, C., & Jacobson, N. (2001). How nurses manage time and work in long-term care. *Journal of Advanced Nursing, 33*(4), 484-491.

Brassil, D. F. (2002). Using humor in our daily lives. *Urologic Nursing, 22*(3):144+

Brumm, J. (2002a, March 4). Put time on your side: part 1. *Nursing Spectrum*. Retrieved November 10, 2002, from http://www.nursingspectrum.com/MagazineArticles

Brumm, J. (2002b, April 1). Put time on your side: part 2. *Nursing Spectrum*. Retrieved November 10, 2002, from http://www.nursingspectrum.com/MagazineArticles

Bryant, C., Fairbrother, G., & Fenton, P. The relative influence of personal and workplace descriptors on stress. *British Journal of Nursing, 9*(13):876+

Bureau of Health Professions, Division of Nursing (2000). *The Registered Nurse Population: National Sample Survey of Registered Nurses*. Rockville, MD: Department of Health and Human Service. Retrieved November 23, 2002 from, http://bhpr.hrsa.gov/nursing/sampsurvpre.htm

Buxman, K. (2002). Say it with a smile. *Nursing Management, 33*(1):49+.

Carruth, A. K., Steele, S., Moffett, B., Rehmeyer, T., Cooper, C., & Burroughs, R. (1999). The impact of primary and modular nursing delivery systems on perceptions of caring. *Oncology Nursing Forum, 26*(1):95-100.

Chambers-Clark, C. (2002a). A nurse's sourcebook of complementary therapy. *Nursing Spectrum*. Retrieved November 21, 2002, from http://www.nursingspectrum.com./Articles

Chambers-Clark, C. (2002b). Stress management. *Nursing Spectrum*. Retrieved November 21, 2002, from http://nsweb.nursingspectrum.com/ce

Charles, R. (2000). The challenge of disseminating innovations to direct care providers in health care organizations. *Nursing Clinics of North America, 35*(2):461-470.

Cherry, B., & Jacob, S. R. (2002). *Contemporary Nursing: Issues, Trends, & Management, 2nd ed.* St. Louis: Mosby, Inc.

Coffman, J. M., Seago, J. An., & Spetz, J. (2002). Minimum nurse-to-patient ratios in acute care hospitals in California. *Health Affairs, 21*(5):53-64.

Cook, J. K., Green, M., & Topp, R.V. (2001). Exploring the impact of physician verbal abuse on perioperative nurses. *AORN Journal, 74*(3), 317-331.

Cosentino, B.W. (2002). Stressed out. *Nursing Spectrum*. Retrieved November 21, 2002, from http://community.nursingspectrum.com

Craig, A. E. (2002, November 11). Personal digital assistant use: practical advice for the advanced practice nurse. *Topics in Advanced Practice Nursing e-Journal, 2*(4): 6 pages. Retrieved November 23, 2002, from http://www.medscape.com

Cranston, M. (2002). Clinical effectiveness and evidence-based practice. *Nursing Standard, 16*(24):39+.

Cumbie, S. A. (2001). The integration of mind-body-soul and the practice of humanistic nursing. *Holistic Nursing Practice, 15*(3):56-62.

Cymerman, E. H. (2002). Nurturing yourself: A luxury or necessity? *Nursing Spectrum*. Retrieved November 21, 2002, from http://community.nursingspectrum.com

Danis, S., Forman, H., & Simek, P. P. (2002). The nurse-physician relationship: can it be saved? *Nursing Spectrum.* Retrieved November 21, 2002, from http://www.nursingspectrum.com./Articles

Detmer, S. S. (2002). Coaching your unit team for results. *Seminar for Nurse Managers, 10*(3):189-196.

Domrose, C. (2003). Fruitful strides in self-care. *NurseWeek.* Retrieved January 25, 2003, from http://www.nurseweek.com

Dowling, J. S. (2002). Humor: a coping strategy for pediatric patients. *Pediatric Nursing, 28*(2):123-131.

Dunbar, C. (2002, June 3). Time management for Alice and other new managers. *Nursing Spectrum.* Retrieved November 10, 2002, from http://www.nursingspectrum.com/Magazine Articles

Dwyer, D., Holloran, P., & Walsh, K. (2002). "Why didn't I know?" the reality of impaired nurses. *Connecticut Nursing News, 75*(1):20+.

Dykes, P. C., & Wheeler, K. (2000). Evidence-based practice. *Nursing Spectrum.* Retrieved December 26, 2002, from http://www.nursingspectrum.com

Eliopoulos, C. (2001). *Gerontological Nursing.* Philadelphia: Lippincott Williams & Wilkins.

Ennen, K. A. (2001). Shaping the future of practice through political activity: how nurses can influence health care policy. *AAOHN Journal, 49*(12):557-571.

Franko, F. P. (2002). Circling the wagons. *AORN Journal, 76*(1):176-181.

Gates, D. M., Fiztwater, E., & Meyer, U. (1999). Violence against caregivers in nursing homes: expected, tolerated, and accepted. *Journal of Gerontological Nursing, 25*(4):12+.

George, V., Burke, L. J., Rodgers, B., Dithie, N., Hoffmann, M. L., Koceja, V., et al. (2002). Developing staff nurse shared leadership behavior in professional nursing practice. *Nursing Administration Quarterly, 26*(3):44-59.

Gordon, S. (2000). Nurse, interrupted. *The American Prospect, 11*(7):1.

Gray, L., & Warrington, G. (2002). When the unexpected happens. *Nursing BS, 34*(1):7-9.

Greggs-McQuilkin, D. (2002). Nurses have the power to be advocates. *MedSurg Nursing, 11*(6):265-266.

Griffin, H. (2002). Embracing diversity. *Nurse Week.* Retrieved January 25, 2003, from http://www.nurseweek.com/news/features/02-12/diversity.asp

Griffith, J. (1999). Substance abuse disorders in nurses. *Nursing Forum, 34*(4):19-28.

Haddad, A. (2002). Ethics in action: an ethical view of burnout. *RN, 65*(9):25-28.

Hageseth, C. (1988). *A Laughing Place.* Fort Collins, CO: Berwick Publishing Company.

Hart-Wasekeeikaw, F. (2003). Profiles in caring. *Reflections on Nursing Leadership, 29*(1):18-21.

Harter, T. W. (2001). Minimizing absenteeism in the workplace: strategies for nurse managers. *Nursing Economics, 19*(2):53-55.

Hartley, L. A. (2002). Using the primary care assessment survey in an ambulatory setting. *Nursing Economics, 20*(5):235, 236, 248.

Hayward, M., & Porter, E. (2001). Educating the next generation of health professionals. *Community Practitioner, 74*(2):68+.

Herbert, M. (Winter, 1999). Leading from the edge. *Nursing Administration Quarterly, 23*(2), 23-27.

Hinderer, D. E., & Hinderer, S. R. (2001). *A Multidisciplinary Approach to Health Care Ethics.* Mountain View, CA: Mayfield Publishing Company.

Hogstel, M. O. (2001). *Gerontology: Nursing Care of the Older Adult.* Albany, NY: Delmar.

Hood, L. J., & Leddy, S. K. (2003). *Conceptual Bases of Professional Nursing.* Philadelphia: Lippincott Williams & Wilkins.

Howard-Ruben, J. (2002). Side by side: study says collaboration key to quality care. *Nursing Spectrum.* Retrieved November 21, 2002, from http://www.nursingspectrum.com./Articles

Hunt, R. (2001). *Introduction to Community-Based Nursing.* Philadelphia: Lippincott.

Jackson, P. L., (2002). A systems approach to delivering clinical preventive services. *Pediatric Nursing, 28*(4):377-381.

Jech, A. O. (2003). The healing power of humor. *Nursing Spectrum.* Retrieved February 12, 2003, from http://nsweb.nursingspectrum.com

Joint Commission on Accreditation of Healthcare Organizations (JCAHO) (2002, October). JCAHO proposes solutions to nusing shortage. *Healthcare Financial Management, 56*(10):11.

Kalina, C. M., Haag, A. B., Tourigian, R., & Wassel, M. L. (2002). What is the difference between absence tracking and case management? *AAOHN Journal, 50*(7):300+

Keegan, L. (2001). *Healing With Complementary & Alternative Therapies.* Albany, NY: Delmar.

Kersey-Matusiak, G. (2002). An action plan for cultural competence. *Nursing Spectrum.* Retrieved November 21, 2002, from http://nsweb.nursingspectrum.com/ce/ce255.htm

Kerfoot, K. (2001). The leader as synergist. *Pediatric Nursing, 27*(1):108-109.

Kerfoot, K. (2002). Leading the leaders: The challenge of leading an empowered organization. *Nursing Economics, 20*(3) 133-134+.

Kohn, L., Corrigan, J., & Donaldson, M. (1999). *To Err is Human: Building a Safer Health System.* Washington, DC: Institute of Medicine, National Academy Press.

Kozlowski, D. (2002). Returning to school: an alternative to "traditional" education. *Orthopedic Nursing, 21*(4):41-47.

LaDuke, S. (200). How to ace risk management 101. *Nursing, 32*(10):55+.

Lafferty, S., & Baird, M. (2001). *Tele-Nurse: Telephone Triage Protocols.* Albany, NY: Delmar.

Lanza, M. L. (2000). Nonlinear dynamics: chaos and catastrophic theory. *Journal of Nursing Care Quarterly, 15*(1):55-65.

Ledger, S. D. (2002). Reflections on communicating with non-English-speaking patients. *British Journal of Nursing, 11*(11):773+.

Lewis, J. A., & Kruckenberg-Scofer, K. K. (2000). New roles for nurses. *Surgical Services Management, 6*(8):13+.

Lowden, C. (2001). Eeek! It's another growth opportunity! *Nephrology Nursing Journal, 28*(2):270+.

Ludwick, R., & Silva, M. C. (2000). Nursing around the world: Cultural values and ethical conflicts. *Online Journal of Issues in Nursing.* Retrieved December 26, 2002, from http://nursingworld.org/ojin/ethicol/ethics_4.htm

Makhija, N. (2002). Spiritual nursing. *Nursing Journal of India, 93*(6):129+.

Manion, J. (2002). Life at the crossroads. *NursingCenter.* Retrieved November 23, 2002, from http://www.nursingcenter.com/Career Center/articles.asp

Marquis, B. L., & Huston, C. J. (2003). *Leadership roles and management functions in nursing: Theory and application.* Philadelphia: Lippincott Williams & Wilkins.

McCaffree, J. (2001). Techno-tools for tracking outcomes. *Journal of the American Dietetic Association, 101*(11):1310-1311.

McElhaney, R. (2002). Conflict management. *Nursing Spectrum.* Retrieved November 21, 2002, from http://www.nursingspectrum.com

Mee, C. I. (2001). Going for the gold. *Nursing, 31*(3):8+.

Mee, C. L. (2002). Battling burnout. *Nursing, 32*(8):8+.

Milstead, J. A. (1999). *Health Policy and Politics.* Gaithersburg, MD: Aspen Publishers, Inc.

Mintzer, B. (2001). The power of a vision: the nurse's journey through health care. *AAOHN Journal, 49*(10):478-483.

Mischenko, J. (2002). A framework for self-managed teams. *Community Practitioner, 75*(6):218-225.

Mooney, N. E. (2003). The therapeutic use of humor. *Orthopedic Nursing, 19*(3):88-92.

Murphy, K. J. (2002). Forensic Nursing. *Nursing Spectrum.* Retrieved November 21, 2002, from http://nsweb.nursingspectrum.com/Articles

Nardini, J. M. (2000). Enriching our practice through culturally competent care. *Nephrology Nursing Journal, 27*(4):353-354.

Nazarko, L. (2002). A catastrophe waiting to happen. *Nursing Management, 9*(3):30+.

Nies, M., & McEwen, (2001). *Community Health Nursing Promoting the Health of Populations.* Philadelphia: W. B. Saunders.

NurseWeek (2002). Career advancement tool. Retrieved December 20, 2002, from http://www.nurseweek.com

O'Grady, T. P. (2000). Laughter lightens our load. *Nursing, 30*(7):6+.

Pesut, D. J., & Herman, J. (1999). *Clinical Reasoning: The Art and Science of Critical and Creative Thinking.* Albany, NY: Delmar Publishers.

The Pew Health Professions Commission. (1991). *Health America: Practitioners for 2005, An Agenda for Action for U. S. Health Professional Schools.* San Francisco: Author.

Pindus, N. M., & Greiner, A. (1997). The effects of health care industry changes on health care workers and quality of patient care: summary of literature. *Urban Institute.* Retrieved November 23, 2002, from http://www.urban.org/health/pindus.htm

Rankin, A. L. (2002). A descriptive study of registered nurses' experiences with web-based learning. *Journal of Advances in Nursing, 40*(4):457-465.

Ray, M. A., Turkel, M. C., & Marino, F. (2002). The transformative process for nursing in workforce redevelopment. *Nursing Administration Quarterly, 26*(2):1-14.

Redding, D. A., & Anglin, L. T. How many is too many? Collaboration of multiple nursing organizations for professional development. *The Journal of Continuing Education in Nursing, 33*(3):126+.

Restifo, V. (2002). Surviving and thriving with conflict on the job. *Nursing Spectrum.* Retrieved November 21, 2002, from http://www.nursingspectrum.com/Articles

Rideout, E. (2001). *Transforming Nursing Education Through Problem-Based Learning.* Sudbury, MA: Jones and Bartlett Publishers.

Roberts, S. J. (2000). Development of a positive professional identity: liberating oneself from the oppressor within. *Advances in Nursing Science, 22*(4):71-82.

Robinson, D., & Kish, C. P. (2001). *Core concepts in Advanced Practice Nursing.* St. Louis: Mosby.

Rojak, J. (2000). How to get your career going. *Nursing, 30*(6):76-77.

Sanon-Rollins, C. (2002). Surviving conflict on the job. *Nursing Spectrum.* Retrieved November 21, 2002, from http://www.nursingspectrum.com/Articles

Schardt, C. M., Garrison, J., & Kochi, J. K. (2002). Distance education or classroom instruction for continuing education: who retains more knowledge? *Journal of the Medical Library Association, 90*(4):455-457.

Schenk, S., & Hartley, K. (2002). Nurse coach: healthcare resource for this millennium. *Nursing Forum, 37*(3):14-20.

Scherrer, C. S. (2001). Outreach to community organizations: The next consumer health frontier. *Journal of the American Medical Library Association, 90*(3):285-293.

Schroeter, K., (2002). Ethics in perioperative practice: patient advocacy. *AORN Journal, 75*(5):941-949.

Shannon, S. E., Mitchell, P. H., & Cain, K. C. (2002). Patients, nurses, and physicians have differing views of quality critical care. *Journal of Nursing Scholarship, 34*(2):173+.

Shaw, A. Lessons in empowerment. (2002). *Nursing Times, 98*(26):36-37.

Sheehan, J. P. (2002). A liability checklist for clinical pathways. *Nursing Management, 33*(2):23-25.

Sherman, F. T. (2002). Nurses, nurses, nurses: you can't live without them. *Geriatrics, 57*(12):7.

Sherry, D. (2002). Time management strategies for the home care nurse. *Home Healthcare Nurse, 20*(5), 340-341.

Shi, L., & Singh, D. A. (1998). *Delivering Health Care in America: A Systems Approach.* Gaithersburg, MD: Aspen Publishers, Inc.

Shneiderman, B. (2002). *Leonardo's Laptop: Human Needs and the New Computing Technologies.* Cambridge, MA: The Massachusetts Institute of Technology Press.

Simms, C. (2000). Stopping the word war. *Nursing Management, 31*(9):65-71.

Simpson, R. L. (2002). IT alleviates health care's "healing crisis." *Nursing Management, 33*(7):8-10.

Sloan, A., & Vernarec, E. (2001). Impaired nurses reclaiming careers. *RN, 64*(2):58-64.

Smith, A. P. (2002, Jan/Feb.) In search of safety: an interview with Gina Pugliese. *Nursing Economics, 20*(1):6-12.

Smith, A. P. (2002, Nov/Dec). Responses to the nursing shortage: policy, press, pipeline, and perks. *Nursing Economics, 20*(16):287+.

Smith, S. B., Tutor, R. S., & Phillips, M. L. (2001). Resolving conflict realistically in today's health care environment. *Journal of Psychosocial Nursing & Mental Health Services, 39*(11):36-43.

Smith-Higuchi, K. A., & Donald, J. G. (2002). Thinking processes uses used by nurse in clinical decision-making. *Journal of Nursing Education, 41*(4):145+.

Snyder, M. (2001). Overview and summary of complementary therapies: are these really nursing? *Online Journal of Issues in Nursing, 6*(2). Retrieved December 26, 2002, http://nursingworld.org/ojin/topic15/tpc15ntr.htm

Snyder, M., & Lindquist, R. (2001). Issues in complementary therapies: How we got to where we are. *Online Journal of Issues in Nursing, 6*(2); Retrieved December 26, 2002, http://nursingworld.org/ojin/topic15/tpc15_1.htm

Steefel, L. (2002). Hands-on collaboration. *Nursing Spectrum.* Retrieved December 26, 2002, from http://www.nursingspectrum.com/ Articles

Stein, A. M. (2001). Learning and change among leaders of a professional nursing association. *Holistic Nursing Practice, 16*(1): 5-15.

Strasser, P. B. (2002a). Managing during times of uncertainty: Part I, short term strategies. *AAOHN Journal, 50*(4):165-166.

Strasser, P. B. (2002b). Managing during times of uncertainty: Part II, long term strategies. *AAOHN Journal, 50*(8):351-352.

Tappen, R. M., Weiss, S. A., & Whitehead, D. K. (2001). *Essentials of Nursing Leadership and Management.* Philadelphia: F. A. Davis Company.

Tiedje, L. B. (2000). Moral distress in perinatal nursing. *Journal of Perinatal & Neonatal Nursing, 14*(2):36-43.

Tingle, J. (2002). Health professionals keep making the same mistakes. *British Journal of Nursing, 11*(7):414+.

Trossman, S. (2001). Illinois RNs win workplace safety measures. *American Nurse, 33*(1):1+.

Tryens, E., Coulston, L., & Tlush, E. (2003, January). Understanding the complexities of herbal medicine. *Nursing Spectrum Southern Edition,* 26-30.

Ufema, J. (2002). Help for beleaguered staff. *Nursing, 32*(5):65-66.

U.S. Department of Health and Human Services. (2000). *Healthy People 2010: National Health Promotion and Disease Prevention Objectives, Full Report With Commentary.* Washington, DC: U.S. Government Printing Office.

United States Department of Labor. (2001). *Occupation Outlook Handbook, 2000-2001.* Washington, DC: United State Government Printing Office.

University of Iowa. (1999). Center for Nursing Classification & Clinical Effectiveness. Retrieved June 16, 2003, from http://www. nursing.uiowa.edu/centers/cncce

Wakefield, M. R. (2002). Turning up the volume to battle chronic illness. *Nursing Economics, 20*(5):229-231.

Wenckus, E. (2002). Working with an interdisciplinary team. *Nursing Spectrum.* Retrieved November 21, 2002, from http://www.nursing spectrum.com./Articles

West, M. M. (2002). Early risk indicators of substance abuse among nurses. *Journal of Nursing Scholarship, 34*(2):187+.

Wieck, K. L., Prydun, M., & Walsh, T. (2002). What the emerging workforce wants in its leaders. *Journal of Nursing Scholarship, 34*(3):283-290.

Williams, T. (2002). Patient empowerment and ethical decision making: the patient/partner and the right to act. *Dimensions of Critical Care Nursing, 21*(3):100+.

Wolf, Z. R. (2002). Preventing medical errors: Florida requirement. *Nursing Spectrum.* Retrieved November 21, 2002, from http://nsweb.nursingspectrum.com

Wolfe, L. C., & Selekman, J. (2002). School nurses: what it was and what it is. *Pediatric Nursing, 28*(4):403-407.

Young, K. M. (2000). *Informatics for Healthcare professionals.* Philadelphia: F. A. Davis Company.

Zurlinden, J. (2002). Opportunities in case management. *Nursing Spectrum.* Retrieved November 21, 2002, from http://nsweb.nursing spectrum.com/Articles

INDEX

A

absenteeism, 138-139

accommodation approach, 52

acupuncture
as alternative therapy, 113
as alternative to methadone, 116

advance directives, 153

advanced practice nursing, 194

advocacy
burnout/moral distress and, 159
dealing with opposing loyalties, 160-161
from moral distress to moral work/action, 159-160
leadership skills for professional, 159
nurse responsibility for, 150, 159
by nurses for each other, 161
patient, 160-161, 190
for patient empowerment, 161
for specific age groups, 161

AFL-CIO (American Federation of Labor Congress of Industrial Organizations), 143

African American nurses, 123, 124

AHCPR (Agency for Health Care Policy and Research), 37

AHEC (Maine Area Health Education Center), 76

allopathic (biomedicine) medicine, 112

alternative therapies. See CAM (complimentary and alternative medicine)

AMA (American Medical Association), 144

ambulatory care settings, 192

American Association of Critical Care Nurses, 60

American Nurses Association, 35, 86, 94, 142

American Nurses Foundation, 124

ANA Code for Nurses, 94, 160

anxiety levels, 170

Area Agencies on Aging, 150

assault (threat to harm), 149

assessment
cultural nutrition, 127-128
nurses'/patient's cultural, 127
quality, 89-91
self-assessment, 1

asynchronous learning, 174

autocratic/authoritative leadership, 58, 59

avoidance approach, 52-53

ayurvedic medicine, 112

B

back injuries, 137

battery (touching without consent), 149

bedside (point-of-care) systems, 26

behavioral theories, 59

brainstorming, 103

British National Health Service, 34

burnout, 159

business/corporate nursing careers, 193-194

C

CAM (complimentary and alternative medicine)
categories of therapies in, 113t
classifications of therapies in, 113
defining, 111
dietary supplements as, 114
healing therapies/traditions using, 112-113
herbal therapies as, 114-115
legal dilemmas of, 115
NCCAM study of, 115
nurse education on, 117
nursing and use of, 116-117
patient self-care choices for, 109-111
payment for, 115-116
reasons for selecting, 110-111
safety issues of, 115
See also patient self-care choices

career management. See nursing career management

care provider role, 190

case management
application to nursing practice, 88
background of, 87-88

case managers, 194

CDC (Centers for Disease Control and Prevention), 76

CDC Web site, 37

CE Evidence-Based Medicine course, 174

change agent role, 28-29, 190
See also innovation

chaos
challenges of living with, 12
relationships and, 13
as state of the world, 11
See also thriving on chaos

chaos theory
  application to health systems, 13-14
  application to nursing practice, 14-16
  described, 12-13
chaotic relationships, 13
charting
  organizing your, 26-27
  as part of legal case, 151-152
  See also documenting patient care
Chi Eta Phi, 124
Chinese medicine, 112
CINAHL, 35-36
civil law, 148-149
classification systems
  listing of some established medical, 37-38
  nursing, 38-39
clinical pathways, 79-80
clinical setting
  application of communication skills in, 24-25
  decision-making in, 64, 86-87
CNAs (certified nursing assistants), 135
coaching relationships, 62-63
Code for Nurses (ANA), 94
cognitive ability, 172
collaboration approach
  to multidisciplinary health care, 102-103
  negotiation element of, 102
  to resolving conflict, 53
collective bargaining
  formal negotiations involved in, 143-144
  pros and cons of, 144
  purpose of, 143
communication
  application in clinical setting, 24-25
  challenges of, 23
  circular process of, 22*fig*
  compassionate, 24
  culturally respectful, 23-24, 128
  dealing with verbal conflict, 27-28
  effective, 23
  as essential to learning new nursing roles, 191
  importance of, 21-22
  verbal/nonverbal processes of, 22
  used as voice for professional change, 28-29
community-based practice
  described, 78
  models for care, 78-79
  modular nursing in, 79
  as nursing employment setting, 192*t*
  partnership model of, 79
community education, 150, 193
community nursing centers, 193

compassionate communication, 24
competition approach, 52
compromise approach, 53
computer technology
  business/institutional systems of, 35
  CPR (computer-based patient records), 39-40
  learning to use, 34
  See also information technology (IT); technology
confidentiality issues, 149, 161-162
conflict
  cultural competence and ethical, 128
  resolving, 52-53
  solutions to, 53-54
  sources of, 52
  verbal, 27-28, 104-105
consulting, 194
coordinator role, 190
coping statements, 203
coping strategies, 203
counselor role, 190
CPR (computer-based patient records), 39-40
criminal laws, 148
critical thinking, 86
cultural assessment, 127
cultural competence
  barriers to, 123
  caring for persons from different cultures and, 126-129
  demographic trends requiring, 122-123
  ethical conflicts and, 128
  health in context of cultural values/beliefs, 124-125
  introduction to, 122
  nursing challenges of, 121-122
  respectful communication and, 23, 128
  understanding cultural beliefs on sickness/cures, 128
  See also organizational cultures
Cultural Competency Staircase Model, 127
cultural nutrition assessment, 127-128
Current Medicare Beneficiary Survey, 91

D
dandelion, 114-115
decision-making
  leadership/management, 64
  quality care and clinical, 86-87
democratic/participate leadership, 58, 59
demographics
  of health care workers, 123
  trends of U.S., 122
  of violence, 123
deterministic relationships, 13
dietary supplements, 114
dietitian, 101

discharge planning, 87-88

distance education, 173-174

division of labor, 50

documenting patient care

    appropriate forms of, 26-27

    as part of legal case, 151-152

    patient/family teaching included in, 27

    purposes of health records, 25

    sources of information/records, 25-26

    See also charting

Donabedian model, 91

DRGs (Diagnosis Related Groups), 37, 79-80

DSHEA (Dietary Supplement Health and Education), 115

DSM-IV (Diagnostic and Statistical Manual of Mental
    Disorders), 38

durable power of attorney for health care, 153

E

early adopters, 16, 17

early majority adopters, 16

Earth Summit (1992), 126, 220

education

    asynchronous learning, 174

    community, 150, 193

    distance, 173-174

    documenting family and patient, 27

    on nurse impairment, 141-142

    See also learning readiness; nursing education

educator role, 190

effective communication, 23

EHR (electronic health records), 26

elderly patients, 24

emotional readiness to learn, 170-171

employees

    collective bargaining by, 143-144

    sexual harassment of, 136

    staffing patterns/work hours of, 137-141

    workplace safety issues of, 134-137

    See also health care workers

empowerment

    application to nursing practice, 63

    impact on nursing work environments, 61-63

environment

    achieving healthy personal/work, 219-221

    empowerment impact on nursing work, 61-63

    staffing patterns and work, 138

    thriving on chaos of work, 12

    UN efforts to improve global, 126, 220

    workplace safety issues and physical, 137

ethical caring, 162-163

ethical practice

    advocacy and, 159-162

    Code for Nurses (ANA) on, 94

    confidentiality issues and, 149, 161-162

    cultural competence and, 128

    International Code for Nurses on, 126

    nurses and challenges of, 157-158

    overview of, 157

    participating in research and, 162

    public and health policy ethics and, 158

evidence-based practice

    application to nursing practice, 93-94

    barriers to implementation of, 94

    described, 93

experiential readiness to learn, 171-172

F

Faculty Loan Repayment Grants, 139

false imprisonment, 149

family education documentation, 27

FDA (Food and Drug Administration), 115

flight nurse, 195

FMEA (failure mode effect analysis), 152

forensic nursing, 193

frame of mind, 171

Framework Convention on Climate Change (1992), 126

G

gate-keeping functions, 87

Geriatric Nurse Training Grants, 139

ginkgo, 114

ginseng, 114

global positioning satellites, 34

Good Samaritan laws, 149

group decision-making, 64

H

HCPCS (Health Care Financing Administration Common
    Procedures Coding System), 38

healing therapies

    categories of, 113*t*

    classifications of, 113

    defining alternative, 112

    traditions of alternative, 112-113

healing through humor, 211

health

    international perspectives on, 124-126

    Internet as source of information on, 35-37, 222

    relationship between humor and, 210-211

    whole personal wellness approach to, 217-219

health care

    redesigning/reengineering, 49-51

    transdisciplinary, 99-106

    See also nursing care

health care advice lines employment, 194

health care delivery

    challenges of, 71-72

choosing a model for nursing, 80-81
clinical pathways approach to, 79-80
community-based practice, 78-79
current state in U.S., 72
health literacy element of, 75-76
hospitals and, 73-75
in other countries, 72
strengths/weakness of U.S., 72-73
systems approach to preventive, 77
See also nursing care delivery model
health care organizations
culture/climate of, 45-47
empowered, 61-63
evolution of processes in, 50
formal structures of, 48-49
informal structures of, 49
types of, 47-49
health care workers
CNAs (certified nursing assistants), 135
demographics of, 123
preventive practice by, 149-151
relationships between nurses and physicians, 99, 104-
    106
transdisciplinary, 101-102, 105*t*
types of laws affecting, 148-149
workplace issues for, 133-144
See also employees
health insurance
NEPs (needle exchange programs) and, 125-126
payment for alternative therapies by, 115-116
health literacy, 75-76
health policy ethics, 158-159
health systems, application of chaos theory to, 13-14
healthy environment
importance of achieving, 219-220
joint work space and, 220-221
noise pollution and, 126, 220
Healthy People 2010, 110
HEDIS (Health Plan Employer Data and Information
    Set), 93
herbal therapies, 114-115
holistic medicine. *See* CAM (complimentary and alterna-
    tive medicine)
Holmes-Rahe scale, 201
Home Health Care Classification, 38-39
homeopathic medicine, 112
hospitals
comparing public and private, 74
comparing voluntary and propriety, 73-74
disciplinary actions by, 142
as nurse employment setting, 191*t*
staffing patterns/work hours in, 137-141

types of services by, 73, 74-75
workplace safety issues and, 134-137, 142-143
humor
challenge of using appropriate, 209
healing through, 211
positive, 210-211
role in nursing practice, 211-213
value of laughter and, 210
hypothesizing, 65, 86

I

ICD-9 (International Classification of Diseases), 37
ICIDH (International Classification of Impairments,
    Disabilities, and Handicaps), 38
ICN (International Council of Nurses), 126
if-then thinking, 65, 86
Illinois Nurses Association, 135
impaired nurses. *See* nurse impairment
Individuals with Disabilities Act of 1975/1997, 77
Industrial Revolution, 219-220
informatics nurse specialist, 194
information
advantages of using standardized language, 37-38
challenges of managing, 33
sorting database, 36
sources of patient health, 25-26
technology impact on sharing, 33-34
using technology to organize, 37
WWW (World Wide Web) as source of, 35-37, 222
information technology (IT)
CPR (computer-based patient records), 39-40
used for nursing education, 40-41, 172, 173-174
as source of health information, 35-37, 222
See also computer technology
innovation
accepting, 16-17
impact on nurses/health care professionals, 17
managing, 17-18
promoting professional changes and, 28-29, 190
See also change agent role
innovators, 16, 17
Inova Health System, 13
institutional quality of life, 89
insurance
NEPs (needle exchange programs) and health, 125-
    126
payment for alternative therapies by health, 115-116
professional liability, 150-151
insurance/managed care companies, 193
International Code for Nurses, 126
international nursing, 126
Internet, 35, 222
interviewing skills, 183-184

IOM (Institute of Medicine), 143
IRBs (Institutional Review Boards), 162
ISP (Internet service provider), 35

J

JCAHO (Joint Commission on Accreditation of Healthcare Organizations), 100
Johnson & Johnson, 140
joint work space, 220-221

K

knowledge readiness, 172
knowledge work, 86

L

laggards, 16, 17
laissez-faire/hands-off leadership, 58, 59
late majority adopters, 16, 17
latex allergy, 135
laughter. *See* humor
laws
    defining and creation of, 148
    ethics of public and health policy and, 158-159
    types affecting health care workers, 148-149
    See also legal issues
leader role, 190
leadership
    application to nursing practice, 59-60
    challenges of, 57-58
    comparison of management and, 61, 62*t*
    decision-making and, 64
    modeling and role modeling theory and, 66-67
    problem-solving and, 65-66
    professional advocacy and, 159
    synergy model of, 60-61
    traits in emerging/entrenched, 61*t*
leadership theories, 58-59
learning readiness
    conditions required for, 169-170
    emotional readiness and, 170-171
    experiential readiness and, 171-172
    knowledge readiness and, 172
    See also education
legal issues
    of CAM (complimentary and alternative medicine), 115
    common litigation areas, 151-152
    hypothetical solution to, 153-154
    nurses and challenges of, 147
    nurses as targets of lawsuits, 147-148
    risk management applied to, 152-154
    See also laws
level of aspiration, 171
liability insurance, 150-151

libel (written word), 149
life balance
    achieving health environment for, 219-221
    challenges of maintaining, 217
    maintaining total wellness and, 221-222
    whole person wellness and, 217-219
lifestyle changes
    health benefits of, 202
    strategies for, 202-203
Lincoln Hospital (New York), 116
living wills, 153

M

male nurses, 123-124
malpractice
    common areas of litigation, 151-152
    legal definition of, 149
    preventive practice to avoid, 149-151
    professional liability insurance and, 150-151
    risk management to avoid, 152-154
managed care employment, 193
management
    application to nursing practice, 59-60
    challenges of, 57-58
    changing attitudes toward workplace violence by, 135
    comparison of leadership and, 61, 62*t*
    decision-making and, 64
    defining, 58
    problem-solving and, 65-66
management theory, 58
manager role, 190
mandatory overtime, 140-141
Mayo physician liaison program, 103
MCOs (managed care organizations), 87
Medicaid reimbursement, 140
Medicare Prospective Payment System, 92
Medicare reimbursement, 140
medication
    risk management to avoid errors in, 152
    study on defective administration of, 143
MEDLINE, 35
Mercer Medical Center, 13-14
Metrowest Community Health Care Foundation, 140
Milstead model, 125
mind-body connection
    life balance and, 219
    stress and, 200
minority nurses, 123-124
modular nursing, 79
moral distress
    described, 159
    moving to moral work/action from, 159-160

motivation to learn, 171

MRM (modeling and role-modeling), 66-67

multi-voting technique, 103

myths about time, 2-3

N

NACGN (National Association of Colored Graduate Nurses), 123

NALS (National Adult Literacy Survey), 75

NANDA (North American Nursing Diagnosis Association), 38

National Committee for Quality Assurance, 93

National Health Interview Survey, 91

National Health Service, 152

National Hospital Discharge Survey, 91

National Institute for Occupational Health and Safety, 137

National League of Nursing, 36

National Library of Medicine, 35

National Nurse Service Corps, 139

National Student Nurses Association, 124

NCCAM (National Center for Complementary and Alternative Medicine), 115

needlestick injuries, 136-137

NEPs (needle exchange programs), 125-126

NIC (Nursing Interventions Classification), 39

NOC (Nursing Outcomes Classification), 39

noise pollution, 126, 220

nonverbal communication, 22

Nurse Education Act, 139

nurse entrepreneurs, 194

nurse impairment

 common indicators/risk factors of, 141

 disciplinary actions due to, 142

 increasing education on, 141-142

 patient safety and, 142-143

 protecting whistle-blowers on, 142

 public policy ethics and, 158

 recovery from, 142

Nurse Reinvestment Act, 139

nurses

 advocating for each other, 161

 becoming voice for professional change, 28-29

 benefits of humor for, 211-212

 broadening vision as, 47

 challenges of transdisciplinary health care for, 99

 challenging of managing technology/information, 33-41

 communication skills needed by, 21-25, 128

 conflict/resolution strategies for, 27-28, 52-54

 cultural assessment of, 127

 decision-making and, 64

 employment settings for, 192*t*

 empowerment and, 61-63

 impact of innovation on, 17

 impairment suffered by, 141-143, 158

 leadership traits of emerging/entrenched, 61*t*

 learning about CAM, 117

 modeling and role modeling by, 66-67

 preventive practice by, 149-151

 problem-solving by, 65-66

 recruitment of minority, 123-124

 responsibility to advocate for patients, 150, 159-162

 shortage of, 139-141

 staffing patterns/work hours of, 137-141

 transdisciplinary health care relationships of physicians and, 104-105

nurse to patient ratios, 140

nursing care

 combined therapies and, 116-117

 cultural competence and, 23, 121-129

 health literacy promotion element of, 75-76

 primary health care activities included in, 75

 spiritual, 116-117

 See also health care

nursing care delivery model

 choosing a, 80-81

 clinical pathways approach to, 79-80

 community-based practice, 78-79

 See also health care delivery

nursing career management

 beginning your, 180

 challenges of, 179-180

 at the crossroads of, 180-181

 interviewing and, 183-184

 opportunities and, 192-195

 overview of, 179

 planning your future/SWOT analysis of, 181-182

 professional portfolio used in, 182-183

 résumés used in, 183

 self-development strategies for, 184-186

nursing education

 on CAM (complimentary and alternative medicine), 117

 CE Evidence-Based Medicine course, 174

 challenges of continuing, 167

 delivery options for, 173-174

 educational material design used in, 172-173

 formal and informal, 167-169

 information technology (IT) used in, 40-41, 172, 173-174

 as nursing employment setting, 192*t*

 readiness to learn and, 169-172

 See also education

nursing homes
    litigation over, 152
    as nursing employment setting, 192*t*
    workplace violence in, 135-136
nursing opportunities, 192-195
nursing practice
    application of case management to, 88
    application of chaos theory to, 14-16
    application of communication skills in clinical, 24-25
    application of CPR (computer-based patient records) to, 40
    application of empowerment to, 63
    application of quality care to, 89-90
    application of shared leadership to, 59-60
    application of time management to, 4-5
    available opportunities in, 192-195
    changing/reengineering health care systems and, 50-51
    changing roles/opportunities in, 189-195
    ethical, 94, 126, 128, 157-164
    impact of changes on, 51
    international, 126
    managing innovation to improve, 17-18
    managing your career in, 179-186
    modular, 79
    preventive, 149-151
    professional practice standards of, 94-95
    quality care as core value of, 85
    role of humor in, 211-213
    school nurses and primary care, 77-78
nursing roles
    coaching as new, 191-192
    communication as essential to learning, 191
    emerging, 189-190
    managing changing, 190-191
    seven major, 190
    traditional, 189
nursing shortage
    impact on staffing by, 139-140
    mandatory overtime due to, 140-141
nursing time management skills
    combining tasks, 5
    minimizing time for required tasks, 4
    pacing work, 5
    prioritizing work, 4-5

O

OAM (Office of Alternative Medicine), 115
obesity, 110
occupational health employment, 194
Occupational Safety and Health Act (1970), 134
occupational therapist, 102
Omaha system, 38

Online Journal of Nursing Informatics, 36
optically scanned records, 26
organizational climate
    challenges of, 45-46
    described, 46
    values/beliefs/goals influencing, 46-47
organizational cultures
    challenges of, 45-46
    overview of, 45
    values/beliefs/goals making up, 46-47
    See also cultural competence
orientation, 172
OSHA (Occupational Safety and Health Administration), 134
osteopathic medicine, 112-113

P

pacing work, 5
paper records, 25-26
paralanguage, 22
partnership model, 79
pastoral representative, 101
patient advocacy, 160-161
patient education documentation, 27
patient health records
    CPR (computer-based patient records), 39-40
    future health care technologies for, 34
    purposes of, 25
    sources of information on, 25-26
patients
    benefits of humor for, 212
    cultural assessment of, 127
    efforts to establish minimum ratios of nurse to, 140
    empowerment of, 161
    nurse as advocate for, 150, 160, 190
    nurse impairment and safety of, 142-143
    participating in research studies, 162
    risk management during care of, 152-154
Patients Bill of Rights, 160
patient self-care choices
    background of, 110
    nursing challenges of, 109
    reasons for selecting alternative therapies, 110-111
    self-care healing processes and, 111
    See also CAM (complimentary and alternative medicine)
Patient Self Determination Act (1990), 153
personal self-development, 184-185
Pew Health Professions Commission, 86
pharmacist, 100-101
physical therapist, 101
physician liaison program (Mayo clinic), 103

physicians
>challenges for nurses working with, 99
>negative effects of verbal abuse by, 104-105
>pursuing issues of verbal abuse by, 105-106
>transdisciplinary health care relationships of nurses and, 104-105

PNDS (Perioperative Nursing Data Set), 161
point-of-care (bedside) systems, 26
preventive health services, 77
preventive practice, 149-150
primary health care activities
>described, 75
>by school nurse, 77-78
prioritizing work/tasks, 4-5
problem-solving, 65-66
professional changes
>change agent role in, 28-29, 190
>political activism for, 29
professional liability insurance, 150-151
professional portfolio, 182-183
professional practice standards, 94-95
professional self-development, 185-186
Prospective Payment System (Medicare), 92
prototype identification, 65, 86
PSM (personal status monitor), 34
public policy ethics, 158-159
PubMED, 35

Q

quality
>indicators of, 88-89
>TQM (total quality management) approach to, 50, 90
quality assessment
>described, 89-90
>outcome measures and, 90-91
quality assurance, 90
quality care
>application to nursing practice, 89-90
>case management and, 87-88
>challenges of, 85
>as core value of nursing, 85
>cost-efficiency and, 92
>critical thinking/clinical decision-making and, 86-87
>evidenced-based practice and, 93-94
>indicators of, 88-89
>micro and macro views of, 88
>professional practice standards and, 94-95
quality manager, 195
quality outcome measures
>Donabedian model on, 91
>sources of data on, 91
>tools to collect data for, 90-91
quality report cards, 92-93

R

random relationships, 13
RCA (root cause analysis), 152
reflection check, 86
reflexive comparison, 86
reframing, 65, 86
Rehabilitation Act of 1973, 77
relationships
>between humor and health, 210-211
>between nurses and physicians, 99, 104-106
>chaos and, 13
>coaching, 62-63
>deterministic, 13
>random, 13
relaxation techniques, 202
researcher role, 190
research participation, 162
resident approach to time management, 4
respectful communication, 23-24, 128
respiratory therapist, 101
résumés, 183
risk management
>advance directives used in, 153
>durable power of attorney for health care as, 153
>living wills used in, 153
>three parts/strategies of, 152-153
risk taking, 171
Robert Wood Johnson Foundation, 139
role modeling theory, 66-67
Rotterdam NEP program, 125

S

safety issues
>of CAM (complimentary and alternative medicine), 115
>nurse impairment and patient safety as, 142-143
>regarding health care worker workplace safety, 134-137
St. John's Wort, 114
sales representatives, 194
Sealantic Fund, 124
self-assessment
>activity log for, 1
>challenge case study, 1
self-care healing processes, 111
self-contracting, 7-8
self-development strategies
>personal, 184-185
>professional, 185-186
>values of developing, 184
self-management assessment, 1
self-talk, 86
September 11th, 15

sexual harassment, 136

slander (spoken word), 149

Social Readjustment Rating Scale, 201

social worker, 101

special care centers, 192-193

speech-language pathologist, 102

spiritual nursing, 116-117

staffing patterns

absenteeism, 138-139

managed care impact on, 139

nursing shortages and, 139-140

overview of, 137-138

work environment and, 138

stress

challenges of handling, 199

defining, 200

as "false alarm," 201

increasing tolerance for, 203

living with, 203-205

measuring your, 201

mind/body interactions during, 200

personality, disease, and, 200-201

sources of workplace, 199-200

stress-reducing options

challenge of developing, 201

developing coping strategies, 203

lifestyle changes as, 202-203

relaxation techniques, 202

support systems, 170

SWOT analysis, 181

synergy model, 60-61

systems approach, 77

T

Tacoma NEP program, 125

task approach

combining, pacing, sequencing tasks, 5

minimizing and prioritizing tasks, 4-5

to time management, 4

team-building strategies, 103-105

technology

application to continuing education, 40-41, 172, 173-174

computer literacy and, 34

CPR (computer-based patient records), 39-40

future health care, 34

impact on sharing health information, 33-34

Internet and WWW (World Wide Web), 35-37

used to organize information, 37

See also computer technology

telehealth, 193

telephone triage employment, 194

thriving on chaos

challenges of, 12

in chaotic work environments, 12

managing innovation, 17-18

relationships and, 13

responding to innovation, 16-17

See also chaos

time awareness, 2

time management

controlling time wasters, 2

critical self-assessment of, 1

myths about time, 2-3

time awareness, 2

time management strategies

application to nursing practice, 4-7

self-contracting, 7-8

time tools, 4

time myths, 2-3

"time traps," 2

time wasters, 2

To Err is Human: building a Safer Health System (IOM), 143

TQM (total quality management), 90

transdisciplinary health care

background and history of, 100

collaboration/negotiation required for, 102-103

described, 99

nurse-physician relationships in, 104-105

nurses and challenges of, 99

nursing coordinator role in, 190

planning patient care using, 105*t*-106

team-building strategies used in, 103-105

transdisciplinary health care partnership

comparing patient planning by individuals in, 105*t*

dietitian's role in, 101

occupational therapist's role in, 102

pastoral representative's role in, 101

pharmacist's role in, 100-101

physical therapist's role in, 101

respiratory therapist's role in, 101

social worker's role in, 101

speech-language pathologist's role in, 102

type A personality, 201

type B personality, 201

U

UAN (United American Nurses), 143

UN environment conference (1972), 220

UNEP (United Nations Environment Program), 126

UNLS (Unified Nursing Language System), 39

U.S. Department of Labor, 181

V
verbal communication, 22
verbal conflict
 handling, 27-28
 negative effects identified in study on, 104-105
 pursuing issues of physician abuse and, 105-106
verbal tracking, 22
Veterans Administration, 140
violence demographics, 123

W
WebMD site, 201
wellness
 analysis model for maintaining, 221-222
 as approach to health, 217-219
 decision-making model for maintaining, 221
 maintaining in work settings, 222
wellness programs, 219
whistle-blowers, 142
whole personal wellness, 217-219
WHO (World Health Organization), 38
workers' compensation employment, 194
work hours, 137-138
workplace issues
 achieving healthy environment as, 219-221
 challenges for nurses, 133-134
 collective bargaining as, 143-144
 described, 133
 joint work space as, 220-221
 maintaining total wellness as, 221-222
 nurse impairment as, 141-143, 158
 safety as, 134-137, 142-143
 staffing patterns/work hours, 137-141
 stress/stress reduction, 199-205
workplace safety issues
 back injuries as, 137
 employee safety as, 134
 government agencies addressing, 134
 latex allergy as, 136
 needlestick injuries as, 136-137
 nurse impairment and patient safety as, 142-143
 physical environment and, 137
 sexual harassment as, 136
 workplace violence as, 134-136
WWW (World Wide Web)
 used in continuing education, 40-41, 172, 173-174
 described, 35
 evaluating sites on the, 36
 selecting information from the, 36-37

PRETEST KEY

Surviving and Thriving in Nursing

1.	c	Chapter 1
2.	c	Chapter 2
3.	a	Chapter 3
4.	d	Chapter 4
5.	b	Chapter 5
6.	a	Chapter 6
7.	c	Chapter 7
8.	d	Chapter 8
9.	b	Chapter 9
10.	c	Chapter 10
11.	a	Chapter 11
12.	d	Chapter 12
13.	b	Chapter 13
14.	c	Chapter 14
15.	a	Chapter 15
16.	c	Chapter 16
17.	b	Chapter 17
18.	d	Chapter 18
19.	c	Chapter 19
20.	a	Chapter 20

Western Schools® offers over 2,000 hours to suit all your interests – and requirements!

Note
Advanced level courses are denoted by the letter **A**.

Cardiovascular
Cardiovascular Nursing: A Comprehensive Overview ....32 hrs
Cardiovascular Pharmacology...11 hrs
A The 12-Lead ECG in Acute Coronary Syndromes ....42 hrs

Clinical Conditions/Nursing Practice
A Advanced Assessment...35 hrs
Airway Management with a Tracheal Tube ....1 hr
Asthma: Nursing Care Across the Lifespan ....28 hrs
Chest Tube Management...2 hrs
Clinical Care of the Diabetic Foot ....8 hrs
A Complete Nurses Guide to Diabetes Care..................................37 hrs
Diabetes Essentials for Nurses..30 hrs
Death, Dying & Bereavement ....30 hrs
Essentials of Patient Education ....30 hrs
Genetic & Inherited Disorders of the Pulmonary System...............3 hrs
Healing Nutrition ....24 hrs
Holistic & Complementary Therapies ....18 hrs
Home Health Nursing (2nd ed.) ....30 hrs
Humor in Healthcare: The Laughter Prescription.....................20 hrs
Immunization Review ....2 hrs
Management of Systemic Lupus Erythematosus ....3 hrs
Orthopedic Nursing: Caring for Patients with
    Musculoskeletal Disorders ....30 hrs
Osteomyelitis...2 hrs
Pain & Symptom Management..1 hr
Pain Management: Principles and Practice ....30 hrs
A Palliative Practices: An Interdisciplinary Approach ....66 hrs
    — Issues Specific to Palliative Care............................20 hrs
    — Specific Disease States and Symptom
        Management ....24 hrs
    — The Dying Process, Grief, and Bereavement. ....22 hrs
Pharmacologic Management of Asthma.....................................1 hr
Pulmonary Rehabilitation ....3 hrs
Seizures: A Basic Overview ....1 hr
The Neurological Exam ....1 hr
Wound Management and Healing..30 hrs

Critical Care/ER/OR
Acute Respiratory Distress Syndrome (ARDS) ....20 hrs
Basic Nursing of Head, Chest, Abdominal, Spine
    and Orthopedic Trauma...20 hrs
A Case Studies in Critical Care Nursing.......................................46 hrs
Critical Care & Emergency Nursing ....30 hrs
Hemodynamic Monitoring ....18 hrs
Lung Transplantation ....3 hrs
A Practical Guide to Moderate Sedation/Analgesia ....31 hrs
Principles of Basic Trauma Nursing ....30 hrs
Traumatic Brain Injury ....3 hrs

Geriatrics
Alzheimer's Disease: A Complete Guide for Nurses ....25 hrs
Alzheimer's Disease and Related Disorders ....3 hrs
Cognitive Disorders in Aging ....2 hrs
Early-Stage Alzheimer's Disease ....10 hrs
Nursing Care of the Older Adult (2nd ed.) ....25 hrs
Psychosocial Issues Affecting Older Adults ....16 hrs

Infectious Diseases/Bioterrorism
Avian Influenza...1 hr
Biological Weapons...5 hrs
Bioterrorism & the Nurse's Response to WMD ....5 hrs
Bioterrorism Readiness: The Nurse's Critical Role ....2 hrs
Hepatitis C: The Silent Killer (2nd ed.) ....3 hrs
HIV/AIDS ....1 or 2 hrs
Infection Control Training for Healthcare Workers ....4 hrs
Influenza: A Vaccine-Preventable Disease ....1 hr
MRSA ....1 hr
Pertussis: Diagnosis, Treatment, and Prevention ....3 hrs
Smallpox ....2 hrs
Tuberculosis Across the Lifespan ....3 hrs
West Nile Virus (2nd ed.) ....1 hr

Oncology
Cancer in Women ....30 hrs
Cancer Nursing (2nd ed.) ....36 hrs
Chemotherapy and Biotherapies ....10 hrs

Pediatrics/Maternal-Child/Women's Health
A Assessment and Care of the Well Newborn ....34 hrs
Birth Control Methods and Reproductive Choices ....4 hrs
Birth Defects Affecting the Respiratory System ....3 hrs
Diabetes in Children ....30 hrs
Effective Counseling Techniques for Perinatal Mood Disorders ....3 hrs
Fetal and Neonatal Drug Exposure ....3 hrs
Induction of Labor...8 hrs
Maternal-Newborn Nursing ....30 hrs
Menopause: Nursing Care for Women Throughout Mid-Life ......25 hrs
A Obstetric and Gynecologic Emergencies ....44 hrs
    — Obstetric Emergencies ....22 hrs
    — Gynecologic Emergencies ....22 hrs
Pediatric Health & Physical Assessment..................................15 hrs
Pediatric Pharmacology ....10 hrs
Perinatal Mood Disorders: An Overview ....3 hrs
A Practice Guidelines for Pediatric Nurse Practitioners ....46 hrs
Respiratory Diseases in the Newborn ....3 hrs
Women's Health: Contemporary Advances and Trends (3rd ed.)..24 hrs

Professional Issues/Management/Law
Documentation for Nurses ....24 hrs
Medical Error Prevention: Patient Safety ....2 hrs
Management and Leadership in Nursing ....20 hrs
Ohio Nursing Law: How Practice is Regulated ....1 hr
Surviving and Thriving in Nursing ....30 hrs

Psychiatric/Mental Health
A ADHD in Children and Adults ....8 hrs
Attention Deficit Hyperactivity Disorders
    Throughout the Lifespan..30 hrs
Basic Psychopharmacology ....5 hrs
Behavioral Approaches to Treating Obesity ....13 hrs
A Bipolar Disorder ....10 hrs
A Child/Adolescent Clinical Psychopharmacology ....12 hrs
A Childhood Maltreatment ....10 hrs
A Clinical Psychopharmacology ....10 hrs
A Collaborative Therapy with Multi-stressed Families ....30 hrs
Counseling Substance Abusing or Dependent Adolescents ....3 hrs
Depression: Prevention, Diagnosis, and Treatment ....25 hrs
Disaster Mental Health ....3 hrs
A Ethnicity and the Dementias ....25 hrs
A Evidence-Based Mental Health Practice.....................................22 hrs
A Geropsychiatric and Mental Health Nursing.................................40 hrs
Group Work with Substance Abusing & Dually Diagnosed Clients ....3 hrs
A Growing Up with Autism ....21 hrs
Harm Reduction Counseling for Substance Abusing Clients ....4 hrs
A Integrating Traditional Healing Practices into Counseling ....35 hrs
A Integrative Treatment for Borderline Personality Disorder ....21 hrs
IPV (Intimate Partner Violence) (2nd ed.) ....1 or 3 hrs
A Mental Disorders in Older Adults ....25 hrs
A Mindfulness and Psychotherapy ....25 hrs
A Multicultural Perspectives in Working with Families ....27 hrs
A Obsessive Compulsive Disorder ....9 hrs
Post-Divorce Parenting: Mental Health Issues and Interventions....4 hrs
A Problem and Pathological Gambling ....9 hrs
Psychiatric Nursing: Current Trends in Diagnosis ....30 hrs
Psychiatric Principles & Applications ....30 hrs
A Psychosocial Adjustment to Chronic Illness in
    Children and Adolescents ....8 hrs
A Schizophrenia ....5 hrs
Schizophrenia: Signs, Symptoms, and Treatment Strategies ....3 hrs
Substance Abuse ....32 hrs
Suicide ....21 hrs
A Trauma Therapy ....11 hrs
A Treating Explosive Kids ....14 hrs
A Treating Substance Use Problems in Psychotherapy Practice ......24 hrs
A Treating Victims of Mass Disaster and Terrorism..........................6 hrs

Visit us online at westernschools.com for additional CE offerings!

REV 5/7/09